The Wines of Australia

FABER BOOKS ON WINE
General Editor: Julian Jeffs

Bordeaux (new edition) by David Peppercorn
Burgundy by Anthony Hanson
French Country Wines by Rosemary George
German Wines by Ian Jamieson
Italian Wines (new edition) by Philip Dallas
Port by George Robertson
Sherry by Julian Jeffs
Spirits and Liqueurs by Peter Hallgarten
The Wines of Greece by Miles Lambert-Gocs
The Wines of Portugal (new edition) by Jan Read
The Wines of the Rhône by John Livingstone-Learmonth and Melvyn C. H. Master
The Wines of Spain (new edition) by Jan Read

Drilling for Wine by Robin Yapp

THE WINES OF AUSTRALIA

===

OLIVER MAYO

===

new edition

faber and faber

LONDON · BOSTON

First published in 1986
by Faber and Faber Limited
3 Queen Square London WC1N 3AU
This edition first published in 1991

Phototypeset by Intype, London
Printed in Great Britain by Clays Ltd, St Ives plc

A CIP record for this book is available from
the British Library

ISBN 0–571–16395–5 (cased)
ISBN 0–571–16396–3 (pbk)

Contents

Maps

Diagram

Acknowledgements

Writing a book about an industry which spans a continent, even the smallest continent, is not easy. It is a pleasure to thank all of the following for advice, information, criticism and encouragement: J. Baldwin, A. Berry, G. Boboc, B. B. Carrodus, B. G. Coombe, C. L. Cowan, B. Croser, D. Davidson, M. J. Detmold, G. Due, I. R. Franklin, E. Franks, J. Gladstones, J. Greenshields, R. J. Hague, S. Hamilton, T. W. Hancock, J. Jeffs, C. Kay, C. H. Kay, J. Kilgour, M. Lake, M. C. Lamey, A. L. C. Ligertwood, E. J. A. Mayo, J. Mayo, M. G. Mayo, J. Middleton, G. Pinney, B. C. Rankine, M. Rives, M. Robson, M. Schubert, A. A. Simpson, J. H. Simpson, K. Smith, J. D. Sobey, T. C. Somers, J. Thomson, G. Wiltshire and A. Wynn. I thank A. D. Powell for permission to quote the passage from *To Keep the Ball Rolling* reproduced on p. 36 and J. K. Galbraith, Houghton Mifflin Company and André Deutsch Ltd for permission to quote that from *A Life in Our Times* reproduced on p. 54. I am most grateful to J. Durham, B. Goldsmith, K. Kain and S. Suter for expertly typing this book. Finally, I thank my wife for putting up with endless discussion of presumption, nervosité and other important properties of wine, and my children for growing up with it.

Preface
to the Second Edition

In the first edition of this book I tried to give a picture of the industry as it now is, to explain how it got that way, and, perhaps most importantly, to give readers some idea, short of physically stimulating their senses of taste and smell, of the special charms of Australian wines, their variety, their liveliness, above all the intensity of their flavour.

In rewriting the book for this edition I have tried not to change the book's own flavour, while covering developments over the five years since the first edition was published. New wineries, recent vintages, amalgamations, changes of direction – all are treated in as much detail as space permits. The Australian wine industry is a dynamic one, trying to blend the best of traditional practice with the newest technology, so any portrait of it must be a little blurred, no matter how fast the shutter speed. For example, even before the first wines are on the market from new plantings on terra rosa at Bordertown, north of Coonawarra in South Australia, I have heard it said that this area will be a new Coonawarra, a rival to Australia's largest area devoted solely to fine wine production; with no real information available one cannot comment further, yet the wines will soon be hotly debated.

A number of readers have asked about the significance of the Australian Aboriginal words that are place names and vineyard names in many parts of Australia, so I have added a brief note in the Appendix.

I have corrected as many mistakes as possible and no doubt made a few new ones. Otherwise, the book is as before, perhaps five years matured in the head.

Oliver Mayo
26 October 1990

Introduction

When the Commonwealth of Australia was established in 1900, by the agreement of the people of New South Wales, Victoria, South Australia, Queensland and Tasmania (Western Australians later), it was determined in the Constitution that the Constitution of each state should continue as before, as would the powers of their parliaments. The founding fathers further recognized the distinctness of the states in section 113 of the Constitution: 'All fermented, distilled, or other intoxicating liquids passing in to any state or remaining therein for use, consumption, sale or storage, shall be subject to the laws of the state as if such liquids had been produced in the state.' The manufacture and consumption of intoxicating liquids had had such different histories in the different colonies that it would not have been possible to form a united Commonwealth without this special provision. The Australian wine industry today reflects these differences.

Australia is a very small nation, no more than about 17 million people, spread thinly around the western, southern and eastern margins of an island continent 7,687,900 square kilometres in extent. It is one of the most highly urbanized nations on earth, some 88 per cent of the population living in less than a dozen cities. Virtually all of these cities lie close to land suitable for vineyards. In every one of the colonies which combined to form the Commonwealth, therefore, a wine industry grew up almost as soon as the first settlers arrived. Only in the Northern Territory, once part of South Australia and soon to become a state in its own right, where the climate is mostly unsuitable for wine production, and where beer consumption is prodigious, has no wine industry been developed.

Each state's wine industry was different, those with more generous climates producing wine more readily and coming to dominate the

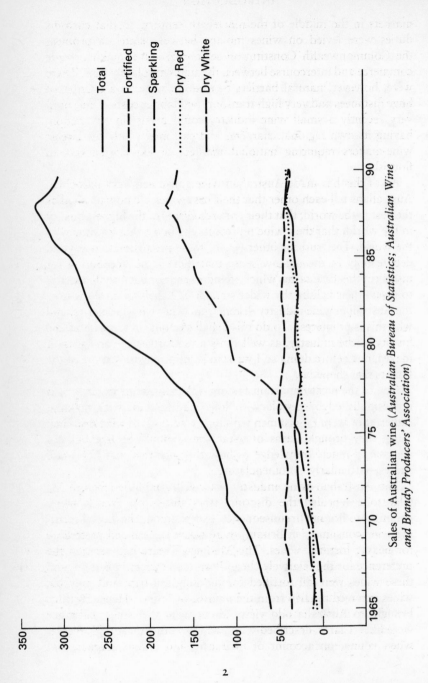

Sales of Australian wine (*Australian Bureau of Statistics; Australian Wine and Brandy Producers' Association*)

markets in the middle of the nineteenth century, so that customs duties were levied on wines moving between states, a problem the Commonwealth Constitution set out to solve, making 'trade commerce and intercourse between the states absolutely free'. There were, however, natural barriers to trade in wine, in a country of huge distances and very high transport and labour costs. Thus, until very recently a small wine industry could persist in any region, having its own regional character and customers, only the largest wine-makers requiring national markets or export markets to flourish.

All of this has made Australian wine consumers very parochial. Australians tell each other that their best wines are now as good as the best in the world, that their *vin ordinaire* is of the highest quality in the world, that their wine represents the best value for money in the world. The truth or otherwise of these propositions is beyond debate only in the narrow sense that there is no accounting for tastes (in this case tastes which I tend to share), but I shall attempt to assess their validity by wider standards. I shall try to show how the Australian wine industry differs from other wine industries, and why this is of interest. To do this I shall examine in some detail the history of the industry, as well as its present structure and what it makes, but before doing so I want to scrutinize closely some of the factors that shaped it.

One of the most important factors is that this wine industry was not established by people with long traditions of wine-making; rather, they were Englishmen with long traditions of wine drinking. Thus, they brought ideas of what wines should be like but not necessarily much knowledge of how they got that way. This still shows, particularly in nomenclature.

The Australian wine industry was well established before Mr Gladstone repealed the discriminatory duties on French wines coming into Britain. In consequence, except among the most discerning wine consumers in Britain, there was a determined preference for heavy, fortified wines. The Methuen Treaty had secured the preference for the relatively cheap Portuguese wines in Britain, and these wines were all fortified for the long sea trip; and only big wines survived the trip from the interior of France. Hence, Britons brought to Australia odd views about what the wines of France were like. 'Claret' described wines which were almost undrinkable when young, on account of their acid and tannin content, and

3

'Burgundy' described wines that were softer, richer in flavour, lower in acid, and much higher in alcohol. These ideas determined the development of the two Australian Claret and Burgundy styles, which have disappeared only in very recent years, makers and consumers alike recognizing that the Bordeaux and Burgundy styles relate to climate and variety rather than to strength and softness.

It was natural that the English should also use German names, Hock and Moselle, for white wines that were predominantly dry and firm or floral and softer. Similarly, French white wine names, such as Chablis and Sauternes, were used where deemed appropriate. These names have persisted to some extent, though Hock is rarely seen on a bottle today, and White Burgundy has become popular only in the last forty years, led largely by one white wine from Western Australia, Houghton's White Burgundy. In a new departure, White Bordeaux was the remarkable appellation used by a wine-maker from the upper Hunter Valley in New South Wales for a wine made largely from Sauvignon Blanc in the early 1980s. Under protest from consumer organizations, the company withdrew this label and reissued the wine as Hunter River White Bordeaux, which was acceptable to the advertising standards authorities of New South Wales. The Clare wine-maker, the Stanley Wine Company, similarly introduced, in the mid-1970s, the term Beaujolais for a light red wine which could be kept in the refrigerator, but soon took it off the market. Later, many makers decided almost simultaneously to abuse this term once more, sometimes using the Australian carbonic maceration process (described briefly in Chapter 2) which is similar to the method of wine-making used in Beaujolais, sometimes not. The wine-makers of Beaujolais have understandably sought legal redress. One wine-maker in the Hunter Valley, Mark Cashmore, has described his odd Cabernet Sauvignon–Pinot Noir blend as 'not Beaujolais'.

As this Beaujolais story illustrates, Australian wine descriptions are a shambles. In general, for a wine to be described by the name of a particular variety, or as having come from a particular region, it should contain 80 per cent of grapes of that variety and 80 per cent of grapes from that region. Thus, a 'Hunter Valley Chardonnay' need legally consist of Chardonnay from the Hunter Valley to the extent of 60 per cent only. Even these requirements are not policed, however, as are the *Appellation Contrôlée* or *VDQS* descriptions in France.

In this book, except where the European terms are necessary in a historical context or because they are brand names, I shall try to use the names of varieties, whether by themselves or in blends, or otherwise describe the wines in relatively objective terms. But, of course, copying of styles has been, indeed remains, an important influence on what is made.

The Australian wine industry is small, about the sixteenth largest in the world. At the moment the inhabitants of the Commonwealth drink no more than 20 litres per head per year, rather less than one-fifth of the amount consumed per head in France or Italy, and of course the population is less than one-third as large. Furthermore, as in most other countries, the wine industry that is perceived by the wine-writing and wine-reading public is quite different from that perceived by the wine-drinking public. Most of what is written relates to a tiny fraction of the production.

Few people want to read about the problems of growers or co-operatives in the Midi when they can be reading about the Dukes of Burgundy or the Châteaux of Bordeaux. I want to give a comprehensive picture of the Australian industry, but shall inevitably dwell on its more interesting and attractive aspects rather than simply on its power to intoxicate.

It is not an industry which has always had a good press overseas, partly because of the merchants in whose hands it put its wine. Many years ago when I was living in Edinburgh, far from the red dust under the purple grapes, my brother went into the Chesser Cellar, at that time one of the few enterprising wine merchants in Adelaide, to send me some wines to brighten the grey Christmas we were about to endure. He had read an advertisement which said that wine parcels could readily be despatched to any address in Britain, and paid for in Australia. He wandered about for a while, making a list, then sought out the proprietor. 'These are what I want to send to my brother in Edinburgh,' he said.

'A very good choice too, if I may say so,' said the proprietor. 'Now *these* are the wines held in London which you can actually get to him.' There were no wines common to the two lists.

In recent years, with traditional firms like Berry Bros & Rudd Ltd beginning to put Australian wines on their lists, and others, like Alex. Findlater, having really good Australian lists, there has been some improvement – though not comparable to that extended to the resolutely parochial expatriate Australian beer drinker, who can find Foster's lager everywhere. However, the reputation Australia has of exporting only its worst wines has died hard. If we look back to the origins of this reputation, it is not hard to see why. In a report on the wine trade to the Victorian Minister of Agriculture in the 1890s, Hans Irvine of Great Western wrote:

I was introduced by a member of the Australian press, in England, to an historical hotel, 'Ye Cheshire Cheese'. I was unacquainted with the proprietor, and he, upon learning that I was an Australian and identified with the wine trade, at once volunteered to let me taste one of, what he called, the best Australian wines in England, and which he had laid down in his cellar to improve for some time. I thanked him, and the cellarman was straightway despatched to bring up a bottle. In the meantime another gentleman entered the apartment, to whom I was promptly introduced. I was told that he was the friend of Mr. — —, a leading light in the wine trade. While conversing with him, the wine sent for had been brought and poured out. Judge then of my astonishment, when, before I had taken my glass in hand, to hear the friend of Mr. — — exclaim – 'I say, Charlie, this is vinegar!' and I was able to fully endorse the statement without having tasted it, the aroma being quite sufficient to condemn it, and proclaim it 'acetic'. The look of disgust on the countenance of our host was comical to witness, and his air of wounded vanity I shall long remember as he remarked – 'I prided myself that you would be able to taste a glass of wine that would please you, and that would do Australia credit. That wine has been in my possession for years. I thought I would lay it down to improve with age, and it turns out like this! We get no encouragement to buy Australian wines – they will not keep.' I looked at the brand, and to my amazement found it was one of the most expensive and best advertised samples of Australian wines sold in England, and if any wine ought to have been good and have given good results this certainly should have done so.

By 1906 at least twelve different merchants were selling Australian wine in London, from P. B. Burgoyne and Company through Emu Wines and the Army and Navy Stores' own brand to de Castella & Rowan and Penfold. Their main advantage was higher strength without fortification. E. Burney Young, who had managed the South

Australian Wine Depot in London, was asked about the growing demand for Australian wines in Great Britain and said:

> one reason for this is that Australian wines are kept well advertised, and another is that they are largely used by anaemic persons, who are relatively more numerous in England than in Australia. The full bodied and generous character of the wines is more palatable in a climate like that of England than the thin acid wines of the continent.

Only in Victoria, after phylloxera had destroyed most of its wine industry at the turn of the century and competition with the lower-cost South Australian vineyards had ruined much of the rest, did wine merchants in the English sense have much influence, buying, blending and bottling for the relatively large and affluent Melbourne market.

This lack of informed intermediaries meant that wine-makers in South Australia in particular, and to a lesser extent elsewhere, could not afford to specialize, to search for what they could do best, since customers would ask for a range of wines. As a result, one of the major differences between the practice in the traditional high-quality areas of wine-making in Europe and that in Australia is that almost no Australian wine-maker, however small, makes only one wine. Indeed, Virgin Hills at Kyneton and Prince Albert at Geelong in Victoria are the only such of which I am aware, though there are a number making two or three, such as Redman at Coonawarra in South Australia who makes a Cabernet Sauvignon and a Shiraz. Some of the newest growers in the Margaret River area of Western Australia have planted only one variety, for example Riesling, but it is not clear to what extent they are yet influencing the wine industry in any real sense.

The annual cycle of wine-making at Roseworthy Agricultural College in South Australia illustrates the extraordinary diversity in products and resulting activities of a relatively small producer. Roseworthy is different in that it is Australia's main centre for oenological education so that much of its wine-making is for teaching purposes, but it is still remarkable how many different wines are made from a total crush of less than 100 tonnes.

Start in March: sultana juice is bought and sterilized for use as the yeast propagation medium during vintage. Pinot Noir and Sauvignon Blanc juice is bought from Lindeman at Padthaway in the south-east of South Australia. The Pinot Noir will be used by students to make bottle-fermented sparkling wine. Frontignan fruit from Nuriootpa in the Barossa Valley is obtained and crushed, Cabernet Sauvignon from Upper Hermitage in the Adelaide Hills, Pedro and Gordo from the College itself, and Colombard from Berri on the River Murray.

In April, Grenache is obtained from Lyndoch in the Barossa for 'port', and Pinot Noir from the Eden Valley to be crushed for a private grape-grower. Also a large quantity of Chardonnay from the Eden Valley is crushed for commercial production, as is Riesling from the Eden Valley, Shiraz from Upper Hermitage, and Cabernet from the Eden Valley.

During these two months, the previous year's Adelaide Hills Cabernet is racked into wood, and a Shiraz cold-stabilized to prepare a 'tasting pack' useful for demonstrating particular faults or characteristics in red wines. At this time there is a range of activities: Sauvignon Blanc and Chardonnay being made ready for wood maturing: racking tanks of various wines and fining with bentonite where sufficient clarity has not been obtained; cleaning Colombard and Frontignan for settling: filtering the base wine for a dry 'sherry' ready for introduction into the solera; and other minor works.

In June and July, red wines are racked to wood storage, possibly with filtration on the way, and the Pinot Noir sparkling wine base is cold-stabilized ready for transfer to bottles. The Colombard is cleaned up and bottled. The previous year's Cabernet Sauvignon and current Sauvignon Blanc are transferred for cold-stabilization. The current Chardonnay and Riesling, which have fermented very slowly, are fined. Some fortified wines are bottled at Roseworthy, and some despatched for bottling.

Over the next two months, some bottling will be done at the College, other wines despatched for contract bottling. The Chardonnay will be moved from stainless steel to new wood, and a Sémillon Riesling blend prepared for stabilization. Some fortified wine such as a bulk tawny port style is prepared, drawing various stocks from wood stage, and other fortified wines are bottled.

Everything is made ready for vintage, at the beginning of February, with a crushing of Frontignan from Lyndoch for a sweet white table wine, and Pedro Ximenez from the College for the base for a *flor* sherry.

The cycle is complete: perhaps thirty different varieties have been received and vintaged – for I have not mentioned the small lots used by students for projects, nor some of the minor varieties crushed for experimental purposes. Perhaps fifty different products have been released on to the market, with very varying degrees of success, and the wine-maker, who is also the cellar manager, has to consider pricing, storage and stock management. It is not surprising that he has no teaching duties.

With this diversity of products goes a diversity and a flux among producers.

It is impossible to be sure of including all Australian wineries in this book. Quite apart from the new ones which are opening their doors, others are closing. It is alleged that Charles Babbage, the inventor of the stored-program computer, read Tennyson's lines in 'The Vision of Sin': 'Every minute dies a man,/ Every minute one is born,' and wrote to Tennyson correcting them: 'Every moment dies a man,/ And one and a sixteenth is born.' Thus it is with Australian wineries.

Altogether, however, there are not many wineries. In the tiny Rhône appellation Côte-Rôtie, on 100 hectares there are over eighty-five individual growers, of whom thirty make and sell their own wine. Licensing laws in Australia are such that a man can make 1,000 litres or so for his family provided they drink it, not sell it, but if he wishes to sell it he must apply for a licence and then pay a tax which varies from state to state but which in Victoria is as high as 25 per cent of the retail price. Furthermore, he must meet all manner of regulations about opening hours, lavatories and the like. Thus, despite the flowering of vineyards in Australia, there are not many licensed – only 500 – and they open and close like a humming-bird's wings.

Driving to the Barossa some time ago, to refresh my memory of the extraordinary stonework of Château Yaldara and the Browning-Hamelin facade of Bernkastel, I noticed a sign, 'New Winery'. The little winery, in old stone buildings built by Germans more than a century ago, had been open for two weeks. Other than from the clean new gravel of the driveway and from the sign, one could hardly have told that Barossa Settlers had not been in business for centuries. Its Shiraz comes from vines planted in the 1880s, and its Riesling from well-established vines.

On the other hand, comparing at dinner the 1980 Pinot Noir–

Shiraz and the 1981 Pinot Noir from Akeringa,[1] I was saddened by the thought that Akeringa, which was near Willunga in the Southern Vales region of South Australia and was in production for a number of years, no longer exists. It is a pity, for the wines are showing both that Pinot Noir can stand on its own in McLaren Vale and that in a blend with Shiraz it produces wines cleaner and fresher than the traditional Shiraz, yet full of fruit and likely to gain elegance with time. Akeringa was one of many small wineries set up in the 1960s and 1970s by medical practitioners.

The strong links between the medical profession and the wine industry in Australia have long been remarked, and of course the health-giving properties of wine were identified much earlier, by St Paul among others. Perhaps Rabelais was the first medical practitioner of note to cultivate his vineyard, but one remembers him for other reasons. More recently it was reported in the Lancet that there was 'a strong and specific negative association between ischaemic heart disease deaths and alcohol consumption wholly attributable to wine consumption'. This was based on a comparison of heart disease rates and various dietary factors across a large number of countries, and aroused a great deal of controversy. With a colleague, I attempted to make a contribution to the controversy in the Lancet, but in the event this appeared in the Medical Journal of Australia, perhaps more appropriately given the relative size of the wine industries in the two countries. Most of the discussion had been about whether the association was a real one, but we wished to suggest a hypothesis for the origin of association. We pointed out that the potassium:sodium ratio in grape berries, and consequently in 'undoctored' wine, is far higher than in any other beverage, natural or synthetic, and thus far more healthy, having regard to the diet of our remote and probably arboreal ancestors.

As I shall discuss elsewhere, modern technology, at least as applied to cheap wines, has removed some of this potassium, replacing it with sodium, so that the best wines are healthier than the cheapest wines.

However, the many medical practitioners who have contributed successfully to the Australian wine industry, from Drs Kelly, Penfold and Lindeman to Drs Middleton, Lake and Cullen, have not been

1 Many Australian wineries and vineyards have taken their names from Australian Aboriginal languages. A table listing some of these words is given in Appendix 6.

doing so to ensure that the potassium intake of the wine-consuming class is maintained at a proper level. They have done so mostly to make good wine.

In a survey of ninety small wineries, Robin Bradley, a prolific Australian wine writer, noted that eighteen had been established by medical practitioners. The connection between wine and medicine is indeed close. But then, so is the connection between ocean-going yachts and medicine, between futures speculation and medicine, between investment in films and medicine, at least in Australia. Until very recently there were substantial taxation advantages accruing to the public-spirited person who was willing to undertake the development of a vineyard, and therefore many people with a high cash flow took this opportunity to convert income into capital. When universal medical insurance was introduced by a new government in 1972, one of its effects was to add fuel to the vineyard development boom. Whatever the other effects of (what is called) Medibank, this one seems to have been almost completely beneficial, except for its contribution to the wine glut of the 1980s.

Australian agriculture has historically proved itself highly successful at producing a surplus of whatever commodity was in short supply a decade earlier. Wine is no exception. The ending of Imperial Preference when Britain joined the European Economic Community in the early 1970s came at about the same time as the end of an internal wine boom; hence there was a glut for some years. As Australia is a high-cost producer it is usually not competitive on price, and as the total production is only of the order of that of Bordeaux and is mostly bulk wine for swigging or quaffing (but very good for both swigging and quaffing), it cannot compete significantly in the high-quality markets. It should therefore be able to find a niche in the value-for-money part of the export market, and this was indeed the case when the Australian dollar collapsed in the mid 1980s.

Australia's high costs relate partly to the small size of its market, which has historically made protection of its manufacturers almost universal, hence increasing the cost of goods needed by primary producers. More important, however, is the price of labour in a country where only 2 per cent of the work force are engaged in agriculture – so that agriculture does not affect the demand for labour and hence wage rates – and where there has never been a peasantry, like that of southern Europe.

Since the industry has these difficulties, and since in the end it will be growers and not marketeers who are bankrupted, and since many of the growers are soldier–settlers or descendants of soldier–settlers who grow grapes because the government settled them on smallholdings in irrigation areas after the Second World War, governments have been reluctant to tax wines as heavily as beers and spirits.

Even before John Gorton, one of Australia's most erratic and interesting prime ministers, introduced a tax on table wines, the problem of such a tax haunted the wine industry. It was introduced in 1969, abolished with a change of government in 1972, reintroduced in the early 1980s and has remained an annual worry ever since. Between March and June each year, wine-makers lobby politicians hectically and the premier of South Australia, of whatever party, reminds the prime minister (party again irrelevant) of the damage the Commonwealth wine tax does to South Australia's chronically depressed economy. Each July, wine-makers remind their mail-order customers of the disaster in the impending Federal Budget. Each August, for more than a decade, panic buying has occurred, causing a small increase in annual consumption, for most wine is not a consumer durable and what is bought in a panic is soon consumed. Bringing part of the budgetary disclosures forward to May, as happened in the mid 1980s, did not really change anything, since individual excise or duty rates can always be changed individually. In 1982 the large wine companies made their forward plans on the basis of 12 to 15 per cent tax, in 1983 15 to 17 per cent; in neither case were they quite right. However, an excise on fortifying spirit was introduced in 1983. The 1970 tax was 50 cents a gallon, the 1983 excise $2.61 a litre (when first introduced), and it was of significance in the areas where fortified wines are of real importance – north-eastern Victoria and the irrigated areas.

The tax on fortified wine stayed at $2.61 a litre for a month, after which it was lowered to $1.50. Four months later it was increased to $1.56, and four months later still, in June 1984, it was removed entirely. From August 1984 a sales tax of 10 per cent was imposed, levied at the point of wholesale disposal or at the cellar door for wine-makers' own retail sales. This kind of tinkering confirmed the growers' worst suspicions of the motives and competence of the Federal Treasury; like all farmers, they were never in doubt about the politicians themselves. In addition to this Federal tax, sales and licensing taxes of various kinds are levied by all the states. In South Australia, for example, the tax in 1984 was at the rate of 11 per cent of declared stocks at wholesale price. Many small growers absorbed the 10 per cent Federal tax, lowering their profits to ensure that they cleared their stocks. Large companies increased their advertising budgets. The consumer therefore did not feel the full effects of the tax immediately, though when it was doubled to 20 per cent the producers had to pass it on to their customers. It appears to be permanent, since the government which imposed it has been handsomely returned to power twice since then, owes little to rural interests and may have motives of public health as well as revenue-raising in mind.

When there had been an earlier excise related to fortified wines, imposed over 15° Baumé (i.e. sugar corresponding to 15 per cent alcohol by volume in the wine), many big wineries had concentrated the must and made their wines differently. They had a concentrator, useful for fortified wines only, of course, because it cooked the must as the water was extracted. The first run of concentrate might be taken up to 30° Baumé, then the vat would be filled with later runs of only 15°. The excise man would follow the hoses and scratch his head: 'I know you're diddling me, but how?' Then he would climb up and lower his sampling bottle into the less dense concentrate sitting on the top of the more dense concentrate, and it would test out at 15°.

This is not practicable when the tax is on spirit purchased by wineries for fortification. The 1983 tax were therefore very hard to avoid, and was paid years before the product would be sold. An easy tax to collect, it had no other merits.

Consumption of fortified wines has hardly changed over a twenty-year period, and that of white table wine has risen remarkably, as the graph shows. Red wine sales rose steadily for a decade and have been static for another decade; the earlier decade was the red wine boom. More recently, consumption of red wine has begun to grow slowly once more. This change in consumer tastes has been accompanied by a proliferation of wineries, as I have already emphasized, and of styles of wines. Consumer guidance has come mainly from advertising and from wine writers closely involved with the industry. The other source of information is performance in shows.

Each capital city has a wine show, with a bewildering range of prizes and trophies and basic bronze, silver and gold medals, scored on a points basis, for an extraordinary range of classes. In addition, the Hunter, Griffith, Lilydale and other areas have shows, and at the McLaren Vale and other festivals prizes are also awarded. As always, wines are scored out of 20 – 3 for appearance, 7 for smell, and 10 for taste. Problems occur in the laboratory when these scores are used to try to determine the relative merits of different trellises or soils; in the shows the problem is compounded by the sheer stamina required of the judges.

In the tenth Hunter Valley wine show, in 1983, fewer than ten judges had to assess over 800 wines in two days. When one considers that many of the red wines showed excessive volatility or hydrogen sulphide, one can only stand back and admire judges as a breed apart.

The results are important in business terms. The Jimmy Watson Trophy is presented for the best young red wine each year at the Melbourne Wine Show. A then young European wine-maker, Wolf Blass, who makes wine in the Barossa with good fruit from everywhere, made a reputation in the early 1970s by winning the trophy three years running. Then interest turned to wondering when a Victorian wine would first win the trophy: one did in 1978. Mildara, masterly blender from the River Murray in northern Victoria, won it in 1982 with a mixture of Coonawarra Cabernet Sauvignon and Eden Valley Shiraz. Then, in 1983, it was the turn of a new Western Australia area: a Cabernet from Cape Mentelle took out the trophy. Yet Mildara could advertise in the *Australian Financial Review* that its entry had won more points (56 to 55). Confusion reigns.

So does conflict of interest. As Jane Cadzow wrote in *Good Weekend* (the *Sydney Morning Herald* magazine) for 20 May 1989 (p. 16):

> some of the writers and judges are financially involved in the industry, either as producers themselves or as paid consultants to the wine companies. Unknown to the hundreds of thousands of readers who rely on them for impartial reviews and recommendations, some of Australia's leading wine columnists are moonlighting as publicists for wine companies.

Andrew Barr, in his enjoyable *Wine Snobbery*, goes further: 'Wine tastings are bunk.'

Despite this, the shows, like history, serve a useful purpose: the judges discover faultless wines; it is rare for a gold medal winner to be undrinkable. Equally, it may be merely faultless, a good wine being the sum of more than the absence of ill qualities. More positively, in the words of Bryce Rankine, a show judge for more than twenty-five years, 'wine-makers write all manners of things on labels extolling the virtues of the product but the quality assessment by a panel of judges in a show gives an independent evaluation of the product, however imperfect.' As Rankine was then Dean of the Faculty of Oenology and Viticulture at Roseworthy, Australia's oldest agricultural college, this is not a partisan view, but its final modest phrase is better reinforced by reading what actually appears on labels. For example, on a 1982 Sémillon Chardonnay from Richmond Grove in the Upper Hunter, one finds: 'This limited release wine is a blend of 64% Sémillon and 36% Chardonnay. Cold temperature skin-juice contact has resulted in optimal flavour extractiveness and development: Alcohol 12.9% v/v pH 3.31 Acid 7.1 g/l Mark Cashmore Wine-maker.' Or take Penfold, one of Australia's oldest and largest wine-makers. It has been advising the members of a long-established club for which it has been making a fine Cabernet–Shiraz blend since 1970 that 'the wine should be stored on its side in a cool cellar, where it should improve in the bottle for many years.' Yarra Ridge, on its brilliant 1989 Pinot Noir, tells one that ten clones were tried and only the best of four contributed to what is in the bottle. Finally, Ursula Pridham of Marienberg informs readers of her 1978 Cabernet Sauvignon that 'this is the classic Australian style – full bodied, deep crimson in colour, rich in flavour with a superb tannin/acid balance. A wine which will live for many, many years.'

Thus, the shows are important, the prizes important: the single-bottle buyer, bewildered by the offerings of 350 wineries, has to start somewhere, and a trophy-winner offers something identifiable yet intangible.

A wine may say on the label:

Silver Medal	1979 Brisbane	Class	5
Silver	1979 Melbourne		15
Bronze	1979 Melbourne		6
Bronze	1980 Sydney		10

One wishes to compare it with another which says:

Gold	1981	Melbourne	Class 40
Gold	1981	Brisbane	52
Silver	1980	Perth	18
Silver	1980	Adelaide	18
Silver	1981	Perth	33
Bronze	1980	Adelaide	18
Bronze	1981	Adelaide	17
Bronze	1981	Sydney	15
Bronze	1981	Melbourne	17

The two wines are predominantly Cabernet Sauvignon, one from Clare, one from central Victoria, both from 1969. There is no overlap in their awards, but the second should be better. All one can do is draw the corks and try the wines.

To show how all this arose, I shall go back to the beginning of the industry. I shall then discuss, non-technically, the technology of wine-making and viticulture in Australia to draw out its distinctive attributes. This I shall follow with a state by state review of the wine-growing areas, because even where climate and soils are very similar, political and social differences between the states have influenced the development of the industry. Distance has been just as important.

For each area I shall give an indication of the size of each distinct winery by the size of its crush. A tonne of grapes makes between 500 and 750 litres of table wine, depending on variety, ripeness, whether or not the fruit was grown under irrigation, and how hard the grapes were pressed (in the case of black varieties). Thus, a tonne of fruit will make between forty and ninety cases of twelve 75-centilitre bottles, the standard size in Australia. If a small grower makes fortified wine he will buy in his fortifying spirit, so his case sales will not represent entirely his own production. Where information is available on fruit bought in, I shall try to provide an indication of this. The figures for tonnes crushed will be the most recent available, and will be the maker's desired stable production level where this has been established. However, the figures given are only indicative of the present relative sizes of the different producers, given the industry's permanent state of flux.

I shall also try to indicate the range of wines produced, namely red and white table wines, sparkling wines and fortified wines. Since almost all the vignerons of Australia grow, make or sell Cabernet Sauvignon and Riesling, I shall not list varieties for each winery, but it can be assumed that in almost all cases a Cabernet of sorts and a Riesling of sorts are sold; I shall indicate where this is not the case.

Finally, I shall also try to indicate, where appropriate, vineyards of outstanding merit. Failure to include a particular vineyard in this category may be taken to reflect bias or ignorance on my part, but I am not attempting a classification of Australian wines along Bordeaux lines. This was tried in about 1970 by the wine merchant and writer Dan Murphy, just before the very fine wines of the old southern Victorian areas and the new south-western Western Australian areas began to appear on the market. For those seeking such a classification, Robin Bradley's *Australian Wine Vintages* provides one, together with the opportunity to argue indefinitely. I do not think that there is sufficient stability in the industry for such a classification to be more than a current market guide.

I have tried to avoid bias. When I was discussing the first edition of this book with one Australian wine-writer, he asked, fairly abruptly, 'Don't the publishers want to sell the book in Australia?'

'Of course it's a market. Why?'

'No connection with the trade.'

'Perhaps they want someone disinterested.'

'Hm.'

I

Very Early History

Stumbling around in the increasingly deep mud, one full bucket at arm's stretch, one empty bucket over his head to ward off hailstones the size and shape of crown seals, the grower reflected that the drought was over. But the yield was down to one fifth of the previous year's delivery, in the absence of any supplementary watering. He supplied very good fruit, finishing harvest two hours. and three inches of rain, into the storm, but some of the other growers were delivering a mouldy pulp the next day.

The size of the cheque would make the 'Vineyard Relations Officer's' congratulations on delivering good fruit in such a season a dubious joke, but at least the risk inherent in not paying the helicopter to spray against downy mildew had paid off.

The gentle Clare hills turn green quickly when the break in the season comes, perhaps as early as March. It is easy to see how Edward Gleeson, bankrupted in Adelaide, was successful in the hills 90 miles north, and called the new town after a part of his native country. In this particular autumn, however, brown and black predominated. Easing the truck over the roads slippery with red mud and black with the soot of the fires, between tall scorched red gums which would soon sprout brilliant green instead of their usual drab grey-green leaves, the grower could see, now that the torrents had subsided, that some of the other growers had had the flood through their vines as well as the fire. Not a good year for wines, 1983. If a harsh climate is needed to make good wines, Australia can deliver it.

As can be seen on the map, only in the far south of Victoria and in the west of Tasmania is rainfall not very variable, the range of observed values being much smaller than the average. The lower

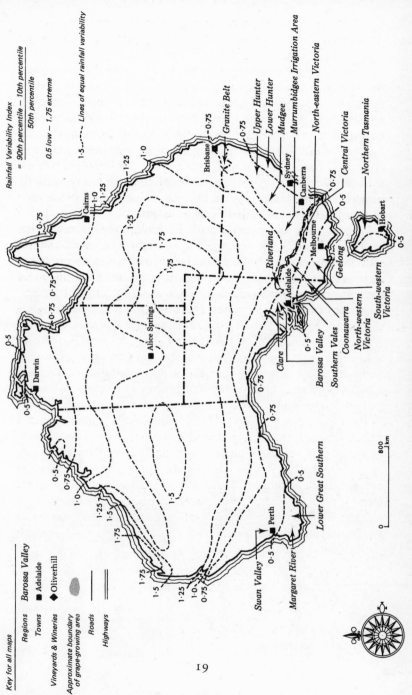

Key for all maps

Regions   Barossa Valley
Towns   ■ Adelaide
Vineyards & Wineries   ◆ Oliverhill
Approximate boundary
of grape-growing area
Roads
Highways

Rainfall Variability Index
= 90th percentile − 10th percentile
        50th percentile

0.5 low − 1.75 extreme

······ Lines of equal rainfall variability

Wine-growing regions of Australia

19

the average, the greater the variation, but the early settlers did not know this.

Wine was in demand in the earliest days of the first colony. We see from the first issues of Australia's first newspaper, the *Sydney Gazette and New South Wales Almanac*, that some dozens of casks, of 120 or 150 gallons, of Madeira and Constantia were sold at between 7 and 9 shillings a gallon. In the same few issues, a 'Method of preparing a piece of land for the purpose of farming a vineyard' was published, 'translated from the French'. However, this was before the days of scientific agriculture, and in the issue of 12 March 1803 the reader was told that 'the pruning is to be performed in January and February', which had not been translated from the French. Furthermore, liming was recommended for orchards, without qualification; Australia's old, dry, unworked soils are rarely excessively acid.

Rum, of course, was even more in demand, and it was many years before the labour-intensive luxury of a wine industry was properly established. Even in the 1860s, an English writer, T. G. Shaw, could say:

> So far as I can learn, Australia is not well adapted, either by soil or climate, for growing wine, and this opinion seems confirmed by the unsuccessful efforts of many years.
>
> So long ago as 1835 [*sic*; obviously wrong] I sent many hundreds of vines to Adelaide, by desire of a very intelligent wine merchant; but no good came of it. Even if soil and climate were favourable, the fact of its being a thinly peopled land must prevent the cultivation and making of fine qualities. It is almost literally true that the vine requires daily manual labour from the 1st of January to the 31st of December, and this can be done only in old countries, with a large population and low wages.
>
> Australia must wait many years before she is in such a position; and she will, in the mean time, be more profitably employed in cultivating her great natural resources, and exchanging these for the wines of Europe. Being one of our colonies, her produce was charged the same as that of the Cape; but, even with such assistance, the importations of wine never rose above two or three hundred pipes a year.

The first vines planted in Australia were probably trodden into the soil in February 1788, soon after the eleven ships under the command of Captain Arthur Phillip established Port Jackson, now Sydney, as a convict settlement on 26 January 1788. The vines were planted at Farm Cove, in light soil, at the location which is now the Botanical Gardens. So close to the water, the vines grew in very high humidity, allowing the ancient European disease anthracnose to grow luxuriantly on them. Today, control over disease is such that a drinkable wine can be made from Chardonnay only a kilo-metre inland from the sea, but at that time hot winds, rather than a fungus, were blamed for the vines' failure.

Because of this view of the effects of climate, a government farm was established further inland on the Parramatta River, and by 1791 there was a 3-acre vineyard under development together with a private vineyard of 1 acre. It is not known whether wine was ever made from these vineyards.

Captain John Macarthur, who pioneered the Merino sheep indus-try in Australia, was the major identifiable early figure in the development of its wine industry. Macarthur was given a large grant of land, totalling approximately 3,400 hectares, in 1805, and allowed thirty-four convicts to work the land. He was an extraordinarily contentious man, fighting with several successive governors of the struggling colony, and after the removal of Gover-nor Bligh he was forced to return to England for a time. He put this time to good use, from the point of view of the wine industry. In 1815 and 1816, with his sons William and James, both born in Australia, he went to France to investigate the vineyard and wine industries. They returned to Australia with a large number of vines and a wealth of information about vineyards. Meanwhile, Macarthur's nephew Hannibal had bought a Captain Waterhouse's farm, The Vineyard, on the river near Parramatta for £160 in 1813. Thus, the whole family was involved in wine-growing to some extent. William Macarthur was the one who mainly worked on the vine, bringing out German grape-growers as colonists, and winning prizes for Australian wine and brandy in London in the 1840s.

However, there were two other major pioneers of wine in Aus-tralia. Gregory Blaxland had been an explorer, with William Lawson and W. C. Wentworth carrying out the first major inland trip, crossing the Blue Mountains in May 1813 and identifying the rich farmlands of the higher country beyond the mountains. Blaxland took up land at Brush Farm, near Eastwood, and brought vines from the Cape of Good Hope, looking for anthracnose resistance on account of the problems with that disease. From this vineyard near Parramatta he shipped a red wine to London in 1822, and was awarded a silver medal by the Royal Society of Arts in 1823. As noted by Laffer (1949), the Society recorded that the wine was 'by no means of superior quality', but nevertheless awarded the medal by way of encouragement. When he was awarded a gold medal in 1828 for another shipment of wine, one may take it that the wine was much better. Blaxland was a thoughtful and purposeful vigneron, noticing that 'as the vines become matured by age, the wine in every situation is of a much better quality'. The makers of Carruades de Lafite would agree. Furthermore, he found that the best wine was made from the poorest soil, another well-established experience.

Despite Blaxland's persistence and success in wine-growing, he suffered setbacks in other business activities and became morose and embittered, and by the time he committed suicide on New Year's Day in 1853 he had long since ceased to be a major influence on the wine industry, or indeed of much interest to anyone.

James Busby is normally regarded as the father of the Australian wine industry. He arrived in Australia in 1824 with his father, John Busby, who had come out as waterworks engineer to the new colony. The son had studied viticulture in France, and within a year had published in Sydney 'A Treatise on the Culture of the Vine and the Art of Making Wine'. Initially, he worked at the male orphan school near Liverpool outside Sydney, in charge of the school farm and teaching of viticulture. The school had been established by Thomas Bowden, a Methodist lay preacher who was sacked for drinking in 1825, at which time the school was moved. Busby found working conditions unsatisfactory at the orphan school, and having been granted 800 hectares in the Hunter River district, probably began to grow grapes there; certainly he did so later, in 1832. From the vines which he had planted at the orphan school, quite good wine had already been made, wine which he later took to London where it was well received.

In 1831 Busby travelled to Spain and to France, studying techniques and collecting varieties. According to Laffer, Busby collected 678 vine varieties on his travels, of which seventy-four were collected personally by him from France. From the quality point of view, perhaps the most interesting are Pineau Chardonay [sic] and Pineau Noir [sic] from Clos Vougeot. It would be of great interest to know whether the very fine Chardonnay clone which has spread from Mudgee in recent years came from that Clos Vougeot material, and whether the old Pinot Noir of the Hunter has all come from Busby's stock. Busby's collection was maintained on land at Farm Cove but destroyed after his departure for New Zealand, so that it is impossible to trace his vines further. This is particularly unfortunate because Busby's vines were the most important in establishing the Australian industry, the bulk of Macarthur's having been unsatisfactory, for as Kelly said (1861): 'By the carelessness or knavery of the parties through whom they were transmitted to the colony, these wretched kinds were substituted for a collection of the best varieties grown in France.'

In March 1832 Busby was appointed British resident in New Zealand. He was not successful there, mainly because he had very little to do, and very little power. He was involved in the rather ludicrous attempt to establish the 'United Tribes of New Zealand' in 1835, and stayed in New Zealand after he had been superseded. The Treaty of Waitangi, from which modern New Zealand may be taken to date, was in fact largely of his drafting, but though he remained in Auckland until his death in 1871, his influence was much the same in his second colony as in his first: he imported vines and within a few years was making enough wine to sell to the troops. The New Zealand wine industry is not within the scope of this book, however.

James Busby's property, Kirkton, was taken over by his father, and was inherited by his brother-in-law William Kelman, and then by Kelman's son-in-law C. F. Lindeman, son of Dr H. J. Lindeman. Kirkton, like many other early vineyards, is no longer a vineyard, but it is still the name of a wine. Busby's attitude to Kirkton was ambivalent. William Kelman had been a fellow passenger on the *Triton* when it brought the Busby family to New South Wales, and Busby took a keen interest in what Kelman was doing. Yet he was not certain that Kirkton should be a vineyard. He wrote to another member of the family in 1837: 'I am sorry Kelman is disappointed with his wine this year, but not surprised. I always told him he had little or no chance of having a wine fit for anything but his own use. I was a little grieved that . . . he should have gone to the expense of planting eight acres.' And Kelman had had 365 varieties among which to choose from Busby's planting of 1832.

Of this collection, like the other at Farm Cove, little notice was taken until it was lost, soon after the First World War. The last wines were made from Busby's, or Kelman's, plantings in 1924 by Lindeman Ltd, which had owned Kirkton since 1914.

It may be that some of South Australia's earliest vines came from Kirkton, as Busby, although by then in New Zealand, arranged for some to be sent to Adelaide in 1839. Of these too, however, no trace remains. The establishment of South Australian and Victorian wine-growing, which dates from 1838 in both cases, will be discussed in later chapters.

Today, when Australia is drifting towards being a Japanese quarry, it is salutary to recall Dr Kelly's words in 1861:

Amidst the overturns and changes in our internal industry caused by the gold discovery, perhaps no interest has suffered more directly than vine growing. After many years' struggle through unwarranted difficulties, vine culture had begun to take its place as one of the permanent resources, when the attractions of the precious metal, in 1852, drew away from their industrial pursuits nearly the whole of the working population of these colonies. For a time it appeared as if the plough itself were to be abandoned, and our fertile agricultural lands were again to revert to their primitive state of pasture lands. There was for a time, a suspension of all ordinary industrial pursuits, and the eight years that have elapsed since the gold discovery have brought little change for the better in the habits of our working classes.

In New South Wales between 1848 and 1852, about 400 acres of vines yielded an average of something over 400,000 litres of wine and 6,500 litres of brandy, but in 1853 and 1854 vineyards were actually taken out of production, and while the area of vines in South Australia rose from 110 to 300 hectares between 1850 and 1856, in New South Wales vineyards were parts of large estates, profitable with no contribution from wine, whereas around Adelaide they were the small proprietor's livelihood, and when his labourers walked to Maryborough or Stawell or Bendigo or Ballarat, as did one of my great-great-grandfathers, he worked himself harder. (My ancestor found enough gold to buy a pair of boots to replace those which he had worn out on the 400-mile walk, and walked back to Adelaide to sell his last two ounces and try something less uncertain.)

In Victoria during this period, acreage and production also continued to grow, despite the proximity of the goldfields; the extra population and the higher prices obtainable for the local wines offset the lure of gold for the growers, most of whom, as in South Australia, were wine-growers only.

By 1870, when Anthony Trollope visited Australia, the wine industry was an accomplished fact:

> In all the Australian colonies, except Tasmania, wine is made plentifully, – and if it were the popular drink of the country, would be made so plentifully that it could suffice for the purpose. All fruits thrive there, but none with such fecundity as the grape. One Victorian wine-grower, who had gone into the business on a great scale, told me that if he could get 2s. a gallon for all that he made, the business would pay him well. The wine of which he spoke was certainly superior both in flavour and body to the ordinary wine drunk by Parisians. It is wholesome and nutritious, and is the pure juice of the grape.
>
> Accustomed to French and Spanish wines, – or perhaps to wines passed off upon me as such, – I did not like the Australian 'fine' wines. The best that I drank were in South Australia but I did not much relish them. I thought them to be heady, having a taste of earth, and an after-flavour which was disagreeable. This may have been prejudice on my part.

Thus, the first half-century of wine-growing saw considerable success in terms of quality of table wines, a success that was not built on, as we shall see in later chapters, because of changes in export markets and the failure to develop an indigenous love of good wine and food. Only when extensive immigration after the Second World War changed the community's awareness of civilized living did the true potential of the land begin to be realized. Naturally there were wine-makers producing fine wines during this long interval, but few wanted to know about them. Coonawarra, the Hunter Valley and the Yarra Valley were the most notable sufferers, and have since been among the greatest beneficiaries, of these wild swings in consumer preferences.

2

A Few Technical Details

Geography and geology have shaped Australia's wine industry as much as recent history. Lying from latitude 20°S to 43°S, with cold currents sweeping from the great southern ocean, Australia could be covered with vines, most of them producing fruit fit merely for eating. Small areas only have the right combination of rainfall, seasonal change and soil to grow good fruit for wine. Wine-making has had to be adapted to the fruit from this hot old continent with its extremes of temperature and eroded, impoverished soils; Europe's soils are more recently formed and richer.

CLIMATE

By trial and error, over about 150 years, de Candolle and others developed methods to predict the success of viticulture in climatic terms. De Candolle enunciated a rule, which I quote from the translation of James Prescott, pioneering Australian soil scientist and climatologist:

> The cultivation of the vine, for the manufacture of wine, can be undertaken in Europe, on slopes with a favourable exposure, up to those localities which provide a sum of 2,900 day-degrees (centigrade) from the day when the mean temperature first reaches 10°C. until the day when the temperature falls below 10°C. in the shade, provided that at the approach of maturity, the number of days with rain does not exceed a dozen per month.

The figure of 2,900 was the sum of the daily mean temperatures over the period he described. This has been modified to sum the excess over 10°C (or 50°F), which would give for Geisenheim, where mainly white wines are grown, 2,900 on de Candolle's scale or

1,000 on the modified scale. A limit of about 890 on the modified scale is the minimum for reliable annual grape ripening. This rules out a little of south-eastern Australia and much of Tasmania.

However, in Europe grapes are grown on the warm fringes of a cold continent, and in Australia they are grown on the cold margins of a hot continent, so a maximum is also needed. Prescott (1969) showed, on the basis of comparisons between Australia and the Mediterranean region, that the mean temperature for the warmest month should lie between 18°C and 27°C. The table below shows a comparison of most of our viticultural regions with some French and Mediterranean regions. It has been modified from the work of Prescott.

European and Mediterranean localities	°C	Australian localities
Champagne (France), Rheingau (Germany)	18	Piper's Brook (Tasmania)
	19	Geelong (Vic.)
		Coonawarra (S. Aust.)
		Mount Barker (W. Aust.)
Burgundy, Bordeaux (France)	20	Margaret River (W. Aust.)
	21	Stawell (Vic.)
	22	Clare (S. Aust.)
		Mudgee (NSW)
Montpellier (France)	23	Rutherglen (Vic.)
		Berri (S. Aust.)
	24	Griffith (NSW)
		Cessnock (NSW)
	25	Mildura (Vic.)
Tunis (Tunisia)	26	
Izmir (Turkey)	27	
	27	
	28	Roma (Qld)
El Fayum (Egypt)	29	Alice Springs (NT)
Jordan Valley (Israel)	32	

Vines are grown in quite unsuitable places, such as Roma and Alice Springs, just as they are in Britain, for some of the same reasons that people keep Rhodesian Ridgebacks in small city flats. Nevertheless, as the table illustrates (compare the map on p. 19), for the most part the viticultural areas are found where they would be expected on the basis of temperature requirements for growing European vines suitable for making wine.

The other main requirements are soil and water. Water has always been a critical determinant of agricultural activity in Australia. In the 1870s farmers spread north in South Australia, believing that 'rain followed the plough'. Houses were built, crops sown, towns planned, and when the good years ended, they withered away. Farina is a name on a map which symbolizes this failure: the crops which the name suggests never grew, and the town was never built. Even today, in dryland vineyards, one old 'gardener' will say to another, over a chilled glass of ruby port, that four rootlings were planted for every bearing vine in his garden, and the second will nod wisely and agree that drip irrigation is a risk. They feel that when the mechanism fails, the vines will have insufficiently deep roots and will wither in the heat.

John Gladstones of the Western Australian Department of Agriculture pointed out that experience had shown that good wines could be made at latitudes as high as 32° or 33°S, despite temperature summations of considerably more than 1,200 day-degrees. Thus, the European optima might need modification. Hence, without the effects of time and loss of memory, one can see in the development of the south-western Western Australian vineyards what actually contributes to an outstanding vineyard area.

First, consider climate. The requirements are lack of strong winds at flowering, lack of frosts after budburst, low, uniform temperatures, lack of variability in temperature, and reasonable relative humidity so that there is not excessive transpiration followed by excessive uptake of potassium by the developing berry, leading to raised pH (lowered acidity) and all the consequent problems of flat flavour and poor staying power.

Next, consider soils. There are salt and drainage problems in Western Australia, so good drainage is critical. Vines do not like wet feet in spring, and Western Australia has most of its rain in winter, a climatic pattern usually called Mediterranean and found also in parts of Chile, California and South Africa. Growers were advised to seek out gravel or stone, or clay over limestone.

Harold Olmo, an ampelographer from California, identified the Mount Barker area, and made Maurice O'Shea, the legendary Hunter wine-maker, enthusiastic about the south-west just before he died, according to Gladstones, who himself suggested Margaret

River – slightly warmer but safer. In the event, both Olmo and Gladstones have been proved correct.

SOILS

Vines are grown on an extremely wide range of soils. This is because the decision to plant grapes can be based on at least four criteria: where the grower wants to live, suitability of climate, suitability of soil type and availability of irrigation. Soil types on which vines have been grown in Australia include everything from red-brown earths through the highly desirable terra rosa soils to heavy alluvial soils and deep sands. Almost any level of soil fertility is therefore found somewhere in Australian soils used for growing grapes, and in addition to the very pervasive phosphorus deficiency, particular problems may arise with trace elements and, in the highest rainfall areas, potassium deficiency.

Thus, as French experience would suggest, the most suitable soils for growing vines are generally regarded as those such as terra rosa, as found at Coonawarra, and red-brown earths or sandy loams with underlying limestone, found in many areas.

Terra rosa is a red soil overlying hard limestone which in turn overlies deep clay with a high calcium content. It is well drained, which is vital for vines, and relatively easily worked. The water table is usually about 3 metres below the surface, but the extreme use of irrigation in the Coonawarra area in particular can be expected to lower it over the years now that more than 2,000 hectares have been planted. The terra rosa area is no more than 15 kilometres long and less than 2 kilometres wide throughout its length. Eighty kilometres north is Keppoch, where there is also considerable usable terra rosa soil. Driving past the Hardy Vineyards at Keppoch in the early evening in November after a fairly wet spring, one can see the setting sun glinting on the irrigation flood between the vines. At this time of year the worry is frost, for the vines are flowering. However, putting so much water into the soil makes for high yields, perhaps 10 to 12 tonnes per hectare for Shiraz, for example.

These very high yields seem hardly compatible with the very highest quality wines, and many commentators have noted that the oenologists of Petaluma, one of Australia's most scientific wine-makers, have carefully tested the effects of reducing yield by severe pruning and the elimination of irrigation. The results suggest that the unirrigated fruit makes far better wine.

Australian soils, as has been discovered by agricultural practice and research, are quite extraordinarily variable, and large vineyards planted in one season generally show very erratic performance for a number of years until cultivation, nutrition and pruning render them relatively uniform. Even after this, production is very patchy. Few of the viticultural areas are sufficiently long established for the very best land for a particular variety to be determined, as has been the case in such areas as Burgundy, Bordeaux and the Rhineland.

The grower, then, seeks well-drained soil, preferably on a slight slope because of the problem of frost, and perhaps, except in very hot areas, a north-easterly aspect. If the area has phylloxera, or salt, or nematode problems, so that he must plant vines on hybrid rootstocks, he will have to take account of the special problems of the rootstocks themselves; some, for example, do not grow well on calcareous soils, unlike *Vitis vinifera*. Nematodes – minute worms that attack and gall roots – flourish in irrigated vineyards on sandy soil along the Murray, and it has been fortunate that some rootstocks possess tolerance to both salt and nematode.

What the grower would like to know, in assessing likely country which has never grown grapes, is how soil variations affect wine quality. This is an unsolved problem.

Trace elements – the minute quantities of gold, silver, zinc, molybdenum and so on in the soil – are carried into the grape berries. The relative proportions of these elements vary between soils, and so do the proportions in the grape berries. Thus, for any given season and variety, the source of the fruit may be determined with some accuracy. This may aid prosecutions under laws such as the Unfair Advertising Act (1970) or the Trade Standards Act (1979), but not in planning how to make better wine.

In the late 1960s the Australian Wine Research Institute and the Commonwealth Scientific and Industrial Research Organization spent a great deal of money and rather more time trying to associate wine quality with soil type. They concluded that differences in composition could indeed be reliably detected and associated with soil or district, but not differences in quality. The reason was twofold: small lot wine-making, to compare carefully controlled batches of fruit, was unreliable; and the assessment of wine quality was not as precise as the assessment of differences in composition.

A colleague of mine was moved to develop novel statistical methods so that he could show conclusively, what other tasters had suspected, that one of a panel of carefully trained scientific tasters was reliable only for the first part of any trial. This was not because he consumed more alcohol, for he did not; he simply suffered palate fatigue of unknown origin. He therefore had to be excluded from future trials; assessing differences in wine quality between grapes from Sultana vines trellised in different ways, or Crouchen vines pruned long or short, requires reliability above all else.

The relationship of climate and soil to the Vintage Chart (Appendix 2) needs some explanation. Every area has special problems, many of which relate to wine quality but not necessarily to fluctuations in wine quality.

The Swan Valley is too hot, which leads to rapid ripening and coarse fruit. It also has nematodes in the more sandy soils, requiring vines to be grown on hybrid root stocks.

South-western Western Australia suffers from the depradations of birds, occasional severe frost and continual salt-laden wind. Wind can badly affect fruit set, and also means that supplementary watering is essential during the long dry summer.

Clare in South Australia has endemic oidium (powdery mildew, a fungus disease) and a long hot summer which requires supplementary watering. There is a minor problem of excessive vigour on the deeper, more fertile soils.

The Barossa Valley has the same problems as the Swan. Only in the cooler Eden Valley can wines with any real delicacy be made.

McLaren Vale is similar to the Barossa but the sea is a moderating influence, so that some finesse can be achieved with white varieties.

The south-east of South Australia has many erratic problems. A hot start to summer can be devastating as the winds sear through the level vineyards and shrivel late-flowering varieties such as Cabernet Sauvignon. Summer rain leads to fungal disease – grey mould rather than noble rot.

South-western Victoria has problems with both high winds and summer humidity. Further south, at Drumborg and Geelong, frosts are particularly bad, though elevated sites with a north aspect like Anakie miss many of these problems. Although phylloxera was the main reason for the disappearance of the Geelong vignoble, it is not a problem at the moment. Frost and summer rain should be the main problems in the Yarra Valley over the years; since the area's revival, there have been few really disastrous seasons.

North-central Victoria has both phylloxera and an excessively hot summer. For the few vineyards, as opposed to orchards, planted on the Goulburn Valley clays, there is a particular management problem as these soils can be quite impervious to water so that vines suffer moisture stress while being irrigated.

North-eastern Victoria is hot and has phylloxera.

The Hunter Valley has the problems of summer rain and fungal disease, and the converse problem of low spring sub-soil moisture because of the low winter rainfall.

Mudgee is surrounded by agricultural and pastoral land, and so has problems with birds and other pests. Otherwise, supplementary watering meets the usual difficulty of moisture stress.

Tasmania may have an early end to the growing season in some years. Ocean winds are also likely to be a problem quite frequently, as are frosts in many localities.

The Granite Belt in Queensland has the problems of summer rainfall and surrounding pests.

These various difficulties are not all such as to lead to wide fluctuations in vintage quality. Indeed, there is little variation in some of the traditional areas, apart from the occasional exceptionally poor year, like 1969 or 1974 in the warmer South Australian districts. Even these two years were very different in that some 1969 reds have come good whereas 1974 wines show no sign of ever being other than thin, unbalanced and dirty.

In all the newer areas, there are very few mature vines and no old vines. When one sees the difference in character of fruit from ninety-year-old Shiraz vines as against five- or ten-year-old Shiraz in the Clare area, one feels that many current vintage assessments for areas such as south-western Australia or the Yarra Valley will need substantial revision. On the other hand, assessments of vintage more than a decade ago are influenced by the surviving better wines, whereas the recent vintages mainly reflect the quality of the fruit at vintage. The table (p. 244) needs to be used with all this borne in mind. More complex tabulations, such as those in Robin Bradley's very useful book on Australian and New Zealand wine vintages, make an attempt to be encyclopaedic and then disappoint by, for example, excluding the very winery which makes what is in front of you (or excluding a winery of outstanding merit, for no identified reason, as Bradley's 1989 edition excludes Wendouree at Clare).

VARIETIES

As we have already seen, the Australian wine industry has a unique history, and the varieties grown today reflect that history. First, there are large areas of grapes suitable for either wine-making, drying or fresh consumption – Sultana (Thompson's Seedless) is the most obvious. Secondly, there are large areas of grapes suitable mainly for fortified wine production: Mataro, Doradillo, the Muscats, Palomino, Pedro Ximenez. Thirdly, there are increasing areas planted to varieties regarded as being suitable for premium table wine production.

The state of flux in which the industry perpetually finds itself is reflected in the areas not yet bearing and planned to be ripped out, shown in Appendix 1. One can predict that a number of varieties, to be discussed in more detail below, will disappear from the Australian wine-making scene if the exports of wine continue to be only 2 or 3 per cent of production, and if table wine consumption continues to rise at a rate slightly greater than population increase. Some varieties, including strange relics of what early settlers could collect in the Cape Province in South Africa on their way out to Australia, may survive, others may not.

To see just what a strange collection of varieties is used to make Australian wine, let us look more closely at some of them; first the black grapes, where I discuss, in turn, Cabernet Sauvignon, Grenache, Mataro (Mouvedre, Esparte), Pinot Noir, Shiraz (Syrah), Tarrango and Gamay.

As you drive north-east out of Auburn, the little town at the southernmost extremity of the Clare wine-growing area, you are confronted with a large sign which says, among other things, 'The home of the noble Cabernet Sauvignon grape'. Here, in the wine boom of the late 1960s and early 1970s, which was reinforced financially by the nickel boom at the same time, approximately 200 hectares of Cabernet Sauvignon were planted in one year, with every intention of producing the best red wine possible in Australia. The land used had never grown this variety before, if any grapes had been grown there. All over Australia, Cabernet Sauvignon was planted at about the same time. Extensive plantings were even made in the Hunter Valley, where the experience of a century had suggested that it was not a very satisfactory variety. Perhaps with modern methods of disease control and mechanical pruning and harvesting it will perform well in some of the previously unsuitable areas, perhaps not. Meanwhile, in southern Australia it is the main grape variety used to produce the best red wines. The character of the wines varies greatly. From the south of Western Australia, the south-east of South Australia and the cooler parts of Victoria, it produces wines of great complexity, character and elegance, recalling the Bordeaux area whence the variety came originally. From other areas such as Clare, the Barossa and north-eastern Victoria, it produces wines with enormous berry flavour and aroma, and rather less balance. From the irrigated areas, the wines are somewhat similar though with less staying power. It is frequently blended with other varieties, especially the ubiquitous Shiraz and, to a lesser extent, Malbec, Cabernet Franc, Merlot or Grenache.

As the major grape for many successful wines of the port type, Grenache has been very widely grown in both irrigated and dryland areas. When markets changed from a predominance of fortified wines to one of table wines, Grenache was used with varying degrees of success by itself for both red wines and rosés, and in blends of various kinds. Because the grapes acquire colour late relative to their sugar production, they have even been harvested green on quite a large scale for white wine production. Wines made solely from Grenache tend to be unbalanced, with a pronounced nose, showing very little of the rose-petal character which is said to be inherent in the variety, rather full fruit on the palate, and a coarse finish, which may be succeeded by bitterness as the wine ages. Makers like Trentham Estate who still produce a straight Grenache tend to emphasize that it must be drunk young, and preferably cold. As the wine-makers of Châteauneuf-du-Pape have long known, a small proportion of Grenache in a wine is often a very desirable thing, but while Grenache has been very successfully used in this manner in Australia, the more recent Australian fashion for wines made solely from a particular variety has meant that Grenache has been rather neglected. As a former grower of Grenache I have suffered from this problem, having at times had to make wine in the bath with unsold grapes.

In the early 1980s a wine glut led the South Australian Government to assist the industry by instituting a 'vine-pull' scheme, whereby growers were paid up to $3,500 a hectare to grub out their vines, provided that the land was not replanted to vines for five years. Accordingly, growers rid themselves of their oldest, lowest-yielding vines, which were often those giving the best fruit. They also mostly removed unfashionable varieties like Grenache. As a result, dryland growers of Grenache, who received $95 a tonne in 1973 and $190 in 1985, got as much as $500 in 1989. But still no one would plant it now.

Everything that has just been said about Grenache, except that I used to grow it, could be repeated more strongly for Mataro. Most people who have learnt to detect Mataro character seem not to like it, but in small proportions it can add to the complexity of a wine, and hence its interest. Despite this, one expects less and less of it to be used for table wine production. For port, it has continuing prospects, but fortified wines seem unlikely to return to their earlier levels of sales, dependent as these were on Imperial Preference.

Both Grenache and Mataro have been used more than was desirable because of their low price and ready availability.

In the 1890s, sound Australian wine could be bought in a cask in London for 1s 6d to 3s a gallon, and it retailed at great profit for 16s to 40s a case, that is, 1s 9d to 4s 6d a litre.[2] In 1983 it was reported in the *Australian Financial Review* that Orlando (at that time part of Reckitt & Colman) had imported Italian Merlot juice for 35 cents a litre in 1982, had blended it with a small quantity of Australian Merlot juice, and had sold the resulting wine as Orlando Cardinale Italian–Australian Merlot. At about $5.00 retail for 750 ml, the wine was much cheaper in real terms than provided by the reverse trade a century earlier, but one feels that a profit was still available for Reckitt & Colman. The managing director of Orlando, Guenter Prass, was reported as saying: 'We believe by purchasing in such a fashion we can encourage people to grow Merlot under proper conditions.' One hopes that he is proved right, for little Merlot is grown. It is not needed for softness, as in Bordeaux, but while there are promising Merlot and Cabernet–Merlot wines about, mainly from Victoria, there is too little to assess whether in any particular area we have a future St Emilion. In a tasting of 1982 Cabernet Sauvignon–Cabernet Franc from Jeffrey

[2] 1 gallon equals approximately 4.54 litres. At the time of writing, £1 sterling = $A 2.07 = $US 1.70. In pre-decimal currency, £1 = 20s (twenty shillings) in both UK and Australian currency, and 1s = 12 pence

Grosset at Auburn and Cabernet Sauvignon–Merlot from Horrocks Wines but made at Grosset's winery, both showed considerable clean fruit and depth of flavour, but this is the modern style rather than the blending varieties. In 1990, this remained true.

Tradition has it that Pinot Noir, which is shy-bearing everywhere, is unsuitable for Australian conditions. However, as Australia is an island continent, one would expect conditions somewhere to be suitable for this grape. Perhaps the inherent conservatism of those who work on the land and the protected Imperial markets were among the reasons that led to little of this variety being grown for so long. But this shortcoming has been rectified in the last ten or twenty years, and while the acreages planted to this variety are still small, they are increasing and, as will be discussed elsewhere, wine-makers such as Carrodus, Middleton, Tyrrell and Robson are showing what fine wines can be made with Pinot, as did O'Shea many years ago. Still, it is rare with an Australian Pinot to have an experience such as that recounted by Anthony Powell.

That August [1939] we set off once more for France, this time making for Dijon, with the aim of moving about Burgundy, as the previous year through the Gironde. At Beaune, the Hôtel de la Poste (I record, at the risk of being a wine-bore), we drank an Echézeaux '23, about third or fourth on the list of Burgundies, priced at 7s 6d in English money, providing one of the only two occasions when I have experienced the vinous exhalation spoken of in wine manuals, the bursting from the newly opened bottle of the scent of violets.

Perhaps Bannockburn at Geelong and Carrodus's Yarra Yering are closest to achieving a genuine Burgundy style. Diamond Valley is another; the others mentioned already are more Australian.

Shiraz has been used everywhere in Australia, usually with some success. From the earthy (or even dirty), soft, brick-red triumphs of the Hunter to elegant, spicy Coonawarra wines, Shiraz reveals itself in as many forms as Proteus. In Clare in South Australia and north-eastern Victoria, the grape produces table wines as long-lasting as any port, and with much the same character, yet it can also produce light, clean, austere wines which are at their best in a mere five years. The fruit character, emphatic or restrained, is what remains constant. A. C. Kelly commented in 1867:

The Sirrah, or Scyras, largely cultivated in Europe on account of the very deep colour, astringency and body of its wine, which is used for making up wines deficient in these qualities, is remarkable for the same peculiarities, which it possesses in perhaps a greater degree. Our warm sunny climate, where the soil is suitable, produces a wine from the Scyras which is not inappropriately termed inky, from its excess of astringency and colour. M. Cazalis also mentions the grape as an instance of a vine retaining its essential characters, even to the nature of its produce, under all circumstances, so much so, in fact, that the wine of the Scyras, grown under different climates in France, can at once be identified by any one acquainted with it. The same holds good with perhaps every wine which we grow in these colonies: under similar circumstances each will give wine similar in general character to that which it produces in Europe.

Although grown on a minuscule scale as yet, Tarrango is mentioned because it has been bred for certain Australian conditions by the Division of Horticultural Research of the Commonwealth Scientific and Industrial Research Organization (CSIRO). It is one of three named varieties resulting from a plant-breeding programme aimed at producing vines well adapted to the hot inland irrigation areas. That is, they must mature slowly and hold their acid well. The breeding programme began in 1965, and Tarrango was commercially released in 1979 after several years' testing. It was the result of a cross between the prolific multi-purpose white variety Sultana (Thompson's Seedless) and a Portuguese black variety, Touriga. Wines have been made by Brown Brothers, and when very young are bright, light, fruity and fresh. As they age they lose some of their early charm, rather like an early harvest Cinsault (Blue Imperial), but I tried one of the first experimental bottlings, 1974, at Christmas 1988 and it was drinkable, still with a little fruit. Whether the CSIRO's now defunct breeding programme will have long-term benefits remains obscure, but the attempt was courageous. In 1990 Brown Brothers in northern Victoria, the main champions of Tarrango, reported great demand for their fresh, lively version of the wine.

Touriga itself, though a port variety, has been used by makers as different as Coriole at McLaren Vale and Sevenhill at Clare to make light, soft, slightly scented wines which may be chilled for summer drinking.

The Gamay grape, from which Beaujolais is made, ripens about two weeks before Pinot Noir, and yields much more copiously. However, it is not allowed in many *Appellation Contrôlée* Burgundies, only in Passe-Touts-Grains and Beaujolais, following the edict issued by Philip the Bold, Duke of Burgundy, on 31 July 1394. Describing the Gamay vine as 'a very bad and very disloyal plant' which makes 'quite foul' wine, the Duke gave growers eight months to grub out their vines, fining them if they did not. He was also against organic fertilizers, which, he claimed, made wines turn 'yellow and coarse'.

The introduction of Gamay into Burgundy and the use of dung formed part of the replanting and rehabilitation of vineyards which was necessary at the end of the century because of the lack of labour which resulted from the Black Death in 1348. Gamay was a quick and easy way to increase production. However, grown in its appointed area, it makes a light, fresh, fruity wine of a kind ideally suited to summer drinking in Australia and to the 'fast foods' so many family drinkers favour. It is hard to understand why almost no one in Australia has used it successfully. It grows well in various vine-growing regions, and the berries are full of flavour. Philip the Bold's edict seems to linger strangely.

There are other black grapes grown, sometimes with considerable success, like Morris's Durif in north-eastern Victoria, but few apart from Zinfandel are likely to increase in popularity in the near future. Particularly surprising is the almost complete absence of good Italian varieties such as Nebbiolo. Barbera has been tried on a small scale, making attractive tannic wines in Victoria, but on the whole they have made little impact since they became available out of quarantine in the early 1970s. Zinfandel, the Italian variety which California has made its own, has been grown with some success in both South Australia and Western Australia, but it is too soon to say what its future will be. At Mudgee, in New South Wales, Carlo Corrino of Montrose Wines has successfully used Nebbiolo, Barbera and Sangiovese, though on a very small scale. I particularly enjoyed the 1984 Sangiovese, which, containing a little Cabernet Sauvignon, was in the late 1980s a big spicy wine with years ahead of it. Their Monticello, a blend of Barbera and Nebbiolo, is light in taste, high in alcohol, a deceptive wine in more than one way.

White wine is inherently less complex than red. The absence of the flavours associated with the pigments is a problem that has been overcome by the making of magical confections like Sauternes, Tokay and Champagne, and by the use of a vast range of varieties. In Australia this problem has been compounded by the confusion over wine styles. In red wines, as I have mentioned, Australian wine-makers, for the most part from the British Isles, have had the English conceptions of 'Claret' – firm, tannic, complex – and 'Burgundy' – strong and soft – at which to aim, but in whites they have had a plethora of French and German models, elusive moving targets.

The variety to enjoy the greatest vogue after Riesling, Chardonnay was to be found in few areas until recently. There was a fine clone at Mudgee, though not identified as Chardonnay for a long time, and limited plantings in the Hunter. In the last ten years there has been a dramatic increase in plantings, as every maker who has any claim to producing high-quality wines has sought this fruit. In good hands it unquestionably produces white Burgundy-like wines of the very highest quality, whether the fruit has come from northern Tasmania, the Yarra Valley, Mudgee, Cowra, the lower Hunter, or the highest part of the Eden Valley.

Until recently almost invariably called Rhine Riesling, to distinguish it from Clare Riesling (Crouchen), Hunter River Riesling (Sémillon) and other misnomers, Riesling was grown extensively when the modern techniques of cold fermentation came into wide use. For this reason it enjoyed a great boom from the late 1960s to the late 1970s, when a reaction set in against the very light, floral wines which were being produced with considerable residual sweetness but with none of the depth of flavour of German wines. Now, as wine-makers try to use the grapes to make wines with more body, it can be more rationally appraised, and while it may not be the dominant high-quality white grape any longer, it will continue to provide very fine wines from all the southern states.

From the many recent attempts to produce 'Trockenbeerenauslese' wine by artificially inoculating the grapes with *Botrytis cinerea* (noble rot), very small quantities of very high-quality wine are being produced, with great depth of flavour and distinct 'orange peel' character. They are, however, different from their German namesakes.

As Hunter River Riesling, Sémillon has produced (and continues to produce) some of Australia's finest and most distinctive wines.

39

Often aggressive when young, mature Hunter River Sémillon develops a beautiful soft flavour, a delicate lingering finish and a honeyed bouquet; it can improve for fifteen years or more. At their best, these Sémillons have sometimes been compared with the Montrachets; I shall discuss this further in Chapter 5. Like Riesling, Sémillon is being treated with *botrytis* in order to make wines resembling Sauternes or Barsac. Some of these wines are very fine.

When one walks into a cellar and finds the wine-maker selling his wares while wearing a singlet emblazoned 'Robert Mondavi Fumé Blanc', and finds that a 'Fumé Blanc' is indeed on sale, one sees the closeness of the Australian–Californian wine-making connection. However, a range of styles of wine, not just 'Fumé Blanc', is made from Sauvignon Blanc in Australia, as is the case in France. The full-bodied dry kind matured in oak has achieved great popularity as makers such as Enterprise Wines have learnt how to match the oak to the fruit, but very sweet wines have also been made success-fully from Sauvignon Blanc. Blends of Sémillon, Sauvignon Blanc and Muscadelle (or Tokay as it is called in Australia) are as yet very infrequent, but they may appear in the future.

Although Traminer is a well-established variety in Australia, having long been used for blends with Sémillon in the Hunter, only with the advent of low-temperature fermentation has it been able to reveal its true aromatic character. From the cooler areas, it makes spicy wines, full of the varietal character, especially if the grapes have been picked fairly ripe. However, because it so easily makes a very coarse wine, many makers have picked it early, resulting in a loss of character and interest. To make wines even remotely approaching in character the best Alsatian examples will require exceptional skill.

Crouchen has been grown in the Clare area for more than a century, hence its misnomer Clare Riesling. It has been much used to provide fullness of flavour in wines aimed at the White Burgundy style, but by itself makes a wine that tends to be flabby and uninteresting. Although it has a place as a blending variety, it is becoming less fashionable, which is a pity as it has an attractive fruit character when well handled.

Muscat Gordo Blanco, also called Muscat of Alexandria, is responsible for some of Australia's finest wines – the extraordinarily rich raisiny Muscats of north-eastern Victoria, their style generally agreed to be unlike dessert wines from anywhere else in the world.

Perhaps Chambers is generally the best, but they are all very fine. Elsewhere in Australia it makes good dessert wines, though without the intensity, power and finesse of the Rutherglen examples, and it is also used very widely to provide fruit flavour in cheap white wines, both still and sparkling. Enormous quantities are grown in the irrigated areas, and some of this fine wine finds itself misleadingly labelled.

Verdelho, one of the Madeira varieties, has been used successfully for dry table wines in Western Australia for many years, following the example of Jack Mann at Houghton. Recently it has become fashionable in the Hunter Valley. A wine writer, Huon Hooke, described it in 1989 as 'perhaps the only wine grape with potential for fame still untapped in Australia' (the *Sydney Morning Herald Good Weekend*, 7 October 1989, p. 97).

Like the other white varieties of the Rhône, Marsanne is not widely grown at all (a little at Mudgee and a little at Tahbilk, and elsewhere in northern Victoria), but it produces rich, mouth-filling wines of considerable charm when carefully treated. Perhaps Hooke should direct his readers' attention to these varieties ahead of Verdelho. Château Tahbilk has been growing Marsanne continuously for a long time, and makes the most reliable wine from it. In a good year it is lively and smells of fresh grass, and some allege that they can detect the character of honeysuckle.

Sometimes when one opens a bottle of three- or four-year-old Blanquette, it smells of Turkish delight, and the palate can be a little cloying also, but at its best, from the Hunter, it makes a firm, durable, full-bodied white wine only a little less enjoyable than the Sémillon of the same area.

In addition to the varieties already discussed, large quantities of wine are made from the varieties previously grown very extensively for dry sherry production – Pedro Ximenez, Palomino and Doradillo – but even the best of these tend to lack fruit character and interest. If there is a revival in sherry consumption, they will be returned to their proper use.

Ondenc, under the name Irvine's White, was for many years a mainstay of the Great Western area, both for Great Western Sparkling Wines made by Seppelt and for some of Best's wines, both still and sparkling, such as the Bin O Hock. Nearby, other wineries such as Montara use Ondenc to make wines such as 'Moselle', a syrupy wine like a still Spumante.

Chasselas is not a variety widely grown in Australia, and from the few examples which have come to my attention this is not surprising, since by itself it makes clean, boring wines, yellow rather than green with a dull finish. Like Müller-Thurgau, it may find a place in particular areas, but for blending only.

Minor white varieties, like White Frontignan, Tokay (Muscadelle) and Trebbiano (White Hermitage), are used for both table and fortified wine production but seem unlikely to make much of an impact in the marketplace, either in quality or quantity. It is very difficult to ensure that the desired varieties are grown. Constantly one is struck by the grower's inherent conservatism, which, until widespread bankruptcy supervenes, can make nonsense of careful econometric predictions of what will be grown in the future. I noticed it at the butcher's a few years ago.

The grey dusty track led round the front of the new cream brick triple-fronted bungalow to the butcher's shop at the back. Climbing out of the car, I noticed a man with a mattock grubbing out some old vines on one of the steepest parts of the block, where it would be hard to pull a ripper. The ripper had been through a couple of acres on the flat, and beside them was a crop of lucerne, flowering purple in the heat.

'Going to replant down there this winter?' The butcher's wife would know, for they were her vines.

'Mmm.'

'What with? Riesling, Chardonnay, Cabernet?'

'Yes, a bit of Riesling – Clare's. And some Shiraz. And some Pedro.'

'Pedro? But the Co-op isn't taking any this year.'

'No, but there's others that will.' She spoke and smiled equally slowly. 'These new varieties. It's just a fashion. My nephew's got a heap of Sauvignon Blanc, and it's just a heap of trouble.'

'But so are Clare's, and the price hasn't changed for two years.'

'You might get a bit of splitting if you're really tough, but you get tonnes of fruit. Now what did I have for you? Two hoggets? Wife all right? She couldn't get over here?'

WINE-MAKING

Wine-making is an essentially simple and natural process. It was introduced into Australia in the state in which it had remained, subject only to minor modification, for perhaps a millennium or more. Grapes were picked when they tasted right – that is, when they contained sufficient sugar to produce, after fermentation, between 10 and 15 per cent alcohol by volume, this varying with the variety, region, season and desired end product.

The grapes were picked as quickly as possible, taken to the winery, and crushed. White fruit had the skins, pips and stalks removed and was then transferred to fermenting vats, which could be wooden barrels, earthenware vessels or stone tanks, normally open to the atmosphere so that the carbon dioxide, which with alcohol is the main product of the breakdown of sugar by yeasts, could dissipate harmlessly. When the ferment had ceased, the wine could be racked – that is, drained into other vessels, leaving a slurry of yeast on the bottom of the fermentation vat.

With black grapes, on the other hand, the skins, which impart the colour and much of the flavour to red wine, were either not removed or returned to the must after the removal of the stalks (*égrappage*). Writing in the 1860s, A. C. Kelly noted that 'in these colonies the removal of the stalk from the vat has been the universal practice. How far we have been right in the exclusive adoption of this system is exceedingly questionable; and it is advisable that we submit ourselves to the teaching of those whose experience is of old standing, while the results of their practice, as seen in the very high quality of the wines, ought to command our attention.' It is evident from Kelly's discussion and his quotations from French writers that retention of the stalk in the ferment made for much harder, slower-maturing wines, which would eventually be better than those made without stalks; this applied equally to Burgundy and to Bordeaux. Removal of stalks is modern practice in both Bordeaux and Burgundy, of course, especially Burgundy.

Thus, most Australian makers followed the practice which led to softer, more immediately appealing wines. They did not, however, use *macération carbonique*, the recently revived ancient technique which makes very fresh wines. If grapes are simply put in an enclosed vessel, the berries will begin to ferment, especially towards the bottom where they have been crushed by the weight of fruit above. As the fermentation becomes more active, so more berries will be broken, and the fermentation will accelerate. Fermented juice run off black grapes will be coloured by the pigments which have been extracted by the activity of the fermentation, and there will be little of the harsher tannin extracted by hard pressing. If, in addition, the pressure in the fermenter is suddenly released, the carbon dioxide dissolved in the fermenting juice will bubble out of solution, bursting the berries and releasing most of the juice; hence the name of the technique. A modern variant of this process, developed by Stephen Hickinbotham, uses a large plastic bag to contain the fruit, and carbon dioxide additional to that produced in the ferment itself, and has resulted in many good, clean 'ready to drink' wines which have then been mislabelled 'Beaujolais'.

The length of the fermentation was hard to control before refrigeration became available. Kelly quoted a French writer as saying that 'the duration of fermentation is so prolonged in many southern countries that they may well be dismayed by the labour required in beating down the head once a day during fifteen, twenty, thirty days or more. The beating down would no doubt shorten the fermentation but not so much as to compensate for the labour required.' The 'head' or 'cap' was the mass of skins (and stalks, where these were retained) and it was lifted by the gas given off in fermentation to float on the surface of the seething must. It needed to be beaten down or plunged to accelerate the fermentation, to prevent fermentation into vinegar of the alcohol in the cap and, of course, to extract the pigments from the skins.

In the cooler areas, fires might be lit in the winery at night to prevent fermentation from stopping. In the warmer areas, cold water might be added to the wine or run down the sides of the vats, and when ice became available, blocks were thrown in during the day. Roly Birks, wine-maker at Wendouree at Clare for sixty years from the end of the First World War, defended the addition of water as mere replacement of what was lost as the must seethed and frothed. After this treatment, his young wines normally contained more than 12 per cent alcohol, and enough tannin to deprive the unwary taster temporarily of breath, so it was hardly a harmful practice.

After several rackings to improve clarity and brightness, the wines would all be stored for some time in oak vessels of various sizes, usually large (2,000 litres or more). White wines were generally bottled within a year, red wines after rather longer, up to three or four years.

Fortified wines had the spirit added when the ferment had reached the desired stage, with several per cent sugar unconverted to alcohol for port or sweet sherry styles, less to none for the drier sherry and Madeira styles. These wines were also matured in large wood for considerable periods before blending for bottling.

These, then, were the traditional processes, carried out with skill and knowledge which varied widely. Even in the greatest European areas there is wide divergence in practice, so that what is traditional need not be identical in nearby wineries. In Burgundy, for example, the house of Louis Latour ferments its Pinot Noir for six days and pasteurizes the wine, whereas other firms such as Prosper Maufoux ferment the wine for 'as long as it takes', which might be eight or twenty days, and do not pasteurize it.

Vintage is a time of controlled panic for the grower. First of all, depending on whether he has another job (as many of the smaller growers do), he has to arrange his annual holiday for a period that is slightly indeterminate as to both starting date and duration. Next, depending on region, if his vineyard is part of a mixed farming enterprise, vintage may interfere with other seasonal activities, a very late vintage running into lambing, for example, in parts of southern Australia.

Pickers are another problem. Will the usual reliable team be available, or have some of them died or retired? Will the unemployed young people be as good as their elders? Will vintage last long enough to give them the work which they have been promised? In both Clare and the Yarra, Vietnamese refugees have been among the most reliable recent workers, though they have never seen vines before in their lives. However, it is not practicable to depend on recent immigrants, as immigration policies constantly change.

Most of all, the grower is at the mercy of the winery. He has to deliver fruit during the period the winery specifies, and in the few weeks up to full ripeness for any particular variety, the advice of the winery will often change several times. Told that he must deliver his Riesling between 10.5° and 13° Baumé, the grower watches anxiously as the birds begin to attack in earnest with the Baumé just over 9°, and an enormous amount of acid, perhaps 15 gm per litre, still present. (This fruit should be magnificent if the birds leave any, the grower thinks to himself.) Then a cool week, and nothing at all happens except bird damage. The grower may have negotiated a bonus if the fruit is over 13° and still has plenty of acid, and as the last few days of receipt of Riesling at the crusher approach, he has to make a decision whether to hold off for a very high Baumé for an

Auslese wine, should there be noble rot about, or rush them through in these last days of normal Riesling delivery.

At the winery, after jolting several kilometres over the rough metal roads in the hot sun, the grower joins the queue at the weighbridge. Perhaps his load is smaller than the others, for big trucks from the river are delivering 10 to 20 tonnes at a time. So the big growers stroll over and eat a few berries from the small dryland grower's modest few tonnes.

The man at the weighbridge tries to guess the weight, to relieve the boredom of his task, and a further delay results. Finally, the grower watches the deep golden-green fruit spill out of the bin into the crusher, and the big Archimedean screw drags the fruit out of sight. A few minutes later there is a roar as the stems and pips are discharged on to an enormous heap which will be delivered to Tarac in the Barossa for fermentation, distillation and extraction of tartaric acid.

When the final delivery is over there is a tremendous feeling of relief. I remember one year borrowing a large four-wheeled trailer to tow behind a four-wheel-drive vehicle because there was a threat of rain at vintage. As the last load was being driven to the winery, a wheel fell off the trailer. The entire cast of pickers, both in the four-wheel-drive and the following car, sat at the side of the road and laughed, while a messenger ran the last few hundred metres to the winery and brought back the wine-maker and a cellar-hand with a truck and a fresh bin. They too roared with laughter. Only I remained impassive. Growers of the best fruit are better organized.

Farmers in Australia tend to assume that having grown their crop and delivered it somewhere, their produce will be snapped up by a market eager to buy, even feeling it has a duty to buy. Grape-growers are just the same: if the fruit is in reasonable condition, delivered on time and to specification, the winery must buy it and pay the growers. Yet the problems, in the hot areas especially, have only just begun.

When James Busby started drafting his first book on wine-making, on the ship from Scotland to Australia, he very naturally drew on continental writers, mainly French, at both the theoretical and the practical level. Forty years later, A. C. Kelly did the same. Another eighty years on, John Fornachon, first director of the Australian Wine Research Institute, would still quote nearly twice as many writers in French as in other languages in his book on the bacterial spoilage of fortified wines. However, it was Fornachon who first made a distinctively Australian contribution to the science of oenology.

In the late 1920s and early 1930s, as fortified wine production expanded, bacterial spoilage of wine – which had, of course, been studied intensively in France from the time of Pasteur onward – had been thought to affect only wines weaker than about 15 per cent alcohol by volume. However, from about the time of the First World War, wines of more than 20 per cent alcohol were discovered to have been spoilt by bacteria in all the hotter wine-growing areas, including Australia. This was a serious problem for the substantial exports of fortified wine to the United Kingdom, so in the early 1930s the Australian Wine Board asked the University of Adelaide to investigate the problem.

It was a very severe problem. Extraordinary measures were attempted within cellars to stop bacterial spread. A visitor to a cellar would be amazed, as he walked around, by the hessian curtains hung between the stacks of casks containing the maturing wine, and by the strong smell of formalin. If the formalin killed anything, it was the ubiquitous vinegar flies, *Drosophila melanogaster*, not the bacteria. Later, companies such as Penfold tried pasteurizers. As these had iron heating plates and copper fittings they caused major metal problems in the wine, even if the bacteria were killed. Ozonizers were also tried, and a wine of the port or sweet sherry style which had been through this treatment had little left to recommend it.

It was in this atmosphere that Fornachon began his work. He was well aware of most of the European work on bacterial spoilage and also, of course, of the malolactic fermentation which was encouraged in the light, dry European wines from the colder areas, to convert the large amounts of malic acid, which contributes a harsh character to the wine, to lactic acid, which is a softer-tasting acid. However, this had rarely been investigated in Australia, since most of the wine was grown in areas where stopped fermentation was not a problem and where, indeed, little malic acid was present in the must.

Fornachon was able to show that the bacteria responsible for the spoilage of fortified wine in Australia were as expected the rod-shaped lactic acid bacteria, *Lactobacillus*, which include the species responsible for the valuable malolactic fermentation. In fact, he found that some of the lactobacilli which he isolated from Australian wines could bring about the malolactic fermentation in wines containing malic acid.

Following others, Fornachon found that the bacteria causing the spoilage were very fastidious in their requirements for growth. The more acid the wine, the less they grew, but of the two attributes of acid – that is to say the amount present and the degree to which the acid disassociates into ions in solution – the latter, usually described by pH, has a range from 0 to 14, 7 representing neutrality, as with distilled water, and wines have values lying in the range 2.5 to 4.5, with rather few below 3 and rather few above 4. The scale of pH is logarithmic, so that a wine with pH 3 is ten times as acid as a wine with pH 4. Fornachon found that bacteria would grow in wines containing as much as 20 per cent alcohol if the pH was higher than about 3.6. He also found that the bacteria would grow quite rapidly between 15° and 28°C. In unfortified wines, however, bacterial growth could be most rapid at even higher temperatures.

The most important antiseptic, as it was called, in the winery was sulphur dioxide, at that time and indeed today. Fornachon was able to show that, under Australian conditions, virtually no lactobacilli were able to grow in wine containing eighty parts per million of sulphur dioxide, and all were killed by one hundred parts per million. Fornachon therefore recommended that 'When SO_2 is added to fortified wine for the purpose of checking the growth of actively growing bacteria, sufficient should be added to raise the SO_2 content to one hundred and fifty parts per million, and it should be thoroughly mixed throughout the wine. The wine should then be freed from bacteria by filtration or fining and racking.' These very high levels of sulphur contributed to the character of many Australian wines for many years.

It is now recognized in Australia, especially as a result of the more recent work of T. C. Somers of the Australian Wine Research Institute, that sulphur dioxide has two distinct roles in red wine-making, first as an antiseptic before fermentation and then, in red wine conservation, by chemically binding acetaldehyde, a breakdown product of alcohol, in young wine. However, excessive levels of sulphur dioxide react with the anthocyanin pigments, producing the smell, so disliked by many, reminiscent of rotten eggs and caused by reduced sulphur compounds, together with some components of the earthy character liked by equally many in even some of the best Hunter River or McLaren Vale reds.

In white wines, a given quantity of sulphur dioxide will produce much higher levels of free sulphur dioxide in the wine, thereby eliminating free acetaldehyde from the bouquet and maintaining freshness. To get the benefits of sulphur dioxide without the problems it is therefore added at the crush to the extent of thirty to forty parts per million, sometimes even less, and with careful management of low-temperature fermentation this is quite sufficient. Thus, when one walks into a small winery like Jeffrey Grosset's and asks the wine-maker how much sulphur dioxide he is using in his wines, he might well say: 'Well, I'd like it to be only twenty-eight, but these wines are going to last for years, and I'd like my customers to lay them down, so I play it safe and add thirty-five. But when you think that most of the customers probably drink the stuff within a month, perhaps I should use less.'

Such makers ferment everything in stainless steel, which makes for control and cleanliness but is very expensive, especially for a large long-established maker with a substantial investment in plant. For the most part they also obtain from the Wine Research Institute yeasts specially selected for the production of a desired type of wine. This yeast selection arose naturally from the earlier work on faults and diseases of wines. It means that yeasts are available for a range of sugar levels in the fruit, so that a high sugar level can be left at the end of fermentation for a sweet wine, or the wine can be fermented to dryness for any alcohol level. Also, a yeast can be chosen which works best at a given fermentation temperature, or which imparts little character to a wine, or a great deal of character – for example the 'tropical fruit salad' character of acetate esters. A yeast which produces significant quantities of these last components was very widely used with Riesling in the late 1970s and many of these wines are still to be found.

Open fermenters are still used in the colder areas – big open concrete vats paraffin lined just before vintage. As a small boy I can recall watching the cap being plunged at Seppeltsfield, and wondering why it was being done; closed fermentation has brought many improvements, but it makes vintage less interesting. Can you smell the fruit? The wine-maker's face shows worry; he is using closed stainless steel tanks to keep all the flavour in, and inside the winery all you should smell is yeast. At the crusher, the grapey smell is such that varieties are better distinguished by their appearance or by chewing them than by smell, and the bees lurch and stagger away, gorged on sugar, no pollen in their saddle bags.

After the fermentation, or even for the later stages in some cases, oak storage is needed by many wines. In Australia many, perhaps most, white wines and some red wines are bottled soon after fermentation. This applies particularly to cheap wines, which can be rapidly cleared and stabilized by filtration and centrifugation.

Oak is a preoccupation of many small wine-growers, red wine-growers in particular. For many years storage in large oak was the rule, probably very old oak, partly on account of the cost, partly because this was traditional. In this, Australian wine practice used to resemble Italian more than French custom.

When, mainly following the lead of Penfold, wine-makers started to use small oak for about a year to introduce the wood tannins which so enhance the flavour of the best French wines, they immediately began to confront a new range of problems. First, there was the cost. A grower who crushes 70 tonnes will be using about 120 hogsheads to mature his wine. These 65-gallon (300-litre) vessels cost, in 1983, about $400 each. Within the decade, this had trebled. Thus, there is a maturation cost directly attributable to the vessel of about 25 to 150 cents a litre (part of the variation coming from the decisions about how much of the wine is matured in oak and whether it must all be new each year) before one considers interest and other opportunity costs. Using small oak is very expensive.

There are other problems. Should the grower import the casks fully assembled, as is the case at Mount Mary in the Yarra Valley, or should they be reassembled in Australia from numbered imported pieces? Or should growers rely on Babidge or Schahinger, or some other Australian cooper? There are very few Australian coopers, most of them located in South Australia because that is where the industry has been largest for longest, but as Australian costs are so high it may be cheaper to import the barrels. Then, it may be that the oak which reaches Australia, like the cork, is not very good on the average. The best oak from France is used in Bordeaux, or Burgundy or Cognac, the best German oak on the Rhine or Moselle, and the American oak is regarded by most Australian wine-makers as too aggressive, with its strong vanilla-like phenols. (In fact, the best American oak goes to Spain to the sherry producers, so it too is not widely available.)

Small quantities of wine can be given very individual attention with the use of oak. A strange blend of equal quantities of Zinfandel, Pinot Noir and Cabernet Sauvignon, from a high-trellised, drip-irrigated experimental plot on a red-brown earth near Clare, is fermented at a low temperature, 20°C or so, in stainless steel, under a blanket of carbon dioxide, for about two weeks. Pressed in an air-bag press, a hogshead-full is taken off as free-run juice, after a little sulphur treatment. Left to itself, deep purple but quite bright, it loses a little of its acid in the malolactic fermentation. By now it has been moved to another winery, for bottling 65 gallons is hard in a big winery.

The wine-maker who is looking after it screws a huge corkscrew into the bung and bangs the collar up against the handpiece, lifting the bung out through the screen of paraffin wax. His eyes light up. 'Listen to that!' And one can hear the crackle of the ferment without putting ear to bung hole. 'Let's see, it's November now: we'll bottle it after vintage.'

They centrifuge and filter it first, and bottle the tiny quantity with hand-operated equipment. A light wine, rather unlike most Clare wines with surprisingly deep fruit on the palate, it needs a year or two in bottle for the small amount of oak tannins it has absorbed to integrate. The labour it has taken makes it impossible to reproduce.

Not all red wines receive or deserve such care, however.

When the consumption of red wines stopped increasing in the early 1970s, many makers who mainly sought to produce red wines tried various tricks to make red wines interchangeable with white. In essence, an Australian equivalent of Beaujolais was sought. It is worth describing one such exercise, called 'April Red', which was successful technically but not in the marketplace.

The name was chosen because it was to be a wine which could be sold six to eight weeks after vintage. The aim, in the words of T. C. Somers of the Australian Wine Research Institute, was to make light reds with 'bright clarity of colour with an impression of freshness and fruit flavour, and they must be "light in style" '. In his work on the effects of time on wine, Somers had noted that newly fermented red wines with very limited extraction showed these desirable characteristics, which are then lost in conservation. Thus, from a hot area, low alcohol and a pH in the range of 3.4–3.7 are possible because malic acid is still present. If the pH is higher, acid may be added at the crusher. To avoid phenolics, the wines could be taken off skins at 10–11° Baumé, during a cold fermentation with almost no sulphur dioxide. The wines would be promptly racked, and cold-stabilized and fined with bentonite under carbon dioxide or nitrogen blanketing for seven to ten days at −3°C. They could then be bottled with sterile filtration or hot bottled at 60°C.

The pigments in the resulting wines are rather different from those produced by traditional fermentation, and the wines were found to be very stable and fresh in character. However, without the market resources of a Philip Morris, these wines have not captured the public imagination simply on their merits; perhaps their merits were insufficient. Perhaps carbonic maceration will produce the right light dry red wines for drinking in copious quantities in hot weather. Perhaps the Gamay will provide them. Perhaps no one wants them, but this is hard to believe.

VITICULTURE

The grape vine grows vigorously for half the year, and as a true vine cannot support its own weight; it bears fruit on the canes, or new wood, which have grown since the previous winter's dormancy. For both of these reasons, the vine has always required training and pruning.

Left to itself, each bud on the old wood yields a cane with several bunches, so that an unpruned vine will produce large numbers of very small bunches. As each bunch must be removed with a separate cut of the picker's blade, picking time is roughly proportional to the number of bunches. Pruned hard, a vine will produce small numbers of large bunches. Hard pruning, therefore, is the norm. It is frequently stated that ripening is more certain and more even if there are few bunches, all located close to the main branches of the vine, but this may not be true in regions of superabundant sun.

Because a vine, like water, finds its own level, it needs support. It could be pruned as a bush, into a goblet shape, so that four or five arms rose half a metre above the ground and the new wood grew from a few buds left on a couple of spurs on each arm. This was the simplest, cheapest method; growth was contained, bunches were large, the fruit was kept off the ground. Alternatively, the vine could be trained up a post or along a wire. Because of the type of timber available and the prevalence of termites, wires tended to be supported by steel spacers at intervals with wooden strainer posts at the ends of the rows. Initially, such trellising raised the canopy of new growth hardly any higher than that on a bush vine, but it allowed more buds to be left, and more fruit to be supported, since the trellis took the weight. The best method of trellising for any particular variety in any particular area may take decades to determine, in the rare cases where viticulturists conduct experiments. In all states some research is being undertaken, but short-term economic decisions will greatly delay true matching of vines to land. With every cane requiring removal by a separate cut, the number of buds left one winter determines how many cuts will be needed the following winter.

In the vineyard it is dawn, but the sun is invisible, partly because of the low grey cloud coming in from the east, partly because the patch of brightness in the grey has yet to reach the dry-stone dike along the skyline. The pruner groans, rubs his eyes and rolls out of bed. He shrugs on an old boiler suit, pulls on an older army greatcoat and a scruffy knitted woollen cap. He makes tea and fries two eggs and, in ten minutes, unshaven, is hunched up at the end of a quarter of a mile of gnarled bushes, fifteen or twenty canes rising a yard from each one's five stumpy arms.

After half an hour his spare hand is blue with cold, and his nose, acting like a condenser, runs steadily. He has not yet brought out the old Ferguson to weed under the vines, so the Salvation Jane (*Echium*), soursob (*Oxalis pescaprae*) and dock which dominate the weeds along the rows have soaked the skirts of his greatcoat. He has to weed by hand a little at the base of every vine to check that there has been no shooting from the fifteen-year-old wood, and the red-brown earth is slowly transferring itself in larger quantities to his soaked sleeves.

Then the rain begins, and he curses and pulls his cap down closer over his eyes. Rain drips into them, and he cuts the fleshy part of his thumb just a little and curses again. The rain is still a light drizzle, but coming from the east it will get worse. He raises his eyes momentarily and looks across the valley to the light-grey gums above the vines. They merge into the gusting drizzle. He takes a bottle of raisin liqueur Muscat from the deep pocket of the greatcoat and swigs, a big mouthful. Then he bends to his task.

Another hour and the sodden greatcoat weighs a ton and there is a minor torrent down his spine, where the pleats open as he moves, and there is only one thickness of khaki felt. He sighs and plods on.

At noon he stops and stomps back to the house, hangs his coat over an electric heater and, as he heats some tomato soup, reflects that electricity prices have risen 50 per cent in a year. After donning dry clothes and a plastic raincoat with a rip under one arm, he plods out again, but the storm has arrived and he cannot prune where he cannot see a foot. The midweek movie is Ray Milland in *The Lost Weekend*, enlivened by crackles and flashes of lightning.

The storm passes, and as the sun disappears behind the trees on the far slope, the clear, pale-red sky suggests that he may make up time next day. As the moon rises behind the stone wall, he squelches back for a meal of fried lamb chops, potatoes and peas, and the news.

He is not a pioneer; he is a blocker. As J. K. Galbraith wrote:

A more commonplace consequence of an early exposure to agriculture is a deeply valid appreciation of manual labour. It leaves all of minimal sensitivity with an enduring knowledge of its unpleasantness. A long day following a plodding, increasingly reluctant team behind a harrow endlessly back and forth over the uninspiring Ontario terrain persuaded one that all other work was easy.

Yet pioneering was much harder. How hard is difficult to appreciate, almost impossible to experience. The first vineyards in Australia were planted on land cleared by convicts hired out to landowners, and few records exist of how they worked, but manual labour, rarely supported by animals, felled the trees, burnt the stumps, cut and sawed the logs, hoed and dug the unworked soil, collected the stones into heaps or built walls with them and planted and tended the vines.

When we think of the pioneers in New South Wales – Blaxland, Busby, Macarthur – we are thinking of the colonial elite; their land was worked by forced labour, nameless and unremarked. In the other colonies the pioneering vignerons worked their own land or paid free labourers, and they worked hard and thoughtfully, for there was no alternative.

The pruner, Australia's nearest equivalent to the peasant farmer, will go on working his own vines in this dismal fashion indefinitely. However, over the last fifteen years it has become more difficult for larger enterprises to hire satisfactory pruners, and much more expensive to pay them. For this reason, mechanical pruning has become widespread. Even in Bordeaux, of course, similar influences are at work, but a shortage of rural labour has been the norm in Australia for many years.

Mechanical pruning requires mechanical harvesting for best results, since so many more buds are left that hand harvesting would be hopelessly uneconomic.

As with any innovation in an industry where tradition is vitally important, the merits of mechanical pruning, or more properly machine-assisted pruning, have been fiercely argued. The machines used include hand-held cutter-bars, i.e. with reciprocating blades, circular saws, chain saws and band saws. Those with cutter-bars or band saws are much safer than circular saws and may be expected to dominate the industry, whether imported French machines or locally made ones.

Several different approaches to machine-assisted pruning have been made. In some irrigated areas it was initially introduced with no follow-up hand pruning, and the result was a dense tangled hedge of new and old wood, which after three years required extensive hand pruning. Since these early experiences it has been used more judiciously, the vines being first hedged with machines and then pruned by hand. In the irrigated river areas, where vines have massive trellises to support huge loads of fruit, as much as 90 per cent of the pruning can be done mechanically, whereas in dryland areas mechanical pruning is used by many growers simply as a preliminary to the handwork necessary to keep bud numbers adjusted to water availability, whether or not supplementary watering is used. Used in this way, mechanical pruning can reduce the cost of pruning by 30 to 50 per cent, including an allowance for depreciation of machinery. Such a major saving in costs means that mechanical pruning will certainly be a permanent feature of the wine-growing industry in Australia, but, as it requires mechanical harvesting, it will not be universal. This is partly because of the vexed question of wine quality, and partly because the economies of scale in mechanical harvesting are not the same as in mechanical pruning.

Both the CSIRO at Merbein on the Murray and some of the major growers, such as Penfold at Coonawarra, have carried out trials of wines made from fruit from mechanically pruned vines, and could not detect any differences. However, some of this lack of difference may relate to the fact that sensory evaluation of wines is not sufficiently sensitive to detect the small differences that may be occurring, so over a period there may be a consistent small advantage to hand-pruned as against mechanically pruned fruit.

Mechanical harvesting is a different question but, as noted, very closely related. If a contractor can be obtained, and the vineyard has been planned for mechanical harvesting, with long rows so that most of the contractor's time is spent harvesting and not manoeuvring, then as small an area as 1 hectare may be profitably harvested mechanically. More commonly, however, 4 hectares would be a minimum. Anyone who wishes to buy a machine should have at least 40 hectares of producing vines. This is where decisions about mechanical harvesting and mechanical pruning interact. There will also be extraneous factors, such as how easy it is to deliver mechanically harvested fruit, which, having been torn from the bunch by vibration, is even more unstable and likely to oxidize than fruit picked by hand. It is for this reason that most mechanical harvesting is carried out in the cool of the evening, and this too imposes constraints on its use. Crushers must be open at night, or else there must be field crushers available, together with gas blanketing for transport to the winery.

When mechanical harvesting was first introduced, most of the large companies carried out trials, comparing quality of wines made from mechanically harvested fruit and those from the traditional method. There is no general agreement about the effect on the best possible fruit, though most wine-makers seem slightly dubious, but for bulk wines it is unquestionably true that the fruit is of acceptable quality. There are, of course, advantages other than cost. Stems and leaves may be present in the harvested fruit to a much smaller extent, and if suitable arrangements are made to prevent the fruit oxidizing, then it will be received into the fermenters in better condition than fruit which has been picked during the hottest period of the day and trucked in the hot sun to the winery.

Provided that the soil is well drained and rain has not been excessive, so that the machines become bogged, both mechanical harvesting and pruning allow about half a hectare an hour to be covered. Thus, if yields are very high the overall saving may be very great, but shy-bearing vines in low-yielding country will not return such savings. Like all moves towards capital intensity, this mechanization carries its own risks, such as inability to use the machines after very heavy rain. The sight of the ungainly machines trapped like blowflies in gravy at Coonawarra in the wet 1983 vintage would put many off mechanical harvesting for ever.

Apart from exceptional cases like that just described, timing of harvest can be much more precise, given control of the equipment, so that this final advantage may be the critical one for a big company with a large area of vines in an area producing high-quality fruit. Not having to co-ordinate a large team of pickers in a relatively remote location allows a vineyard manager to make more precise decisions under less stress and uncertainty. In Burgundy, the house of Prosper Maufoux now uses mechanical harvesting wherever possible and after two years' trial identified a further advantage, though not one which is hoped for or expected every year. If early rain has caused bunch rot, but there has been a dry period before vintage, the rotten berries will have dried and shrivelled on to their stalks, so that only the sound berries are shaken off.

Fungal diseases may more generally be controlled by mechanization. It is possible to spray from the air precisely when the weather and vines require it. For some of the more humid regions, frequent spraying with heavy metal or sulphur compounds may cause oenological problems, but these are soluble in principle.

Phylloxera has a different cause, but one which is also preventable. It is the worst insect pest of grapes and vines. A root louse, it used to be called *Phylloxera vastatrix*, a much more descriptive name than its present correct name: *Daktulosphaira vitifoliae*. (It was for a time called *Phylloxera vitifoliae*, taxonomists enjoying little games.) As is well known, it is a native of North America, confined to the area east of the Rocky Mountains where it exists in small numbers on the various North American relations of *Vitis vinifera*, such as *V. riparia, V. rupestris* and *V. labrusca.*

Examples were brought to Europe for scientific investigation in about 1860 but, whether from these or as illegal immigrants on American vines brought to Europe, the insect was first noticed just north of Avignon on *V. vinifera* in 1865. By 1872 it was found from the west of Montpellier to north of Valence to south-east of Marseille. By 1880 virtually every important vignoble was affected.

The devastation of this very important industry was such that an extraordinary variety of remedies was tried, but by the late 1870s various French scientists had suggested grafting *V. vinifera* on to North American rootstocks such as *V. riparia* and *V. rupestris*, which were resistant to the root louse. (The study of grafting has reached a fine art, or indeed science, in France, but Australia has luckily so far been spared the necessity of mastering that art.)

It was about the same time that phylloxera was first reported in Australia, near Geelong. Soon afterwards it was found near Melbourne, then in central and north-eastern Victoria, reaching Sydney by 1900, where the Minchinbury champagne vineyards were devastated, as were those around Albury and Corowa on the Murray. The movement of the louse was not systematic, following as it did human error, but it seemed inexorable. Nevertheless South Australia seemed to remain invulnerable.

Grafted vines were very expensive and, since South Australia had already come to dominate wine production, in many areas wine-growing was simply abandoned. Around Rutherglen, in north-eastern Victoria, resistant rootstocks were used quite extensively, but half a century after the first discovery of phylloxera at Rutherglen the area under vines was still not back to what it had been in 1899.

The virtual abandonment of Geelong and Bendigo as wine-growing districts between 1900 and the mid 1920s probably reflects the economic difficulties which growers had as much as the problems of phylloxera. These areas have been re-established on the basis of small production of very high-quality wine, so that they do not compete with the *vins ordinaires* produced on an enormous scale by the national marketing companies.

None of this means that the problem of phylloxera has been solved. It still lurks near Sydney, in the Goulburn Valley, and further east in Victoria. Where the wine industry was kept going with resistant rootstocks, phylloxera was able to survive on the roots and not be a problem. It is thus waiting to devastate large plantings of vines on their own roots, or even on hybrid roots, for there is evidence that in California over the period 1983–89 the resistant rootstock AXR-1 has become susceptible. Phylloxera is a particular problem on heavy clay soils that crack, and there is much clay soil along the Goulburn River. Some of the vineyards there have suffered very severe losses recently, since young vines can become almost totally unproductive after only three or four years of infestation.

Phylloxera has not moved much in the last eighty years. In fact, it has never reached South Australia or Western Australia, though it was found in Queensland late last century. Just why it did not get to South Australia is uncertain. Interstate plant quarantine was introduced very early, and continues to the present day, but there are always irresponsible people who feel that they know better than legislators, so that it cannot simply be the result of plant quarantine. There are also considerable areas of vines on their own roots in heavy clay soils in South Australia. Whatever the reason, it has contributed to South Australia's dominance of the wine industry, at least as regards quantity, for approximately a century.

EDUCATION FOR WINE-MAKING

At the time of the establishment of Roseworthy Agricultural College (1883), the free colony of South Australia had been in existence for only forty-seven years, and the University of Adelaide was only nine years old, yet in many ways the Agricultural College should have come first. South Australia had been the granary of Australia, on account of the good yields of wheat obtainable on the plains to the north of Adelaide, during the period of rapid population growth which followed the discovery of gold in the eastern states. However, yields of wheat had started to drop dramatically by the early 1870s, and other agricultural problems had also become evident.

The early directors of Roseworthy had a very difficult time, through being both principal of the College and having to teach agriculture, but the fourth principal, A. J. Perkins, was appointed to Roseworthy as government viticulturalist in 1892 and had had twelve years' South Australian experience before he became principal in 1904. A graduate of Montpellier in France, he introduced studies in viticulture and oenology soon after his appointment and established the College's wine cellars in the late 1890s. In fact the dux of the course in 1896 was Leo Buring, a man who had a profound influence on the Australian wine industry until his death in 1962.

Thus, scientific investigation of problems in oenology and viticulture had begun well before Australia became an independent nation, but it was not until the early 1930s that general agreement arose within the wine industry that a special course, adapted to the needs of Australia, should be mounted at one of the universities or agricultural colleges. Initially there was no agreement as to the site of the course, some saying that it should be within the University of Adelaide, others that it should be somewhere along the River

Murray since this was where the most profitable grape-growing was at the time. Luckily, A. R. Callaghan, the College principal, was an extremely vigorous and persuasive advocate for Roseworthy Agricultural College, and in November 1935 the South Australian Winemakers' Association sent a resolution to the Minister of Agriculture urging the establishment of a course at Roseworthy.

The minister accepted this urging because of both the strength of the support and the names of the supporters. Ron Martin of Stonyfell, Les Salter of Saltram, Oscar Seppelt, Thomas Hardy, Carl Angove, W. Smith, Sam Tolley, Ron Haselgrove, Karl Wiedenhofer were among the supporters, and many of them were old students of the College, holders of the Diploma in Agriculture. Quite apart from the political backing, Martin offered a prize for wine-tasting, Leo Buring offered one for the dux of the second year, and the Buring family bestowed a travelling scholarship in memory of one of their number.

It is of some interest that, just about the time that the Roseworthy course was being initiated, Herbert Kay, chairman of the Wine Board, was writing to the Registrar, University of California, Berkeley:

Dear Sir,

I have two sons aged 20 and 22 who are employed in my own wine-making business. They have good knowledge of the practical side of vine-growing and wine-making and they are anxious to have an opportunity of learning something of the scientific side of wine-making.

There is no oenological college in Australia, but I understand that there is one at your University. If this is so would you be kind enough to let me know

1. Can students take up a brief course in wine science – not to gain any degree or diploma but just to acquire knowledge?
    If so, how long would such a course take?
2. What would be the approximate cost of such a course?
3. What would be the approximate cost of living for students?

If my information is wrong and the oenological college is not connected with your University would you be kind enough to send this letter to the college which has such a course. Thanking you in anticipation.

Yours faithfully,
Herbert Kay

Half a century later, Herbert's son, who did not go to Berkeley or even Davis, was surprised to learn of this letter, but meanwhile Herbert's grandson had been dux of the oenology course at Rose-worthy.

When the course was established, teaching was carried out partly by two men bearing names notable in the industry then, and to some extent now. Hickinbotham, father and grandfather of the Hickinbothams now at Dromana in Victoria, was one, and John Fornachon, first director of the Australian Wine Research Institute, was the other. A Burge and a Kelly were among the first four students, a Chaffey and a Seppelt in the second intake (though that particular Seppelt was killed in the Second World War and so is not one of the many Seppelts still in the firm). Wine families have continued to support the College, although not always in the happiest circumstances. For example, when Hugo Gramp, Thomas Hardy and Sidney Hill Smith were killed in 1938 in an air crash on the way to a conference in Canberra, another award was established. More recently, as the College has entered its second century, firms such as Penfold, though no longer family firms, have continued to make substantial donations to support the College.

Some viticultural and related training was provided at Dookie in Victoria for many years, and horticultural research and education are carried out at the Universities of Adelaide and Sydney. The major recent change has been the introduction of strong wine-making courses at the Riverina College of Advanced Education at Wagga Wagga in New South Wales.

This College opened its doors in 1971 but rapidly came to serve both the Murrumbidgee and Murray irrigation areas, with 'study centres' at Griffith on the Murrumbidgee River and Albury-Wodonga on the Murray. At that time the wine industry was expanding strongly and technical innovation was widespread, so that local businessmen involved in the wine industry saw the need for local education in oenology and viticulture. One of these was R. A. Potter, who was engaged in improving wine-making technology at Griffith and who was also on the council of the new College.

As the wine industry grew, Roseworthy was slow to expand its well-established courses, so that pressure for a second centre of wine-making education increased rapidly, especially outside South Australia. This had to be different from Roseworthy, of course, so it was decided at Wagga that they should capitalize on their developing expertise in external studies and in management and applied science. Thus it was from the first planned that students could take their degrees while working full time in the wine industry. A lower-level course in viticulture was later established, in recognition of the lack of basic training in this vital area, and it too was aimed at external students.

The initial success of this new wine school was due partly to the need for more trained people in an expanding industry, but was also attributable to the enthusiasm for and involvement in the wine industry of people such as Brian Croser, Tony Jordan, Max Loder and Don Lester, some of whom I shall be referring to again in subsequent chapters. And the fact that the course could be taken over a number of years while working full time (with occasional residential interludes at the College) meant that even from South Australia, relatively well served for research and training, wine-makers would enrol for the external degree. This particularly helps the proprietors of small wineries like Wendouree at Clare in South Australia, one of whom recently finished this degree.

Thus, just like Roseworthy, Wagga has benefited from the fact that the leaders of the wine industry, unlike the leaders of many Australian industries, recognize the importance of scientific and technological innovation in their trade. It is to be hoped that the absorption of Roseworthy into the University of Adelaide – a shotgun wedding with Federal Government accountants' fingers on the triggers – does not cause long-term harm to the technical progress of the industry, for a university's remit has in Australia historically been usefully distinguished from that of an agricultural college.

3

South Australia

South Australia was established by proclamation on 28 December 1836 in the name of His Majesty King William IV, who died soon afterwards, so apart from the first settlers from HMS *Buffalo*, the colonists were early Victorians. Not far from the spot where the colony was proclaimed, near Glenelg, 7 miles from the centre of the city of Adelaide as it now is, Richard Hamilton established Ewell Vineyards before 1840. He was a wanderer, from Ewell in Surrey (though from a Scottish family), and had spent some time in New York before applying for land in the new colony of South Australia before his arrival.

There is some controversy about whether Richard Hamilton or John Reynell first planted vines, but certainly Hamilton arrived first, in October 1837, and took up land in June 1838, whereas John Reynell arrived in October 1838 and took up land in July 1839. However, this land had been taken up first by Thomas Lucas, and John Reynell married Mary Lucas soon after he arrived in Adelaide, so he could possibly have been in a position to plant vines as soon as he had land.

In the 'Paradise of Dissent', as Douglas Pike, Methodist moderator and first editor of the *Australian Dictionary of Biography*, called the free colony of South Australia, the way of the wine-maker was hard. When Walter Duffield sent a case of white wine to Queen Victoria in 1845 and was rewarded with a medal from Prince Albert, magistrates at Mount Barker in the Adelaide Hills fined him £10 for making wine without a licence. The Distillation Ordinance, under which such licences were issued, was very complex. For example, the building in which a still was housed had to be of stone with the stones laid to a particular pattern, all tubs and pails had to be numbered and the door had to have two sets of locks and keys, one

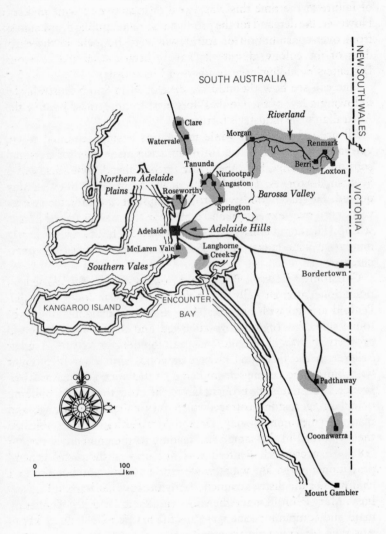

Wine-growing regions of South Australia

for the distiller, one for the government agent. Since a licence cost £50 and was necessary for a wine-maker, given the high frequency of failure at the time this was a real disincentive to wine-makers. However, the demand for the product was there; public drunkenness from over-consumption of spirits was very frequent in the early days of the colony, despite its having been established by pious Dissenters including large numbers of Methodists.

One can see how the industry developed in South Australia by following a few of the families' fortunes. In time, these became the Australian wine industry's fortunes.

All around Adelaide, while it grew as a small colonial town, vineyards were established. In many cases wine was for personal consumption only, but others saw further ahead. One such was a Scottish doctor, A. C. Kelly, from whose works I have already quoted. He made good wine to the south of Adelaide for twenty years until over-expansion and a break in the market forced him to sell up. The commercial acumen of Thomas Hardy, another early immigrant wine-maker, allowed the vineyards to persist and prosper, however.

Christopher Rawson Penfold was probably the second medical practitioner after Dr Kelly to establish a vineyard in South Australia. Penfold arrived with his wife Mary and baby daughter in a 350-tonne ship, the *Taglioni*, in late 1844 and took up a substantial property at Magill, 4 miles due east of the city centre. A great believer in the medicinal powers of good wine, Penfold brought with him grape cuttings from some of the notable wine areas of France. In particular he brought Grenache, from the Rhône. Building or enlarging a stone cottage which they called The Grange and planting vines immediately, Dr and Mrs Penfold also established their vineyard in the same year, leading to the company's slogan: '1844 to evermore'. Penfold was not only a successful general practitioner and a fine wine-grower and businessman, but also first chairman of the district council. Partly because her husband was so busy, Mary Penfold made the wine with the aid of Ellen Timberall, maid and companion. She was thus the first female wine-maker in Australia, a fact not always noted.

Despite the medicinal powers of wine, Penfold died at the age of fifty-nine in 1870 and was succeeded in managing the firm by his wife and his son-in-law, T. F. Hyland. Within ten years of his death the firm had 24 hectares planted in vines, mainly Mataro, Grenache,

Pedro Ximenez and Tokay, and were buying over 200 tonnes of grapes from other growers. The vintage cellar was approximately 20 metres square, the storage cellar rather larger. When Mary Penfold died in 1892, Penfold was one of the largest wineries in Australia.

The Grange Cottage, from which the most remarkable of the Penfold wines takes its name, was almost demolished soon after the Second World War, but was restored as a result of protestations by some members of the family, and opened for a time as a museum in 1949. It is no longer open to the public.

There were still over 100 hectares of vines at Magill at that time, and vintage went on until 1972, when all operations were transferred to Nuriootpa. When Tooth & Co., the Sydney brewer, took over Penfold in the early 1970s, the Auldana vineyard, which had been bought in 1942 from a receiver, was subdivided for 'building blocks', as small areas of land are called in Australia. Most of the Grange Vineyard itself has now gone the same way.

The Swan Valley wine-maker Houghton is making very good wines from a large vineyard of John Roche's in south-western Western Australia. It therefore seems a little odd that the reduction of the Grange Vineyard at Magill from a 35-hectare vineyard, together with the winery buildings and the Grange Cottage itself, to a 10-hectare fragment surrounding the buildings, a development which 'released' 169 building lots, should have been carried out partly by Roche, also a former Lord Mayor of Adelaide. The buildings are on the Register of State Heritage Items, but the vines and the land beneath them were not.

When N. S. Khrushchev made his famous secret speech to the twentieth party congress of the USSR in 1956, he attempted to end the cult of Stalin's personality. He did not fail completely, but in any case there was a recrudescence of the phenomenon in the last years of L. I. Brezhnev. Perhaps a personality cult is unnecessary in a long-established society where the system of government is taken for granted. The Australian wine industry is not yet in this happy state, where the vignerons know what to do in any given circumstance and wine buyers never know their names. The architects of the great cathedrals of medieval Europe are unknown, as (to all but a very few historians) are the great wine-makers who developed Claret, Burgundy, Hock, Sauternes, Champagne, sherry, port and all the others as we know them today.

In Australia, as the struggle to come to terms with a constantly changing market and a hostile climate continues, the wine-maker is a prince at least. Fortunately, because wine is such a civilizing and moderating influence, wine people, even those inflated to three or four times their original size by the press, remain relatively tolerable. Max Schubert is a man resistant to the pressures of publicity. He had to work hard for his success.

His career illustrates much of the history of the wine industry over the half-century that he has been with Penfold, but some aspects of it could have been possible only within a family firm, and a rather old-fashioned one at that. When he joined Penfold, diseased wines were everywhere, and the problem was to keep them drinkable for at least three months, so that they could be sold. I have discussed these problems in the preceding chapter.

Lesley Penfold Hyland gave Schubert his start, sending him to the School of Mines, as it then was, to learn chemistry. After the Second World War he was promoted from laboratory attendant to wine-maker, and visited France in 1949–50. Returning, and given some authority, he was able to make important changes. In viticulture he ripped out the Grenache at the Grange Vineyard itself and, in replanting there and elsewhere, changed the spacing to make the vines work harder. He began experimenting, inspired by what he had seen in Bordeaux. He wanted to use oak in the way the Bordeaux wine-makers use it, to add additional flavour and complexity in the most effective way, with small barrels of new wood no larger than 300 litres, to allow increased area of contact with the timber and hence greater extraction of tannins from the wood.

Although Schubert aimed to make the best red wine in Australia, so that he was expressing his skills as a wine-maker, he also wanted the wine to be sold in relatively large quantities. The target was about 5,000 cases, hardly a third of Château Latour's, but this has been reached only in the best years, with very poor years allowing less than half as much to be made.

In 1952 Kalimna in the Barossa was Penfold's only source of Cabernet Sauvignon, and they could not persuade their contracted growers to plant it. They therefore had to use Shiraz, until then regarded largely as a reliable port variety. They had a number of individual vineyards growing Shiraz with particular reliable characteristics, and Schubert aimed to combine these characteristics. The vineyards included one at Morphett Vale, now covered with housing, others at Coonawarra, Clare, Kalimna and Eden Valley, and of course The Grange itself.

The technique was used to bring the various lots of fruit in, crush them, run the juice off skins, cool in a heat exchanger, and then put the skins back. There had to be a little oxidation, to develop complexity and flavour; totally protecting red fruit from oxidation could lead to instability later. Some sugar should remain when extraction had finished, then the wine would be put into new wood, where the malolactic fermentation would occur. During the development of 'Grange Hermitage', and indeed in all of Penfold's red wine-making, stuck fermentation was not a problem. Initially fermentation would be at 15°C, then rising to 18–20°C, perhaps 18–22° at the end of fermentation. The juice would be left on skins for a week.

While some fruit from Magill has always gone into 'Grange Hermitage', it has gone into other wines as well, 'St Henri' and 'Bin 389' in particular, these two having been (with Grange) Penfold's top three wines, as Magill fruit has always allowed really deep fruit flavour to develop. Initially, 40 to 50 per cent of 'Grange Hermitage' was from Magill. At recent tastings, the second commercial release (1953) has seemed the best, 1963, 1952, 1955 and 1956 following in roughly that order. However, Schubert himself believes that the 1971 and 1976 will, when they are sufficiently old, equal the 1953. From 1983, generally in South Australia an appalling vintage, came the biggest Grange to be recently released. Schubert made the wines to be enormous at first, so that as they aged they would become more elegant, never seeming overweight and always staying alive. In addition to their vast depth of fruit, Schubert has always aimed at achieving absolute balance early on, since he believes that a wine with a fault will stay a faulty wine for ever. Totally different from the much lighter, subtle yet earthy Shiraz wines of the Hunter, or the huge, fruity examples from north-eastern Victoria, 'Grange Hermitage' is a unique and outstanding Australian wine. The Magill Estate wine, made since 1983 from Grange vineyard fruit, Schubert has called, in contrast to the Grange, 'a very feminine wine' (*Australian Financial Review*, 20 September 1985).

In 1909 the metropolitan vineyards of Adelaide were almost 1,000 hectares in extent, from 50 hectares for each of Penfold and Auldana at Magill and Hamilton's 30 at Glenelg to vineyards of less than half a hectare at east Adelaide, almost in the city. Almost all of this has now disappeared; the map gives an indication of the remaining wineries. And there were vineyards in towns such as Maitland, Kapunda, Stansbury, Curramulka and Rhynie where none now survives.

In Australia the years of the First World War were begun by a devastating drought, one of the worst on record at the time, and indeed remaining so. Herbert Kay of Amery in South Australia's Southern Vales wrote to his brother in January 1914: 'My dear Fred, Many thanks for yours of 14 December. Things here are looking very dicky for the vintage, no rain, currants will be a poor crop, wine grapes mostly skin and seeds.' On 5 February he wrote again: 'I start vintage Wednesday 11th February and look forward to a very light one. The Mataro may save the situation but the Shiraz and Cabernet are shocking. Currants will be much lighter crop than last year.' A few days later he was writing again to Fred.

I was much interested in your account of the interview with Burgoyne [a wine shipper]. I hope they will treat us better in future but have no great faith though I do think both Cuthbert and Burney [staff of Burgoyne's] are fairer than the others we have dealt with.

I have sent away the 150 hogsheads to go per *Homeric* and have cancelled the other two shipments – I had to do it to secure hogsheads for the *Homeric*. I am very glad I have done it as the vintage is very early and my hands are full. We start currants tomorrow. Nine pickers are here. I expect two more tomorrow and three on Monday. If they turn up we shall be full handed, which is well and we must hurry if we are to save the Shiraz and Cabernet. The vines look awful, yellow everywhere except in the gullies. I tried Kell's grapes yesterday, nine and a half and beginning to shrivel, I told them to start picking on Monday, the density will be low but there will be some juice in them, of course if rain comes all will be altered but at present it looks bad.

Yields were indeed down: from about 35 tonnes of Cabernet Sauvignon to about 21 tonnes, the vintage starting half-way through February, so that one finds an entry: 'picking suspended until Monday owing to heat'.

For other wineries the war was also a time of change. At Hamilton's the two young brothers Eric and Robert took over a company run down during the war years. It is said that over 1,000 gallons

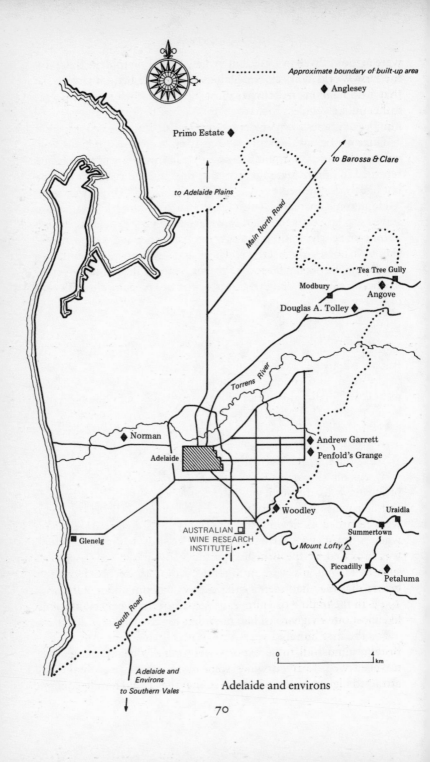

to Barossa & Clare

Anglesey

Primo Estate

to Adelaide Plains

Tea Tree Gully

Modbury

Angove

Douglas A. Tolley

Torrens River

Norman

Andrew Garrett

Penfold's Grange

Adelaide

Woodley

Uraidla

Summertown

AUSTRALIAN
WINE RESEARCH
INSTITUTE

Mount Lofty

Glenelg

Piccadilly

Petaluma

South Road

Approximate boundary of built-up area

0   4
         km

Adelaide and environs

Adelaide and
Environs
to Southern Vales

70

were made at Ewell in 1840, but Sydney Hamilton told me that until the First World War, 18,000 gallons formed the biggest vintage, so that 1,000 gallons from what must have been the first crop seems rather unlikely, unless Richard Hamilton had bought in a substantial number of grapes from unidentified growers.

Three of Richard Hamilton's sons went to Victoria, seeking gold in the gold rush, but found it better to sell provisions to miners and returned to South Australia in due course, their fortunes not made but hardly diminished.

Hamilton's increased substantially in size about 1860, but it stayed a relatively small family winery for many years. Mechanization came early, in the form of what was called a 'horse works' – simply a horse-driven crown wheel and pinion which worked a crusher, labour being far too scarce for treading the grapes, whether by the white feet of laughing girls or the heavy leather thigh boots of Surrey yeomen.

Many remarkable techniques were tried out in the early stages. For example, from a runaway French sailor in the 1870s Hamilton learned how to make a wine resembling the *vin de paille* of the Rhône, where the Grenache and Carignan grapes were laid on straw to dry them and concentrate the juice before crushing. With this technique, smaller quantities of stronger wine could be made, and better control could be exerted, for runaway fermentation was the norm in the hot Adelaide autumn, and huge quantities of spirit were used to stop the ferment. Hamilton's last vintage of this kind was in 1920, about the time a distillery was built.

By this time most of the wines were fortified, both because of the problems with the fermentation mentioned already and because fortified wines were what the market demanded. Beverage wines were regarded as fit only for weaklings. This at least meant that when a lower wine tariff, an effective subsidy to Imperial wines, was provided by the British government in about 1925, wineries such as Hamilton's were in a good position to export. However, before that they had seen a brief post-war boom and a collapse in 1923. In the middle of vintage, in March of that year, Hamilton's, like most other vignerons, had no orders for any wines.

For the first hundred years of export of wine from Australia to Britain, almost all these exports were table wine. Although they travelled well, fortified wines were more expensive to make and attracted higher duties in Britain, so that they could hardly compete with Portugal or Spain. The treaty between Britain and Portugal in 1916, which prevented the use of the words 'port' and 'Madeira' to describe wines not from Oporto or Madeira, was also a great handicap. It was very easy to sneer at a wine labelled 'port type', and to assume that it was a poor imitation. It is no doubt partly for this reason that the inappropriate European names continue to be used throughout Australia, handicapping the development of meaningful regional names as well as inviting complaints from wine writers and European wine-makers.

After the war the Federal Government, through the state government, set up returned servicemen on small farms in many different areas, to aid the policy of closer settlement as well as to rehabilitate the demobilized soldiers. Some took up dairying, others wheat-growing, still others grape-growing, especially in the new irrigation areas along the River Murray. In 1924 the Australian government, noticing that soldier–settlers' blocks were producing a great deal of fruit suitable for fortified wine, introduced an export bounty. This itself was an incentive to export, but when the Empire Preferential Tariff gave its 50 per cent difference in excise for ten years, the possibility of dramatic increases in sales was soon realized. Later the bounty was reduced, in a number of stages, but by then this new Empire trade was well established.

This was despite problems such as that caused by giving six months' notice of intention to reduce the bounty in 1927, an announcement which was followed by wild hunting for cargo space on ships and storage space in London. Imports into England in fact rose from less than 9 million litres in 1926 to 20 million litres in 1927. Apart from creating an over-supply, these shipments did nothing to enhance the reputation of Australian wine for they were not properly treated in bond, and much bad wine was sold. It was, in fact, at about this time that the Australian Wine Board was created, in 1930, and soon afterwards, under the leadership of Herbert Kay, it was arranging for bacterial spoilage to be investigated, as was discussed in the last chapter.

This time of over-supply of poorly cared for wines is described indirectly in *Casanova's Chinese Restaurant*, where the narrator describes how he 'had bought the bottle labelled Tawny Wine (Port flavour) which even Moreland had been later unwilling to drink . . . Following a preliminary tasting, we poured the residue of the bottle down the lavatory.'

During this period when the Australian wine industry was as usual struggling to find an identity and, more important, struggling with the problems of excessive shipments on consignment, a federal viticultural congress was held at Leonay, Emu Plains, near Sydney in New South Wales, and on Friday 4 October 1929 an Al Fresco Luncheon and International Wine Sampling was conducted. The location was symptomatic of an industry not controlling its own destiny; the centre of the industry was Adelaide, far from where important financial decisions were taken. The menu was heroic: 'brandied prunes, salt herrings, hot dogs, mustard dressing (kindly donated by the SPCA and mustard club), sliced fowl – ham – bully beef, Leonay asparagus, sauce vinaigrette (latter item provided by the United Vinegarons of Australia), cheese and salads, dessert, café'. The wine list was even more remarkable: 'Sherry, Hock, Chablis, Sauterne, Claret, Burgundy, Port and dessert wines and some Vin Ordinaire (presented by some ten more or less wine-growing countries of this universe), no restrictions on quantity'.

The Hocks included H. Buring and Sobels Ltd Springvale Riesling 1923, Lindeman Cawarra 1924, Eltviller Taubenburg Rhein 1919, and De Pury Victoria. Among the Burgundies were Burgoyne's 'sent on transport to England during war and subsequently returned' (Victoria), Gevrey Chambertin (France, 1920) and Lindeman 'bottled in Scotland' 1923.

The industry's ability to co-operate was at its best on such occasions.

The 1930s were quite prosperous for the Australian wine industry – what was left of it after the depredations of phylloxera and the hard market times of the Edwardian period and the war – but the Second World War once more damaged it substantially when from 1941 to 1944 virtually no Australian wine at all was shipped to Britain.

When wine was once more re-exported to Britain after the war, it was only 40 per cent of the 1939 level, which had been about 18,000 tonnes. Imperial Preference ensured some Australian exports, particularly of fortified wine, until Britain entered the European Economic Community.

THE BAROSSA VALLEY

The Barossa Valley takes its name from Colonel William Light's participation in the Peninsular War; the mis-spelling no doubt arose because signposts and maps were not being prepared in large numbers by the time Light died, and few of the settlers were familiar with the Iberian Peninsula. Light was the first surveyor-general of the new colony. His old commander and patron, Lord Lyndoch, is commemorated in the name of one of the towns in the Barossa Valley.

The fact that the Barossa was settled very largely by Germans came about in a very curious way.

George Fife Angas, a rich and successful Scottish businessman and landowner who was very active in promoting the South Australian colony in London, saw it as providing 'a place of refuge for pious Dissenters of Great Britain, who could in their new home discharge their consciences before God in civil and religious duties without any disabilities . . . a place where the children of pious farmers might have farms on which to settle and provide bread for their families'. However, the largest single group of 'pious Dissenters' that Angas bought to South Australia consisted of Lutherans, led by Pastor Kavel, who were leaving religious persecution in Prussia following the establishment of the national church there. A Particular Baptist, Angas had to grapple with his conscience before deciding whether to aid Lutherans, but in the event the combination of the opportunities to promote the Colony by bringing out more immigrants and to aid Dissenters was sufficient to sway him. The first group arrived in November 1838, and by the end of 1847 over 2,500 had arrived.

Angas lent them a considerable amount of money, partly so that they could buy 2,000 acres at £10 per acre in the hills which were the sources of the Gawler and Rhine Rivers. (Like many other German place names, this Rhine changed its name and became the Para River at a time of anti-German feeling.)

After the 1848 revolution, the influx of immigrants from Germany increased greatly, in fact more than trebling over the next decade, so that when the colony was twenty years old over 7 per cent of the population were German immigrants. While a considerable number of the Germans were farmers, many were more familiar with mining than with wine and worked alongside Cornishmen in the copper

Penfold's Kalimna ◆

Blass's Bilyara ◆

Greenock ■   Tollana

Daveyston ■   North   Para River

Tarac   Nuriootpa ◆ **1**

Gnadenfrei ◆   **2** ◆

Seppeltsfield ◆   Marananga ■   **2** ◆

Douglas A. Tolley   Dorrien   Saltram ◆

1 ◆   Angaston ■

Peter Lehman   Hardy ◆

4 ◆ **3** ◆   Yalumba ◆

Veritas ◆   **5**

Basedow ◆

Tanunda   **6**   Menglers Hill △

Bethany   Tanunda Creek

Gomersal ■   High Wycombe   **1** Elderton

St Hallet   **2** Penfold-Kaiserstuhl

Château   Rockford ◆   **3** Hoffman's North
Rosevale   Krondorf ◆   Para

4 Bernkastel

Chatterton ◆   **5** Leo Buring

Château   Rowland Flat   **6** Château Tanunda
Yaldara ◆   Karlsburg ◆   Orlando ◆   **7** Charles Melton

Karawirra   Liebich's
Wilsford ◆   Rovalley   Jacobs Creek

The Red Gum ◆

Sandy   Altona
Creek   Lyndoch ■   Pewsey Vale ■

Barossa   **1** ◆
Settlers ■

Adelaide 50 km

0   4
km

Barossa Valley

75

mines of Burra and Kapunda. None the less, the community they created is notable because in it developed Australia's largest single wine-growing region.

Although the Barossa Valley was peopled largely by Germans, they were not from wine-growing localities so it was a very long time before the promise of the higher areas for making good-quality Riesling became evident. Perhaps also the fact that railway workers wore heavy jackets and hats to work in the middle of summer and did not expect anything to be refrigerated, since the means had not been invented, also meant that robust red or fortified wines in fact suited the climate better, whatever their effects on the head. However, soon after the First World War wine-makers such as Rudy Kronberger, an Austrian at Yalumba, and Sydney Hamilton, an Australian at Hamilton's, began to try to make light, relatively dry white wines, feeling that a market for such wines must exist if they could only be made successfully. Yalumba 'Carte D'Or' and Hamilton's 'Ewell Moselle' were the results. For fifty years Yalumba's 'Carte D'Or' Riesling has had a considerable amount of Eden Valley Riesling in it, though the earlier ones, like Hamilton's 'Ewell Moselle', would have had many sherry varieties as their base. These have been reliable wines, blended to a standard for about sixty years, and one feels that they will go on in this way indefinitely, gradually becoming relatively more and more inexpensive compared with the current market favourites. It is in the area of making very reliable wines up to a quality and down to a price that the big Australian wine-makers excel.

Yalumba is one of the three big wine companies still in family hands, the other two being Hardy and McWilliam. However, Yalumba is rather different. It was founded by Samuel Smith, a Dorsetshire brewer, who arrived in Adelaide in 1847, settling first at Klemzig, a German colony near the city of Adelaide. Soon, however, Smith needed to move further afield to establish himself, and he took a job with George Fife Angas 80 kilometres north-east, near what is now Angaston.

Having bought 12 hectares to establish a vineyard, Smith began to develop it at night while working for Angas during the day. It was not, however, that first small vineyard which established his fortune but rather the £300 worth of gold which he got at the diggings in Victoria in the early 1850s. This allowed him to expand the vineyard and build his first winery. Within a decade his wine was starting to sell well, as it has ever since.

The facade of the cellars is an imposing bluestone structure, two storeys high with a large clock tower. It was built in the late nineteenth century, when Samuel Smith's son and grandsons expanded the business. When the grandsons retired, two great-grandsons took over, now with the surname Hill Smith, the Hill coming from the family connection to the same Hills who had produced one of Australia's finest left-handed batsmen, Clem Hill, in the era before the First World War. There are now members of the sixth generation of the family working at Yalumba.

What has distinguished Yalumba from the other family dynasties is that it has kept one base at Angaston, even though it has about 200 hectares of vines on the Murray as well as about the same area in the Barossa. Thus, all its wine-making activities from crushing to bottling and storage are under one series of roofs.

Yalumba has always been successful in blending to a quality, whether in its 'Galway Pipe' port, its 'Galway Vintage' Claret or its 'Carte D'Or' Riesling. The Claret, a blend of Cabernet Sauvignon from Oxford Landing on the Murray, Shiraz from the higher areas around the Barossa Valley and minor quantities of other varieties from the Barossa, is distinguished by the fact that a particular bottling of the 1961 vintage was described in 1966 by the then prime minister, the late Sir Robert Menzies, as the best Australian Claret he had ever tasted. Politicians' jokes tend always to be at other people's expense; few who subsequently bought or tasted the wine concurred with his judgement, though it was indeed a fair wine which lasted well.

In recent years the best parts of Yalumba's 20,000-tonne crush have gone into special bottlings of reds with various family members' and others' signatures on them, and into their Pewsey Vale Riesling and other wines made from a vineyard in the cooler Barossa Hills about 500 metres above sea level. The signatures have included that of a notable racehorse trainer, for the Hill Smiths have strong connections with the racing world. The skill of the makers, and the large range of material from which they choose, was evident in 1974 when Christabel Hill Smith's blend of Shiraz and Cabernet Sauvignon was made. Unlike most wines from that poor year, it had clean, elegant fruit in plenty, and a softness which made it attractive early. Later, better years have produced better, longer-living blends, but not so much better than their fellows with lesser labels. They typify what the Barossa should make.

The sparkling wines, from the widely discounted 'Angas Brut' to the top-label 'Yalumba D', have benefited from the now discontinued association with Champagnes Deutz. 'D' has considerable evidence of lengthy yeast contact, rare in Australian bubbly.

Seppeltsfield is, like Yalumba, a family monument as well as the centre of a large wine empire. In Seppelt's case this embraces other vineyards (and, formerly, Château Tanunda nearby) in the Barossa and vineyards or wineries at Qualco on the Murray and Clare in South Australia, at Great Western and Drumborg in Victoria, and at Barooga in New South Wales.

The huge storage sheds for fortified wines and the old houses, distillery and winery buildings are flanked on one side by enormous car parks for the vast numbers of tourists who congregate at weekends, and on the other by the creek into which winery wastes went a century ago. Well maintained and painted in the Seppelts' tasteful green and fawn, the village has a slightly melancholy air, a hint of Fatepur Sikri at times, because it is no longer inhabited by the vast numbers of workers which the vineyard and winery required when Benno Seppelt was building them up. At vintage time, of course, it feels different, and the only peaceful spot is at the top of the nearby hill. Here stands the eclectically Greek family mausoleum, designed by one of the family, on which I can recall climbing in company with a small Seppelt when as little boys we waited for someone who was working down below.

Although founded by a German immigrant in 1850, Seppelt saw its biggest expansion in a later era, buying Clydeside at Rutherglen just before the First World War and Great Western in western Victoria at its end. Drumborg was planted in about 1960 to provide cold-area fruit, and Clare over a decade later for similar reasons. Today Seppeltsfield is the centre for fortified wines, both sweet and dry, which have consistently been among the best in the country. The 'DP' series of Australian sherries is particularly good, for example. The 'fino' is light, dry, clean and yet full of flavour, having just the right quantity of aldehydes and related compounds. At Château Tanunda a range of very reliable table wines was made. During the many years when such wines were out of favour, the 'Greenock' Sauternes, made mainly from Sémillon, was reliably fruity, though never quite luscious enough.

Not all Barossa wineries are as large as Yalumba, Penfold-Kaiser Stuhl or Seppelt, but some aim to grow very rapidly. Two long-established South Australian beverage companies were brought to the stock market in 1983. A comparison between them illustrates some of the problems of the Australian wine industry.

Woodroofe, a family-owned soft drink company founded in 1878, had a declining market share but good brand acceptance when it was taken over by two vigorous entrepreneurs in 1980. Within three years they had increased the profits from about $250,000 a year to over $1,250,000, and the company was floated off with an issued capital of $8,000,000, the 50-cent shares having an asset backing of 35 cents, forecast earnings of about 17 cents a share and dividends of 9 cents a share. The company was well received by the market, and it later sold off the highly desirable sparkling water assets profitably.

Two very enterprising young wine-makers, Grant Burge and Ian Wilson, had been working together very successfully since the mid 1970s making good wines at the Southern Vales Co-operative, despite its descent into extreme financial difficulty culminating in liquidation. Some time before this they had acquired, with other businessmen, a firm called P. T. Falkenberg, a century-old winery near Tanunda selling wines as 'Krondorf', and had once more begun to make quite exceptionally good wines. Virtually every wine they have made since 1978 has won a medal in a state capital wine show, and most of them have won trophies or gold medals. Their brick-built winery in the Barossa is one of the ugliest, but the unimpressive facade hides some of the most modern equipment for controlled low-temperature fermentation of all wines. It can crush 2,000 tonnes of fruit per annum and is designed to accept mechanically harvested fruit as well as hand-picked fruit. Like many other makers in South Australia, Burge and Wilson grew only a little of their own fruit but bought in good material from Clare, Coonawarra, Eden Valley and elsewhere to make a small range of very fine wine, the Eden Valley Riesling and Coonawarra Cabernet being particularly good. Krondorf also bought Merrivale at McLaren Vale, a financially unsuccessful maker of good, clean wines.

When Krondorf was brought to market it was to have an issued capital of $4,000,000 with an asset backing for each 50-cent share of 36 cents, projected earnings per share of about 12 cents, and dividends of 4 cents per share. Such a profit was indeed achieved for the first year of operation, on sales of about $4,500,000.

Initially the market received Woodroofe far more enthusiastically than Krondorf. Evidently it expected a better financial performance from a maker of carbonated drinks and mineral waters than from a maker of fine wine. This was despite the fact that Woodroofe was competing with enormous companies like Cadbury Schweppes and Coca-Cola, whereas Krondorf, like many other medium-sized makers of fine wines, should have had an established market niche quite separate from that occupied by the major companies such as Penfold. Furthermore, the price of good fruit was then quite low in real terms, so that a winery which did not have to grow most of its own fruit, and therefore to have very large capital investment in land, should have been in a position to perform very well in a financial sense. Twenty years after the wine boom began, everyone recognized that wine-making, for all its charm, was not an easy way to quick fortune. Two years after flotation Krondorf sold its wine assets to Mildara and changed its name, battered by the heavy discounting of even its best wines. Grant Burge bought Krondorf's 70 hectares of vines to make wine under his own name, and other members of the family established the Burge family winery. As a brand name for Mildara, Krondorf is now successful in the medium-priced sector of the market but lacks the individuality of its Burge and Wilson days.

Because the Barossa has been Australia's largest dryland wine-growing region for so long, and also because it has too much sunshine to be regarded as ideal for making the best table wines, it has few very small wineries. Charles Melton (1980), Chatterton (1969) and High Wycombe (1976) are the only ones crushing less than 50 tonnes. Charles Melton makes a big, strong, meaty Grenache–Shiraz that has distinct South Rhône echoes.

In the 50–100-tonne class are Barossa Settlers (1983), Craneford (formerly Holmes Estate 1973), and Gnadenfrei (1980). Craneford is in higher rainfall country outside the Barossa proper and should have good long-term prospects. Gnadenfrei is run by Malcolm and Joylene Seppelt and sits beside the little church where the characteristic palm trees of the Seppelt family begin, a mile before the Seppeltsfield itself. Malcolm was the first Seppelt to stay in the wine industry and establish himself independently of the large family-controlled company B. Seppelt & Sons Ltd, now owned by the South Australia Brewing Company. More recently Karl Seppelt has established Premier Cru Estate at Mount Pleasant in the Adelaide Hills.

Mountadam (1984) is in the difficult middling size, in which national sales are needed but their scale does not support all-out national advertising, but it has been established in the Barossa hills by David and Adam Wynn, father and son who have between them great experience and scientific expertise. Using only 30 hectares of a 1,000-hectare property, the Wynns have enlarged their crush to 200–300 tonnes of Mountadam fruit, a very large proportion of which is Chardonnay, with some Pinot Noir and Cabernet Sauvignon, as well as the Riesling already mentioned, and a similar quantity of bought-in fruit, sold under the David Wynn label. Their Mountadam Chardonnay and Riesling are outstanding, as would have been expected from the quality of wines made from their fruit in the early 1980s by Jeff Anderson at Roseworthy Agricultural College, and of Wynn's High Eden Riesling, established in the Eden Valley nearby by David Wynn when he was running Wynn Winegrowers before its takeover by the Sydney brewer Tooheys. As Adam Wynn put it:

> Good wine-making is being careful, observant and gentle and in a small winery you have the perfect opportunity to apply these principles. What is different about the way we operate is that the winery, although having all the toys and equipment which any wine-maker could ever desire, has been built with gentleness, flexibility and the traditional methods in mind. So this vintage [1984] I was making some Chardonnay in the typical Australian stainless steel manner and some in the barrel-fermented Burgundian tradition. You will get no prizes for guessing which is the vastly superior wine.

There are seven wineries in the 100–500-tonne class: Basedow (1896), Elderton, Hamilton (1839, but the move to Springton in the Barossa hills was made between the two world wars), Karlsburg (1971), Mountadam, St Hallett (1918) and Veritas (1955).

Basedow was a small family-owned winery which was sold to a group of small investors in about 1970, since when it has greatly improved to be one of the best of the traditional Barossa makers. Its reds have little or none of the cooked fruit taste so characteristic of the warmer areas. St Hallett, as a family-owned winery, always made thick, rich ports and other fortified wines which last for many years without a great deal of development. More recently, under new management, it has begun to make a surprisingly well-balanced fruity Shiraz more like a Rutherglen wine than a Barossa wine in its overpowering flavour and longevity.

Elderton is Neil Ashmead, though based on an old Tolley vineyard; the wines may or may not be made by Ashmead or at Elderton, but they are good wines, well sold. The 1983 Shiraz has lasted very well, in 1990 still showing mint and life on the palate despite the horrors of 1983.

In the 500–1,000-tonne class are Bernkastel (1932), Henschke (1850), Hoffman (1870), Karrawirra (1969) and Wilsford (1928).

Bernkastel wines use to be rather light in character. For example, 1970 was a very big year, yet the 1970 Claret (Shiraz and Mataro) was tolerable in 1973 and over the hill by 1975, and the 1970 Cabernet Shiraz Mataro, which was well balanced and clean with some Cabernet character in 1975, was thin and dull two years later. In the mid 1980s Peter Lehmann, renowned for big delicious reds, made some of the Bernkastel wines, and the style became 'best of the Barossa', like most of Lehmann's wines. I recall enjoying the 1986 Cabernet Sauvignon with over-cooked, spit-roasted lamb at a farewell barbecue. The winery is a slightly fantastical castle.

Henschke changed its nature from just another German winery to one of the most interesting in South Australia during the twenty years that Cyril Henschke was wine-maker. Using much less new oak than most other aspiring fine wine-makers, and also aiming at softer wines than most, he made his Shiraz-based 'Hill of Grace' and 'Mount Edelstone' two of the most sought-after wines of the 1960s and 1970s. Despite their softness, some of them have continued to improve for a decade though enjoyable when only two or three years old. His 1968 'Mount Edelstone' comes to mind as a velvety Shiraz in 1978, where it had been spicy five years before. The even years of the 1980s are good drinking at the time of writing and will all improve for years. However, the 1987 'Mount Edelstone' is quite exceptional. It has won many prizes but is much more interesting than most such wines; it has something of the dense yet almost floral richness of a 'Hermitage', not the berry flavour that characterizes almost all Barossa Shirazes. Too good not to lay down, it is too tempting not to take up. So Stephen Henschke has gone on from where his late father left off. Cyril Henschke also made dry

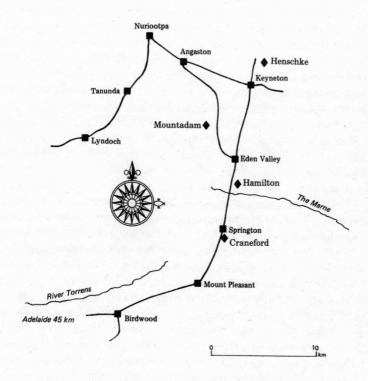

Nuriootpa

Angaston

◆ Henschke

Keyneton

Tanunda

Mountadam ◆

Lyndoch

Eden Valley

◆ Hamilton

The Marne

Springton
◆ Craneford

River Torrens

Mount Pleasant

Adelaide 45 km   Birdwood

0   10
                      km

Barossa Hills

whites of original character and surprising staying power. His 1965 Sauvignon Blanc, for example, still had a fresh, grassy nose, deep flavour and a light, dusty finish in 1973, and the same year's Ugni Blanc, though past its best, was fading slowly and still enjoyable in 1978. The current whites hold less interest, but many will not mind, happy to enjoy the great reds.

Hoffman, like Henschke, reached its fourth or fifth generation of family control. The last family member to be in charge before a takeover was Bruce Hoffman, whom I recall as a gliding instructor rather than a wine-maker. He made reliable table wines and outstanding ports blended of Shiraz, Grenache and Mataro.

In the 1,000–5,000-tonne class are Château Rosevale (1962), Leo Buring (1945), Hardy's Siegersdorf (1921), Krondorf (1860), Liebich's Rovalley (1919), Saltram (1900), Wolf Blass (1973) and Yaldara (1947).

Château Rosevale has been most notable for 'Vin-Spa', a sparkling white sold in beer bottles with crown seals for little more than beer but with more than twice beer's alcoholic strength. It was thus ideal for making a fruit cup or punch absurdly strong by eliminating the need for soda water or lemonade.

Leo Buring's Château Leonay is part of Lindeman, owned for many years by the Australian subsidiary of the American tobacco company Philip Morris but now part of the South Australian Brewing Company. However, the name commemorates a notable figure in the wine industry. Buring came from a wine-growing family, so after being dux of Roseworthy in 1896 he studied further at Geisenheim and Montpellier before starting work in the industry. He worked at Rutherglen and Great Western before joining Penfold in 1902, for whom he made their first bottle-fermented sparkling wines at Minchinbury near Sydney. He stayed with them until 1919. Overall he worked in New South Wales for more than twenty-five years, including a period when he ran Lindeman for a creditor bank, so that when he returned to South Australia in 1945 he was one of the most widely experienced as well as successful people in the industry. The winery he bought from the Hoffman family had been built at about the time he left Roseworthy, but he added the rather ugly castellations as he expanded the business. After his death, Lindeman bought what was by then a substantial but struggling company. It makes better whites than reds, with fruit from Clare and Coonawarra as well as the Barossa. In fact, those made by John

Vickery for more than a decade from about 1963 probably represent the best Australian Rieslings as yet to be made on a large scale. Crisp and fragrant, they have successors in the Leasingham Rieslings of Stanley and many other similar wines, but they have be surpassed by any wines from Clare, Eden Valley or Coonawarra. Tasmania and southern Victoria are another story.

Saltram was begun very early as a partnership between the Salter and Martin families, H. M. Martin of Stonyfell eventually taking it over. While Peter Lehmann was in charge it made exceptional full-bodied red wines, even blends such as Shiraz and Tokay, as made in 1972, but after several changes of ownership it has less of a following. One sees its 'Pinnacle Selection' and its 'Mamre Brook' Cabernet–Shiraz blend, once the flagship of the Stonyfell–Saltram line, quite heavily discounted in bottle shops, such is the competition in the over-supplied red wine market. 'Mamre Brook' is thus good value, but one tends more to recall the reds of the late 1960s and early 1970s which in the early 1980s were fine examples of the old style, having an abundance of fruit, a tannin finish, and a sulphur-derived bottle stink necessitating as much breathing as any wine from the Hunter or McLaren Vale. The whites have usually not been as good as the reds.

Peter Lehmann has continued to make wine very successfully since leaving Saltram. For Masterson Wines (named after a famous television gunfighter), Lehmann has made very reliable wines from grapes which growers have been unable to sell elsewhere – 11,000 tonnes in 1980, a very bad year for small growers – while under his own name and for Primo Caon, an Adelaide wine merchant, he has made rather better wines from Pinot Noir, Cabernet Sauvignon and Sémillon. The Pinot, with none of the depth of flavour of the best examples from southern Victoria, is delightful young, and may age gracefully. His 1982 Sémillon 'Sauternes' was delicious, one of the most golden of the Australian botrytized wines.

Château Yaldara is a family firm which actually has a château, a simulated Georgian–Victorian structure built in stages over the last twenty years. It houses a remarkable collection of Victoriana, including a large academic painting of *The First Tiff* or perhaps *The Reconciliation*, which a cousin of mine inherited but could not house. The wines vary from odd to reasonable and are relatively modest in price. The odd ones include a sweet red table wine, the reasonable a clean, light dry, bottle-fermented sparkling wine.

Seppelt is the only firm in the Barossa crushing between 5,000 and 10,000 tonnes a year. This is about half of its Australian production.

Tollana (1888) and Yalumba each crush between 10,000 and 20,000 tonnes a year. Tollana is the brand name of Tolley Scott & Tolley, which was established for wine-making and distilling by the Tolley family and which after one or two intermediate owners belonged for about twenty years to the Distillers Company of the UK. Tollana does not have a high market rating, so that its well-made but unexciting table wines represent good value for money. Like other big distillers of brandy, the firm had to reorientate itself somewhat when the preferentially low duty on brandy as against other spirits was 'harmonized' about 1970.

Wolf Blass is a German-speaking immigrant wine-maker who might have been expected to improve Australian whites, but who has used his remarkable palate to make and blend prize-winning wines of whatever kind the judges currently seek. As there is general agreement that the standard of Australian wine-making is much improved, some of the credit is probably Blass's. I can recall obtaining in 1976 from a club a special blend of two prize-winning 1974 wines made by Blass, and initially being most disappointed by the brown colour and lack of integration of fruit, tannin and oak, yet over three or four years the wine came together into an outstanding Barossa Cabernet–Shiraz blend. It is now a soft and charming wine, despite a lingering slight excess of oak, a wine that has sat on a high plateau of quality from 1983 to 1990. Blass's gift for publicity has not earned him universal admiration, but he has nevertheless introduced many to the pleasures of better wines than come in flagon or plastic bag; his influence, on balance, has been benign.

Since his company, Wolf Blass Wines Ltd, came to the share market in 1984, it has performed very well; though not all share-holders like their annual reports to wear wing collar and black tie, as has Blass's at least once. Acquisitions have included Enterprise (now Tim Knappstein Wines) and Quelltaler (now Eaglehawk Estate) at Clare, and a vineyard at Marlborough in the South Island of New Zealand. With its oaked sparkling wine and Red, Grey, Black, Yellow and White labels of still wine, the company is well placed to increase market share everywhere except perhaps right at the top since its recent merger with Mildara.

Two wineries crush over 30,000 tonnes: Penfold–Kaiser Stuhl and Orlando (1847). The development of Penfold's red wines I have already discussed briefly, but they deserve further thought. Because of the effects of oak, pressing and a very little oxidation, their firmness, richness and lasting abilities make them atypical of the Barossa, where the best purely local makers have usually sacrificed some intensity of flavour in striving for elegance and an absence of jamminess. Penfold has sought flavour and balance. The 'Grange' sometimes hints at cooked fruit, one bottle of the 1966 tasted in 1979 having this attribute, for example, in contrast to the 1964 and 1965 tried at the same time. By 1985 this jammy taste had departed, however, even when the wine was tried after a day when the ambient temperature had exceeded 40°C, and the 1966 'Grange' was a superb wine, rich, complex, elegant, with a flavour of mulberries and cream. The 'Bin 389' is lighter and always avoids jamminess, though it is considerably less complex and long-lived. Particularly good years have been 1969, 1971, 1972, 1975, 1977, 1982, 1983 and 1986, showing remarkable consistency. The 'Bin 707' is similarly rich in flavour but otherwise different, being made entirely from Cabernet Sauvignon, most of it Barossa fruit. Comparing the 1986 with Mildara's 'Alexanders', Wynn's 'John Riddoch' and Oakridge Cabernet Sauvignon from the same year, over a beef Wellington in September 1989, I found that the two Coonawarra wines were surprisingly ready to drink, whereas Oakridge's Yarra stalkiness had nearly as far to travel as the '707's' chocolate and berries. The cheapest of this set of closely related wines is 'Koonunga Hill'; on sale everywhere and drinkable when only two or three years old, it represents an attempt to make the house style available cheaply without too much loss of quality, an attempt largely successful. Kaiser Stuhl was established in 1931 as the Barossa Co-operative Winery and struggled for many years with the inherent problem of co-operatives: concentration on production rather than marketing. Eventually a decision was made to appoint a really outstanding manager, and in the decade or so that he was there, Keith Smith, with no background in the wine industry, turned Kaiser Stuhl into a financial prize, which was won by the Adelaide Steamship Company through Penfold Wines in 1981, in the face of very strong competition from Thomas Hardy & Sons. The joint company is now part of the South Australian Brewing Company and is being merged with Seppelt, so Kaiser Stuhl's future identity is hard to predict. Nevertheless, several Kaiser Stuhl products are among the top ten of bottled wines in terms of sales throughout Australia, mainly tank-fermented sparkling whites.

Almost the only red wine to make the charts is Orlando's 'Jacob's Creek', a blend of Cabernet Sauvignon, Malbec and Shiraz. A light, fruity wine which has won many prizes in the 'commercial' (that is, high-volume) classes of the shows, 'Jacob's Creek' is blended to a style and a standard from fruit which can originate anywhere. The Gramp family, who established Orlando and guided it through its first 110 years, were early users of cold fermentation, *cuve close* sparkling wine-making, centrifugal filtration, gas blanketing of fruit to prevent oxidation and other techniques for making wines clean, fresh and drinkable very young. Thus, the takeover in the early 1960s by Reckitt & Colman of the UK was more of an aid to marketing than to wine-making. 'Jacob's Creek' is to be found everywhere, even in fast-food chains which have licences. It is now sold in the UK as William Jacob from Colmans of Norwich, but the company is no longer British-owned, as a result of a management buyout led by Robin Day. In 1988 'Jacob's Creek' (Rhine) Riesling was one of the best Rieslings in Australia, a tribute to the company's ability to make good wine on a substantial scale.

As might be expected, Orlando also makes very fine wines in much smaller quantities. Its Cabernet Sauvignon, from various sources, is always good. Its Auslese Riesling is not made every year, but in the early 1970s a few long cool summers allowed wines to be made which are at their peak when a decade or more old, with a rich yet delicate honeyed nose, luscious fruit on the palate and a lingering yet fresh finish. Its White Burgundy, made from Chenin Blanc and Madeira, has been reliable year after year, much better in many years, such as 1967, 1968, 1970 and 1977. The earliest of these was still fine in 1983, though somewhat maderized. Such wines are made from the 5 per cent of its crush which Orlando grows, or from a few selected suppliers in cooler areas.

ADELAIDE

Until very recently, as I have outlined, there were substantial numbers of wineries, and considerable areas of vines, within the Adelaide metropolitan area. However, they have disappeared rapidly, Stonyfell after a change of ownership from Dalgety to Seagram, Hamilton to build a new university, others less notable leaving no trace. Now there are only four, apart from hundreds of backyard makers who probably sell only to their friends. They are Norman (1853) crushing 250 tonnes a year, Patritti (1926) crushing 500 tonnes, Andrew Garrett Champagne Cellars (1904; formerly Wynn's Romalo, later part of Seaview) making over 40,000 cases of sparkling wines a year from base wine fermented elsewhere, and Penfold's Grange, which has been reconstituted to make about 2,500 cases from the 50 tonnes of fruit yielded by the remaining fragment of the vineyard (see map on p. 70). As noted earlier, this wine, 'Magill Estate', is one of the lighter of Max Schubert's inspirations.

Patritti is a family-owned winery with 40 hectares in the Southern Vales (see map on p. 97). It buys in much of its crush and makes a wide range of wines with Italian overtones. It has been innovative in seeking to make a light red wine drinkable soon after vintage, the 'April Red' mentioned earlier, but less successful in selling such wines. I shall discuss such attempts further when looking to the future.

Norman has vineyards at Angle Vale, to the north of Adelaide, with its winery closer to the city. It also takes fruit from other growers and has experimented successfully with varieties such as Traminer and Pinot Noir. The wines are all carefully made and good value for money, but rarely reach peaks of excellence. This has remained true since its acquisition of Chai Clarendon (formerly Light Wines), after control moved away from the family in 1982, but under the new, more pretentious label it sells cool-climate wines of higher quality and price.

Woodley was a fifth Adelaide maker until about 1985 when its parent, Seppelt, was acquired by the South Australian Brewing Company. Woodley had its greatest days as a maker of fine wine when a substantial part of the production of Coonawarra was sold under its elaborate labels, which were among the most attractive in the trade. The proprietors, David Fulton and then Tony Nelson (an Austrian wine-maker with experience in France before coming to Australia to avoid Hitler), were much more alive to what might be done with good fruit than the makers, who drew their fruit from the hotter areas and made mainly fortified wines. However, Woodley belonged for several years to Industrial Equity, a corporate raider, and while the labels of the 'Queen Adelaide' red and white wines are elegant and distinctive, the wines are merely reliable. The facade of the winery was modernized at one of the many inopportune moments for such renovation which the post-war period has offered, so there is little architectural loss in the closure, but yet another part of the history of the industry has ended in a socially impoverishing way.

NORTHERN ADELAIDE

Tea Tree Gully, less than 20 kilometres north-east of Adelaide in the foothills of the Mount Lofty ranges, is no longer regarded as a notable wine-growing area, but in the early 1860s Archdeacon G. H. Farr established a vineyard at Brightlands, his property there. Other neighbours did likewise, and when Dr William Thomas Angove established his practice at Tea Tree Gully in 1886, he emulated his neighbours and planted a vineyard, making his first wines in the archdeacon's cellars. He later bought another property at nearby Hope Valley and built his own cellars at the start of this century. He called his Tea Tree Gully vineyard St Agnes, and sold his wines under this name.

By the time Dr Angove built his own winery, his oldest son Thomas had graduated from Roseworthy, and when all three sons were working for the firm, they took it to the Murray River, first to the Renmark Irrigation Settlement which had been established in the late 1880s, and then to Lyrup, another settlement south-west of Renmark on the river.

As with Yalumba, Seppelt, Lindeman and other large firms, the move to the River was to provide a source of reliable, high-sugar fruit, which could both be made into wine and also provide the base material for distillation. For Angove is most notable for its brandy, its vermouth sold under the name of 'Marko', and other fortified products. Its Shiraz port has many admirers. For example, the 1968 was a rather rough wine when young, as is not unusual, but softened and developed steadily so that from 1978 to 1983 it was rich and yet restrained, drinkable well past mid-winter in Adelaide.

When the state government compulsorily acquired 100 hectares of vineyards at Tea Tree Gully for some additional suburban sprawl, Angove lost its main source of unirrigated material, so that most of its 15,000-tonne crush is now from the river. A family-run vineyard, it has surmounted this obstacle – which will certainly not be the last act of government vandalism perpetrated against the wine industry – by paying close attention to quality of fruit, so that wines such as its melon and lemon 1988 Chardonnay are not simply good value but very good wines as well.

Not far away, in Hope Valley, the Tolley family has a large operation, crushing over 5,000 tonnes, about half of it bought in. The firm was established by Douglas A. Tolley in 1892, and labels its wine 'Pedare', after the sons Peter, David and Reginald Tolley. Possibly the name contributes to the undervaluing of the wines by the market. Whatever the reason, its port is a fine old rich fruity wine which is outstanding value, its Cabernet Sauvignon and Cabernet–Shiraz blend very reliable and its Traminer neither bitter nor blowsy, common faults in Traminers from the warm areas.

Less than 30 kilometres north of Adelaide, on featureless flat plains which receive less than 500 millimetres of rain a year and which, because of over-zealous pumping in the past, have a problem with salt in the water table, is an unlikely group of wineries using the most modern techniques to make some very good wines.

One of these is Roseworthy Agricultural College, where experimental wine has been made for most of the present century. For a long time, under the leadership of Bob Baker, it was noted for its fortified wines, especially *flor*-influenced wines of the sherry type. More recently, as the industry and teaching needs have changed, Roseworthy has changed too, and crushes about 100 tonnes of fruit from almost every area in South Australia for the large range of table and fortified wines and brandy to which I have already alluded. The table wines extend from student project wines, sold in screw-topped bottles and made from odd varieties grown at the State Department of Agriculture's experimental station, to outstanding Chardonnays made from the Wynn family's Mountadam vineyard high in the Barossa Range, before Mountadam's first vintage in 1984.

Primo Estate is probably the most notable. Working closely with Roseworthy, the Grilli family have tried techniques such as double pruning, whereby the vines are pruned after they have flowered so that they flower again, and harvest is up to a month later than normal. This avoids the searing heat of February and March. As well as an excellent Cabernet made by this method, Grilli has produced a very fine botrytis-affected Riesling. In fact, in late 1983 I had a wine circular from a club which offered the 1983 'Primo Estate Beerenauslese' in half-bottles for the equivalent of $180 a dozen bottles. In the same newsletter the 1980 'Château Coutet'

(Barsac) was offered for $150 a dozen. The Primo Estate wine was very carefully made: Riesling and Traminer grapes were sprayed with *Botrytis cinerea* culture, in a contolled atmosphere, after harvest, and the grapes were crushed after the mould had grown for some weeks. The wine was certainly very sweet, and had intense flavour, but to me at least lacked a little acid on the finish to balance the lushness. In consequence, it is hard to see why such a wine should command a 20 per cent premium over one of the best Barsacs from one of the best recent years.

Anglesey Wines was established as Angle Vale Wines in the mid 1960s and took its present name in 1978 after a financial reconstruction. Like Primo Estate, Anglesey crushes between 100 and 500 tonnes a year.

Gordon Sunter established a very small operation in the early 1980s.

One of the most interesting aspects of this area is that because of the salt in the underground water, the vines have to be irrigated with sewage effluent, from the huge sewage treatment works on the coast at the improbably named Bolivar, given this name in a flush of nineteenth-century enthusiasm for the Liberator. Indeed, many of the vineyards have to be irrigated almost continuously in order to keep the salt at bay. For this reason, and because the area is very close to Adelaide and ideal for building Australian dreams – detached single-storey houses each set on one-twentieth of a hectare of land – in enormous numbers, it is unlikely that the area will ever become important. In 1984 a promising newcomer, Gawler River Wines, sank under the weight of its financial obligations – a gloomy portent, perhaps.

ADELAIDE HILLS

The Adelaide Hills form the only high-rainfall cool climate of South Australia. The elevation of 400 to 700 metres and rainfall of 700 to 900 millimetres combine to make grape-growing an exacting task which should reward skill and patience but which was not favoured when palliation of disease and frost was impossible rather than difficult. The land also slopes very steeply and is expensive compared with most potential vineyards. Vignerons will have to be rather different from the old norms.

Petaluma is certainly a different kind of winery. Its location is unusual, in what used to be prime market gardening land at an altitude of about 650 metres, just behind Mount Lofty in the Adelaide Hills, but at first sight it looks conventional enough: well-tended young vines with turf down the rows, olive-green sheds at the bottom of the hill. A closer inspection, however, shows that the spacing between the rows is only a little over 2 metres, compared with the Australian norm of about 3 metres, and the vines themselves only a little over 1.5 metres apart down the rows, compared with almost 2 metres. There is drip irrigation throughout, but the yield of about 12 tonnes per hectare means no sacrifice in quality, since there are twice as many vines per hectare, and they are having to work rather harder than usual to produce the grapes. Pinot Noir and Chardonnay only have been planted, to complement vineyards at Coonawarra and Clare, and make a sparkling wine by the champagne method, originally labelled, rather severely, 'Petaluma Tiers' (the 'Tiers' being the old name of this part of the Adelaide Hills) but now called simply 'Croser', after the proprietor, Brian Croser. The 1986 'Croser' was a firm wine when released in 1988 with lemon and peach on nose and palate, but not enough yeast for a drinker expecting a Champagne simulacrum. No doubt for financial reasons it was sold too young, like most Australian sparkling wines, a compromise rare for Brian Croser. The 1987 is a much better wine with some elegant fruit and attractive yeast, but still sold too young.

When one reaches the winery one notices that it, like the vineyard, is different. A few stainless steel fermenters are visible above the crusher, but most of the stainless steel tanks are shrouded in insulation and covered with plastic-clad pressed sheet steel. Over 20 tonnes of liquid nitrogen and the same amount of liquid carbon dioxide are used each year for cooling, and what one is actually looking at is a totally insulated winery, freed from the vagaries of climate. Grapes can be picked into plastic-lined pallet cases, which can then be held in a cold store so that even the picking and crushing season can be extended, at least for a couple of weeks.

Everything looks very simple but is the result of a great deal of planning. Brian Croser has planned and built a number of wineries, and he had established his label half a decade before he had a vineyard and almost ten years before he had a winery of his own. With his former partner Tony Jordan he established a consulting company, Oenotec, to provide the most advanced advice to about twenty wine-makers. More importantly, they take their own advice. Taking in only the best fruit, and handling it as carefully as possible, they will have expended about $3.00 (in 1983 terms) on a litre of juice by the time that it is fermenting. Such high costs demand absolute control over all stages of the wine-making process, and this is what the insulated winery gives them.

Only a few wines are made: a Riesling, from the best fruit from Coonawarra, Clare and Margaret River in Western Australia; a Chardonnay, first from Cowra in New South Wales, then including Coonawarra fruit, and now Adelaide Hills fruit; a Cabernet, mainly from Coonawarra; and the sparkling wine. The Chardonnay is one of the best on the market, always with plenty of acid to give it time to improve from fine to outstanding.

Fermentation is, of course, at very low temperatures; the red wines are begun at perhaps 10°C and increased to 15°, with the cap of skins, which is held in the middle of the fermenter, controlled so that it does not get too hot (a little over 20°). No sulphur is used in the red wines, and very little in the whites. Croser believes that physico-chemical fining removes flavour, and that the best fining agents are time and gravity, so that the must may be held at very low temperature for some time after crushing in order that it may fine itself. One might ask to what extent this large-scale self-fining replaces the six or seven rackings and finings which are used during the *élevage* of a classed growth Bordeaux, given that Croser's low-temperature undisturbed process is so very different from traditional handling.

Investigation by the Australian Wine Research Institute some years ago showed that about 70 per cent of all Australian red wines spontaneously underwent a malolactic fermentation. Such odds are not good enough for Petaluma. In June to July a malolactic culture of specially selected *Leuconostoc oenos* is seeded into the wine, and the malolactic fermentation is completed. In some years, such as 1979, 1980 and 1982, the wine requires no filtration, but this cannot always be achieved.

The wines that require wood treatment – the Chardonnay and the red – are now being held in French oak barriques in the Ashton cold store, not far from the winery, at 2°C. This is an almost completely new departure in the wine world, but the end results speak for themselves. The reds, when released at about three years old, are dense, vigorous, crimson wines showing tremendous Cabernet fruit and minty herbaceous bouquet, with the oak already well integrated, and yet the wine obviously has the potential to improve for a decade or more. Tasted a couple of years before bottling, they are purple as well as crimson and have the same characteristics but in superabundance. Croser calls them aggressive, but they are too elegant for this word to be appropriate.

The Rieslings have much more of the mouth-filling flavour that one associates rather with German whites than with Australian whites. Although the Riesling boom is over, the wines remain exceptionally good, and for those who do not necessarily follow fashion they are beginning to become more reasonable in price. This is Australian wine-making at its best.

Other wineries and vineyards have recently been established in the Adelaide Hills, mostly near Lenswood in country which has grown apples, cherries and other fruit requiring a cold winter for fruit-set. The vineyards are mostly at altitudes greater than 500 metres with rainfall of more than 800 millimetres a year. Stephen George, whose parents established Skillogalee at Clare, Geoffrey Weaver, Hardy's chief wine-maker, and Tim Knappstein of Clare are among the new growers, most of whose plans were set back by the devastating bushfires of Ash Wednesday 1983. Early wines from Weaver's Ashbourne label and from George have shown great promise, though Weaver's 1981 Cabernet Sauvignon used Coonawarra, not Adelaide Hills material; the skill is there and the fruit is slowly joining it. Weaver's first Stafford Ridge Riesling, made in 1985, was crisp and less fruity than the Riesling he made from Clare fruit in the same year, as expected from the colder climate. Later vintages are confirming the early promise. Wilson's Adelaide Hills sparkling wine is well regarded by many.

Further afield at Mount Pleasant, Nick Seppelt has developed for Seppelt a 270-hectare vineyard called Partalunga. The whites are showing that the move was a good one. Not far away, Karl Seppelt has established his independent Grand Cru Estate. His 1983 Cabernet Sauvignon, from that bad year, did not last, but later wines have been much better.

SOUTHERN VALES

Vineyards were established to the south of Adelaide from 1838 onwards, as we have seen. Further afield than Reynella, around what is now McLaren Vale, Dr Kelly saw the possibilities and moved to exploit them, followed by Thomas Hardy, who was the dominant grape-buyer by the end of the nineteenth century.

The early 1890s saw many successful wine-growers established in business. Growing exports, widespread drought in the pastoral and extensive agricultural country, and the defeat of phylloxera all combined to make grape-growing and wine-making look attractive from many different points of view.

The Kay Brothers' story begins in 'An Australian Rough Diary for 1891 No. 4': on Monday 2 February 1891 we find the entry: 'Entered into possession at Amery Section 514, 515, 516 and 740. Rose, Bert and Fred arrived about 6.30. Stock, brown horse "Darkie", roan horse "Roanie", four swarms bees, six hens, furniture per M. Weber's wagon 19.45.' The property was well established, for there were still mulberries to pick, and on Ash Wednesday, 11 February, we find the entry: 'Counted trees and vines – hill patch 1,829 vines, 101 blanks; flat patch 1,957, 149 blanks; cuttings 1,545.' On Friday 13th one finds 'Began hoeing vineyard'; on Saturday, 'Continued hoeing vineyard.' Sunday was the day of rest for these devout Unitarians. On Monday, 'Finished hoeing hill vineyard and began flat.' On Tuesday: 'Finished hoeing flat vineyard.'

In late July one finds: 'Carted three dray loads of vine cuttings from Tintara 25,800 Shiraz, 5,000 Reisling [sic], 10,000 Carbonet [sic].'Next day, after half an inch of rain; 'Jarvis began plowing hillside vineyard. Began planting in fallow paddock – planted 452 Shiraz.' The planting went on until early September, Frontignan, Mataro and Carignan being among the varieties. On Tuesday 29 March 1892 is the record of the first grape harvest: 'Picked wine grapes and carted to Mill 4¾ cwt. Picked Muscatells [sic] and put partly on cow shed roof and part on house roof. Memo grapes were 4¼ cwt black (Mataro and Grenache), ½ Sweetwater.' The record of the first vintage appears on Friday 15 April: 'Made wine from Doradillo grapes one and a half gallons must.' The 'Mill' to which the grapes were carted in McLaren Vale would have been Hardy's Winery; in April the following year one finds: 'H. K. went to McLaren Vale to arrange with Kelly about grapes, agreed to sell him twenty bushels wheat.' These black grapes were delivered to the mill also, this year over 1 tonne.

The cellars were built in 1894 and 1895 and the first real vintage

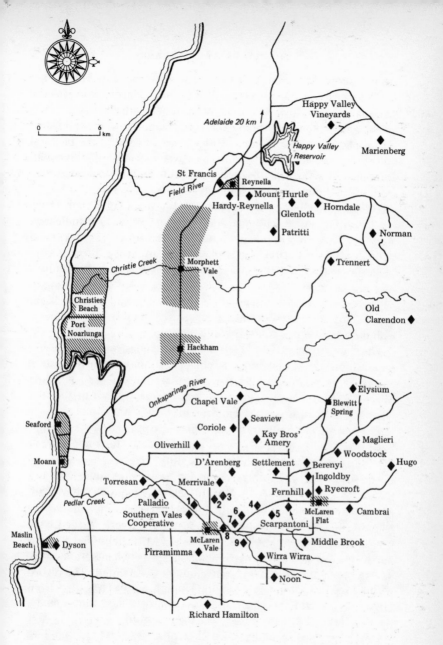

Happy Valley
Vineyards

Marienberg

Adelaide 20 km

Happy Valley
Reservoir

St Francis
Field River
Reynella

Mount Hurtle

Hardy-Reynella

Glenloth

Horndale

Patritti

Norman

Christie Creek

Morphett
Vale

Trennert

Christies
Beach

Port
Noarlunga

Old
Clarendon

Hackham

Onkaparinga River

Chapel Vale

Elysium

Blewitt
Spring

Seaview

Coriole

Kay Bros'
Amery

Maglieri

Seaford

Oliverhill

Woodstock

Moana

D'Arenberg

Settlement

Berenyi

Hugo

Torresan

Merrivale

Ingoldby

Ryecroft

Fernhill

Pedlar Creek

Palladio

Southern Vales
Cooperative

1

2

3

6

4

7

5

McLaren
Flat

Cambrai

Maslin
Beach

Dyson

Pirramimma

McLaren
Vale

8

9

Scarpantoni

Middle Brook

Wirra Wirra

Noon

Richard Hamilton

1 Hardy's Tintara	**4** Tinling	**7** Daringa Cellars
2 Manning Park	**5** James Haselgrove	**8** Maxwell
3 Chalk Hill	**6** Genders	**9** Andrew Garrett

Southern Vales

took place in 1895, with everything scarcely finished by Thursday 7 March: 'Moved press into cellar, burnt out bung holes, took head out of 300 gallon cask, began making plunger, cutting wood, began picking in windmill paddock.' The next day: 'Finished picking in windmill paddock, 4¾ cwt. Shiraz and ¾ cwt Carbernet [*sic*] . . . crushed first cask of grapes.' The vintage was more strenuous then than now, and equally hectic. Wood-cutting, racking off casks, picking, crushing, greasing the dray wheels, and even cleaning up the cellar on the occasional Sunday: so the work went on. Picking finished on 11 April, but work on the wines went on through the autumn and winter. In July, on Sunday 14th, one finds the entry, no more laconic than usual: 'Cellar roof blew off.' The following day: 'Took cellar roof to pieces and carted to pig sties and barn, put iron on roofs of new pig sties and little sty. Began repairing cellar.' In 1896 cellar work was set down as 'before vintage: men 71 days; vintage: men 672 days, horses 24 days; after vintage: men 491 days' – all this for about 50 tonnes of fruit.

The view from Amery, Kay Brothers' homestead, is splendid. Situated on a ridge, it looks south and south-east to the gentle curves of the Willunga hills, a uniform set the tallest of which is Mount Wilson, south-west to the sea. At the bottom of the hill, behind tall pines, is the old Tintara vineyard, planted more than a century earlier, its Sauvignon Blanc grapes contributing to Hardy's fine dessert wines, the 1965 blend with Sémillon still a fine wine in the 1980s, though with rather a bottle stink.

On soil which is mainly red-brown earth over limestone and ironstone, Amery has grown Shiraz, Cabernet Sauvignon, Sémillon and Rhine Riesling successfully for many years. The quiet Cud Kay, of the third generation on the property, has made many fine examples of the staple blend, Cabernet–Shiraz, notably in 1964, 1967 and 1971. More recently his son Colin has begun to make lighter wines, the Pinot Noir (and sometimes Pinot–Shiraz, a blend with a long history of success in the Hunter, not often enough used now) being sound and clean, but the Cabernet–Shiraz remains the wine of choice, 1986 promising well for the future.

Despite the neo-brutalist shed that obscures the old, rambling cellars built down the slope to take advantage of gravity in handling the wine, the vineyard is one of the most welcoming in an area which saw too much whimsy, tax-dodging and general incompetence during the wine boom. The Kays have a kind word for everyone, saying of a straight Mataro made by a competitor, 'Yes, I think that he does about as much as you can with Mataro.' Their own have been grubbed out long since.

Only two Southern Vales wineries fall into the very small (25-tonne) category: Dridan's Skottowe Estate (1975) and Fernhill (1975).

Dridan made some excellent Shiraz wines, the labels an attraction by themselves – for he is one of South Australia's most successful artists – before he moved his interest and his wine-making to the Old Clarendon Winery in about 1983, a gallery, restaurant and tourist trap which also makes and sells a range of red and white wines. The interaction between attracting customers and making good wine has become irrelevant for Dridan with the sale of the whole enterprise.

Fernhill makes one of the area's best Shirazes and a good crisp Riesling.

In the next category (25–50 tonnes) are Berenyi (1964), Daringa (1974), Manning Park (1983), Noon (1969) and Trennert (1971).

Berenyi makes extraordinary red and white wines from Grenache. He picks the grapes when they are very ripe and lets wild yeasts ferment them dry. Volatility and aldehydes give them the character of sherries or Madeiras, and they are very high in alcohol. I do not understand them.

Manning Park, formerly the property of the nearby Merivale which is now part of the Barossa's Krondorf, is almost in McLaren Vale itself. Owned by the proprietors of St Anne's vineyard near Ballarat in Victoria, it offers rich, full-flavoured wines which avoid the sulphurous stink associated with the area.

Makers of 50–100 tonnes are Cambrai (1975), Hugo (1979), Maxwell (1979), Richard Hamilton (1972) and Settlement (1968).

Cambrai has as its wine-maker and proprietor Graham Stevens, who was very successful when wine-making successively for D'Arenberg in the 1960s and Coriole in the 1970s. He is an outstanding wine-maker with an open mind, who has made a rich, deep-flavoured and durable blend of Cabernet Sauvignon and Pinot Noir, uses Grenache well, makes an enjoyable rapid-maturing Zinfandel, uses wood well in his sweetish full-bodied whites, and makes a dense purple port of great quality.

Hugo's wines are among the best in the Southern Vales, with a deep-flavoured, rich yet balanced Chardonnay outstanding for quality and value.

Settlement was set up as a partnership between a medical practitioner and an Italian wine-maker with a flair for publicity and incredibly powerful but balanced red wines, made partly with fruit from the vineyard's own sandy slopes above McLaren Flat, partly from any source of good fruit. In the past this has included Coonawarra, but now Settlement's own vineyard at Margaret River in south-western Western Australia is supplying very fine Cabernet Sauvignon, and these wines should get better and better.

Makers of 100–500 tonnes are Coriole (1967), Genders (1968), Andrew Garrett (formerly Estate, McLaren by the Lake, and Hazelmere 1980), Maglieri (Gully) (1972), Marienberg (1966), Merrivale (1972), Palladio (1974), Pirramimma (1892), St Francis (1970), Taranga (1973), Wirra Wirra (1969) and Woodstock (1970).

Andrew Garrett Wines, in its former incarnation as Hazelmere, like Marienberg and the now defunct Elysium, has had a female wine-maker – not a rarity in Australia but still, unfortunately, relatively unusual. However, at the latter two wineries the makers were also the proprietors. Andrew Garrett Wines now has Andrew Garrett, one of the new entrepreneurs of wine, in charge, but the estate is, like the Old Clarendon Winery, Mitchelton in northern Victoria and various other projects, intended to be a centre of attraction and entertainment, with restaurant and accommodation as important as the well-made Cabernet and Chardonnay. Its first vintages have been very good, but multiple changes of wine-maker and owner occurred only a few years after its establishment so that style and direction have changed with control by Garrett Wines. Andrew Garrett makes wine in many places from fruit from everywhere, and sells it all on his name and its quality.

Pirramimma was a long-established maker of fortified wines which took some time to adjust to the disappearance of this market but which is now making some of the most elegant reds in the Southern Vales, even a carbonic maceration wine for instant consumption. With those of Kay Brothers, Hardy and Osborne, Pirramimma's earlier red wines typified the area's style – rather dirty but with plenty of flavour for those prepared to wait.

Wirra Wirra is established in an ironstone building rebuilt on the ruins of a winery begun in 1902 but successful for only a few years. The Trotts, who run it, are related to the Johnstons of Pirramimma and were among the earliest to begin to make clean, fresh red wines in the Southern Vales, using Shiraz and Grenache well together and making a Cabernet that might well have been mistaken for one from a much cooler area. They also make a 'Hand Picked' Riesling which displays the strength and fruit although perhaps not the sweetness to be expected from a very good Auslese indeed. Whites from the area have always had flavour; they now sometimes have finesse as well.

Woodstock, like most of the larger wineries in the area, makes wine from others' fruit as well as its own, for example one of the more unusual of the botrytis-affected wines of 1984, using Riesling and Chenin Blanc from Clos Robert, a large vineyard without a winery.

In the 500–1000-tonne class are only Chai Clarendon (Light, 1969), D'Arenberg (1928), Kay Brothers (1890) and Ryecroft (Wilkinson) (1895). All are more notable for their red wines than their white, and they hover in the difficult scale where national sales are necessary but national advertising is impossible.

D'Arenberg perhaps reached a peak of quality in 1969, a very difficult vintage, when its Cabernet won the Jimmy Watson Trophy. However, D'Arenberg reds have a devoted following, and the company is one of the few smaller wineries to sell matured wines.

In the 1,000–5,000-tonne class are Reynella (1838) and Seaview (1850). Reynella belongs to Thomas Hardy, the giant of the area, and Seaview to the South Australian Brewing Company. In this category until 1980 was the Southern Vales Co-operative, first established in 1896 as a proprietary winery, belonging to Penfold from 1911 to 1965, expanding by buying the Horndale Distillery from Gilbey in 1968, and then collapsing in 1981. Wine is still made there, from some of the same grapes which Burge and Wilson, later of Krondorf in the Barossa, used so successfully in the mid 1970s, but it is no longer a major winery.

Finally, crushing over 5,000 tonnes of grapes before one counts the contributions of Reynella or Houghton in Western Australia, there is Thomas Hardy. It has stayed family owned and controlled in an era when this has become not only difficult but unfashionable, and has, as is said in Australia (quoting a former rural deputy prime minister, 'Black Jack' McEwen), 'bought back a bit of the farm', acquiring Emu Wines, parent of Houghton and Valencia in Western Australia, from British interests, Reynella from an overseas-

influenced tobacco company, and Stanley of Clare from the H. J.
Heinz Company. Acquisition, by the original Thomas Hardy, at a
low price in 1877 (following a decade of economic difficulty), of Dr
Kelly's pioneering Tintara vineyard had been one of the most
successful investments in the wine industry. Sale of the 27,000
gallons of good wine made by Dr Kelly paid for the entire purchase
as the economy recovered and the population grew. The acquisitions
of a century later seem likely to be just as successful.

Family control has allowed moves into new areas, with management and wine-making gradually incorporating more outsiders. The
wines are consistent, rarely reaching the greatest peaks, though the
company wines win many prizes. Its brand names, such as 'Nottage
Hill' Claret, 'St Thomas' Burgundy and 'Old Castle' Riesling, are
very reliable, and some of its more recently developed whites, such
as the Chardonnay (especially 1982 after a few years in the bottle)
and the Sauvignon Blanc (1984 full of gooseberries, one would have
thought), from Keppoch or Coonawarra in the south-east of the
state, have been very good indeed, though its use of Pinot Noir has
yet to impress. The 1985 Riesling from the south-east, much better
than the painting on the label, won a trophy when young and
by 1990 had developed into a very fine wine indeed, with the
characteristics of the snow on which good King Wenceslas looked
out on the feast of Stephen. The 1987 'Eileen Hardy' Chardonnay,
also made by Geoff Weaver and blended from several different
batches of fruit given slight maturation in a mixture of French and
American oak, was exceptionally good value in 1989 at well under
$20, compared with at least $25 for wines of comparable quality
from such makers as Hickinbotham, Petaluma and Rosemount.
Hardy reserves its 'Eileen Hardy' label for its best, of course, and
unlike the smaller makers has other labels for wines that are merely
adequate or good.

Both Hardy and Reynella have always made very good fortified
wines. Now, in Reynella, Thomas Hardy has a winery which long
made a complex, rich Cabernet Sauvignon with a very small following, a wine which improved for many years, twenty-year-old examples clearly different from, yet not disgraced by comparison with,
similarly aged Clarets of good years. That these wines will still be
made, given Hardy's respect for tradition, one feels certain.

LANGHORNE CREEK

Langhorne Creek is a very small area possessing less than 250 hectares of grapes, no more than a dozen growers and only two vignerons – Potts's Bleasdale, founded in 1862, and Bremer wines, Potts' junior by more than 110 years. None the less, its fruit has long been recognized as having a distinctive character, best described as earthy. Stonyfell has for many years made a powerful, tannic, long-lived wine called 'Metala' from Cabernet Sauvignon and Shiraz grown at Langhorne Creek. Lindeman has similarly made a Shiraz – Cinsault blend, and Wolf Blass has used Shiraz from the area to provide the fruit and tannin for many a prize-winning blend. 'Metala' remains fruity and earthy almost indefinitely, the 1966 hardly changing between 1974 and 1987.

Yet it has been the Potts family with their vineyard Bleasdale (named after a temperance advocate who recommended wine for moderation) which has established both the area's name and its special method of ensuring good yields in a dry area near the slowest-flowing part of the Murray River. They built sluices which allow them to divert the winter floods of the Bremer River, a minor stream, on to the vineyards. It is probably fallacious, though of course appealing, to relate the earthiness of the wines to their annual inundation with silt.

The most interesting Potts wine is the Malbec, at its best soft, scented and fruity, improving for up to eight years. They have also been making an attractive dry wine from Verdelho (or Verdielho, as they label it) for much longer than the variety has been fashionable. It is rather watery and characterless when young but develops a good rounded flavour after three to four years. However, much of their 1,200-tonne crush, half of it bought in, goes into tank-fermented sparkling wines which sell at about half the price of the bottle-fermented product and have been very widely taken mixed with orange juice round swimming pools on Sunday mornings.

Bremer Wines, which grows about two-fifths of its 50-tonne crush, is no threat to the identification, in the wine-buyer's mind, of Potts and Langhorne Creek.

On the Angas River is Temple Bruer, run by the former distillation instructor of Roseworthy Agricultural College.

At Currency Creek, not far away, is Santa Rosa wines, also very small. Its late-picked Riesling is a wine with considerable fruit but

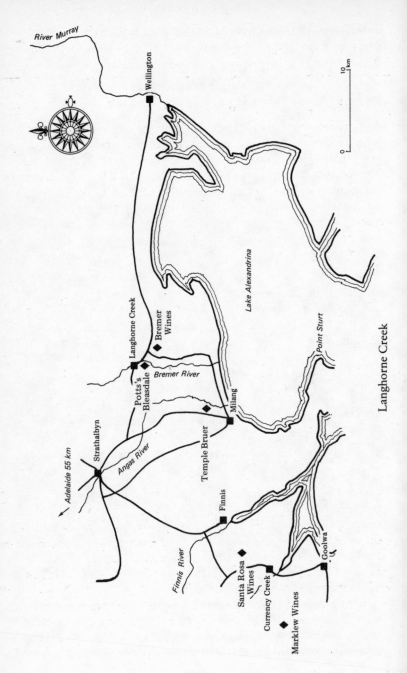

Langhorne Creek

little finesse. The wines have improved recently with the aid of Brian Barry of Clare. Near Middleton and other beaches is Marklew Wines, another small producer begun by a medical enthusiast.

CLARE

As explorers moved north from Adelaide, they also became settlers. John Horrocks, one such employer, had his servant establish a vineyard at Hope Farm, Penwortham, near Clare. Horrocks had been born at Penwortham Hall in Lancashire, and he called his new village after it. He also provided vines in 1840 to George Hawker, an important pioneer of the Merino sheep industry, but Horrocks himself did not live to see the wine industry established for he was shot by his camel in 1846. (It kicked his gun as Horrocks handed the weapon to a servant.) It was probably the first camel imported into Australia – from Tenerife in 1840 – and it gave great trouble in the Clare district, frightening bullock teams and, on the expedition to the north of South Australia on which Horrocks was killed, biting one member of the party and one of the goats taken for provisions. The camel itself was shot after Horrocks' death, Edward Gleeson, who gave Clare its name, being one of those appointed to execute the animal.

Gleeson established another of the very early vineyards at his house, called Inchiquin. The house remains but the name is now attached to a flagon port made by the local co-operative. Gleeson peppered the district with Irish names, so that there is today a Donnybrook Tea Garden, for example.

As well as the Lutherans who left Germany after 1848 and who established the Barossa wine industry, Roman Catholic Germans came to South Australia at about the same time and some headed further north. Austrian Jesuits set up a church at Seven Hills to the south of Clare, and later a college, to educate the many Catholics in the area. One of these Jesuits obtained vines from Bungaree, the Hawker property north of Clare. These were planted in 1851 and by 1858 the 7 acres in production supplied sufficient grapes for 1,000 gallons of wine and 60 of brandy.

With plenty of labour from the congregation, fine stone cellars were built, cut into the side of the hill and roofed with arched stones. Initially only altar wine was made, but over the years, though altar wine remained important, a range of table wines and temporal

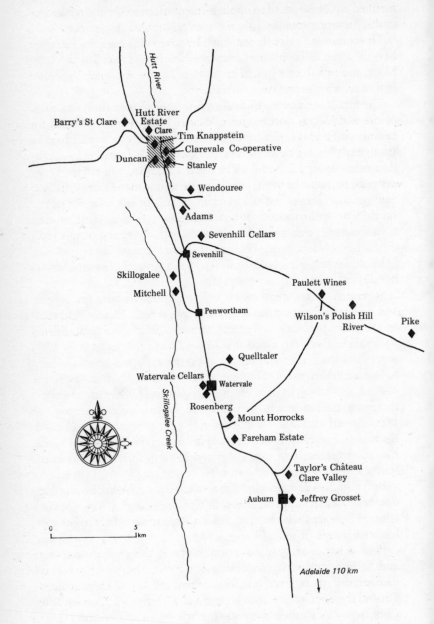

Barry's St Clare

Hutt River

Hutt River Estate
Clare
Tim Knappstein
Clarevale Co-operative
Duncan
Stanley

Wendouree

Adams

Sevenhill Cellars

Sevenhill

Skillogalee

Mitchell

Penwortham

Paulett Wines

Wilson's Polish Hill
River

Pike

Quelltaler

Watervale Cellars
Watervale

Skillogalee Creek

Rosenberg

Mount Horrocks

Fareham Estate

Taylor's Château
Clare Valley

Auburn
Jeffrey Grosset

0   5
km

Adelaide 110 km

Clare Watervale

fortified wines was made as well, fermentation occurring in big slate tanks, the stone coming from the nearby Mintaro slate quarry.

The community has stayed small but there has been a succession of only seven cellar-masters from the first in 1851 to Brother John May, appointed in 1972. The first two were Austrians, then an Irishman, a Swiss and two Australians.

The fine stone church of St Aloysius reminds one that, like most of the wineries of north-eastern Victoria, this one is not open for tasting on Sundays. On other days the visitors can try a range of strange whites, for example a very dry one made from Tokay, in the past often oxidized, and a clean fresh Verdelho, and rather better dry reds, perhaps the most interesting being one made from Cabernet Sauvignon, Shiraz and Grenache, called simply 'Dry Red', a restrained, well-rounded wine faintly like a Rhône wine, with a lightish colour, a deep flavour and a strong finish. In 1976 and 1981 it was particularly good, but it is always reliable. 'Nobel Red' is a light chillable wine made from Touriga, enjoyable in the open on hot days.

Several wineries were set up before 1870, but only the Jesuits' and Treloar's Prospect survive, the latter, established at Watervale in 1865, until recently called Buring and Sobels' Quelltaler. Buring and Sobels, Germans from the Barossa Valley, bought it in 1889 and established a reputation for good sherry, good Riesling and a lighter red than most in the district. Owned for a while by Remy Martin, it is now part of Wolf Blass Wines, but the name has almost disappeared. 'No use flogging a dead horse round the traps,' as Blass himself said after the takeover. But the new name, Eaglehawk Estate, is characterless and unevocative. The wines are well made, but not as interesting as the firm, durable Sémillons made while Remy was in control.

By 1900 the Clare area was defined as the strip of relatively high country from Auburn in the south to Stanley Flat just north of Clare. There was also a vineyard near Riverton, slightly to the east, but it no longer exists.

Four wineries at least were established in the 1890s. Koonowla and St Andrew's were built near Auburn in 1896, but they have disappeared, though the buildings remained, as did a few growers. Only in the 1970s did wineries return to Auburn. The Stanley Wine Company was formed in 1894, the winery in an abandoned jam factory within the Clare town boundary. Alfred Basedow, of the

Barossa wine family, was the first manager and wine-maker. Between 1900 and 1912 one of the proprietors, Joseph Knappstein, rescued Stanley from the effects of a wine slump by travelling to Europe himself to establish a market for the company, and by 1912 it was a Knappstein family concern. It was sold to the H. J. Heinz Company in 1971, though a member of the family was still involved. By then it was becoming very well established for making fine white wines and elegant fruity reds, much of the credit in its last years as an independent company going to Tim Knappstein, who had been dux at Roseworthy, and who has since established his own winery in the old Enterprise Brewery, also within the town of Clare. By the time it was sold, Stanley was very large for the area, its crush of 4,000 tonnes in 1972 being of the same order as the entire crush of Hunter Valley grapes. Under the market-inspired leadership of Heinz, Stanley's production base was changed to irrigated fruit, the major centre located at Buronga in New South Wales. As might have been obvious to anyone concerned with selling wine rather than tomato sauce, the quality of the wines fell, their reputation collapsed, and in 1988 the supermarket suppliers were happy to sell to Thomas Hardy. Not all of the wines made during this dismal time were poor, however, and indeed some of those from the late 1970s and early 1980s, such as the 'Bin 49' and '56' Cabernet Sauvignon-based wine of 1979, were very good, but once a reputation is lost it is hard to recover, as Iago was quick to point out. Hence, Stanley's numbered bins are replaced, at the top of the range, by Domaine Leasingham, good wines typical of the area, sold at reasonable prices because it takes time to revive a name.

Tim Knappstein has rapidly established himself as one of the area's best makers of both reds and whites. His wood-matured Sauvignon Blanc is one of the first of many aimed at the Pouilly Fumé style, and still one of the best, and his Cabernet Sauvignon has more balance and firmness than one expects from this area.

Just south of Clare, A. P. Birks began wine-growing as a hobby on his farm in 1895. By 1903 he was ready to sell his wine and in that year he sold 1,500 gallons. His son Roly had his first vintage in 1917, and in 1977 a big party was held in the cellars to celebrate his sixtieth. However, by then the winery had been sold, first during the mining boom to the Fitzpatrick brothers of Sydney, who also had the Seymour Winery in Victoria. Later, after some financial vicissitudes, more sympathetic proprietors acquired the winery, and it has been during their time that it has stabilized as the last maker of the really big red wines for which the area has been known, so that Wendouree is rather like Bailey in north-eastern Victoria. The Shiraz, at its best, is a complex wine full of smells like crushed ants, blackberries, mint and cedarwood, bright purple in the glass but turning one's teeth black. The year 1976 was a particularly good one for this wine. The 1983 and 1984 also show great promise, the wines being similar to good young 'Hermitage', perhaps less complex than 'Côte-Rôtie'. Since 1983 was generally disastrous at Clare, the 1983 Shiraz is an outstanding achievement. They are among the last to use Mataro unashamedly, in a blend with Shiraz. A rich wine, with perhaps less depth than the pure Shiraz (though it can be drunk with pleasure in a high wind), it matures faster, perhaps taking only five to seven years to get into its stride. As the makers produce these traditional wines with rather more finesse than ever before, they also experiment. One such experiment is the first fortified Riesling to come out of the area – indeed perhaps the first in Australia or anywhere else. Quite a delicate wine, with strong Riesling character and yet a certain grapiness, it is an experiment which should be pursued by someone.

Between 1900 and 1970 only two wineries, the Clarevale Co-operative and Jim Barry's St Clare, were established. The Co-operative, however, was established twice, collapsing within a year and then beginning again just at the start of the Depression, in 1930. The winery, like Stanley's, is in the town, in the old coaching stables of Hill & Company, local affiliate of Cobb & Co., of romantic gold-fields association. The initial members were small grape-growers, mostly returned servicemen on small blocks, debt-ridden and struggling. With government support the Co-operative persisted through the years of rationing during the war, then, after the war when fortified wines were in demand for export, it was more successful, but when the need came to modernize, to make table wines, its debt grew too great to manage and control was taken by Kaiser Stuhl from the Barossa, which itself was then acquired by Penfold, now part of Seppelt.

St Clare, just north of the town, was set up by Jim Barry after twenty-two years at the Co-operative as wine-maker. With careful control over his fruit quality, which had been impossible in the Co-operative, he rapidly established himself as a maker of good, rich, fruity reds, the 1970, 1971 and 1973 Cabernet–Shiraz blends all developing very well into the early 1980s.

In the 1970s, seven wineries were established in the Clare area. Taylor Brothers of Sydney established Château Clare Valley Estate on the Wakefield River near Auburn in 1973, the aim being to make the best Cabernet Sauvignon in the area. They achieved immediate success, just in time to catch the red wine slump and the white wine boom. An extensive grafting programme has achieved a better balance of varieties, but the white wines have yet to demonstrate themselves to be as good as the red. Robertson Wines (later Heritage Wines, now the site of Tim Adams Wines) was established in about 1975 and Skillogalee, Enterprise, Mitchell and Fareham Estate at about the same time or a little later.

Skillogalee and Mitchell, quite near each other, with vines growing at an altitude of about 450 metres above sea level, make elegant whites and robust yet restrained reds. Indeed, the 1980 Mitchell Cabernet is one of the best reds from the area over quite a few years. Skillogalee changed hands in 1989 and a new style has yet to be formed.

In the early 1980s Jeffrey Grosset established himself in a disused butter factory at Auburn, where he is making some of the best Rieslings in the area. At about the same time, the Mount Horrocks Winery and Watervale Cellars were set up a little further north, and Polish Hill River and Paulett's Wines to the east.

The Mount Horrocks wines of Watervale have no connection with the explorer other than that the grapes are grown near the slopes of Mount Horrocks, a modest hillock to the north-east of Watervale. At least one member of the Horrocks family, however, has enjoyed them, as he told me, though he was surprised to see a winery with his name on it. The wines are made by Jeffrey Grosset of Auburn, but later the proprietors, the Ackland brothers, will make their own. (Such co-operation is by no means unusual in this friendly industry.) The Horrocks wines are very similar, therefore, to the Grosset wines. This makes them among the more elegant wines of the Clare area. The 1982 Cabernet Merlot was a purple crimson wine, soft yet with enough acid to make it last for roughly a decade, and with great charm in both smell and taste. The Sémillon shows what can be done with this variety in Clare: drunk in the year of making, it was crisp, fresh, fruity and slightly sweet but with a long acid finish, so that one could be confident it would last.

Taken with Tommy Ruff, a small, slightly sweet South Australia fish, it was far superior to Angelo Puglisi's Sundown 1982 Sémillon from the Granite Belt in Queensland, which was soft and oxidized and seemed to show slightly too much oak treatment.

Apart from the local markets, Penfold–Seppelt and Wolf Blass have substantial plantings in the area, and Clare fruit is used by many other makers, particularly the large blenders like Lindeman, to provide fruit and body to wine from thinner, lighter areas in good years and bad.

Only four wine-makers crush less than 50 tonnes: Watervale Cellars, Paulett Wines, Mount Horrocks and Grosset.

In the next smallest category, 50–100 tonnes, are Fareham Estate, which is also a contract bottler for wine from the McLaren Vale and Coonawarra areas as well as Clare, Tim Adams (formerly Adams & Wray), located on the site of Robertson Wines whose founder was notable for the panache with which he sold a range of wines of limited distinction, and Polish Hill River, whose Riesling is a good example of the area's style.

Enterprise, Mitchell, St Clare, Sevenhill and Wendouree all crush between 100 and 500 tonnes.

Quelltaler and Taylor's Château Clare Valley crush between 1,000 and 5,000 tonnes.

Clarevale and Stanley both crush between 5,000 and 10,000 tonnes, though Clarevale's crush has declined since Penfold–Kaiser Stuhl took over its management and redirected fruit from the river growers to Nuriootpa in the Barossa, where much irrigated material is already handled by the larger company, since Kaiser Stuhl had merged with the Waikerie Co-operative some years earlier.

COONAWARRA

The Coonawarra area was settled by graziers from Tasmania in 1837, the year after the Colony of South Australia was established. However, John Riddoch and his family, the Scottish farmers who established grape-growing at Coonawarra, did not arrive in the south-east of South Australia until 1861. There Riddoch acquired a property called Yallum Park, which he extended by buying land whenever possible until in 1881 he held 50,000 hectares freehold and almost 200 square kilometres leasehold.

Riddoch decided that closer settlement would be very profitable,

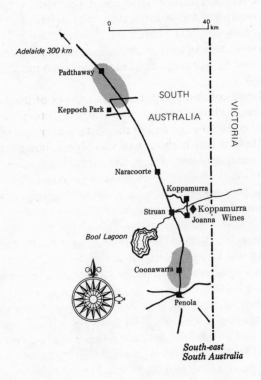

Adelaide 300 km

Padthaway

Keppoch Park

SOUTH

AUSTRALIA

VICTORIA

Naracoorte

Koppamurra

Struan

Koppamurra
Wines

Joanna

Bool Lagoon

Coonawarra

Penola

0   40 km

*South-east
South Australia*

South-east South Australia

and determined to form the Coonawarra Fruit Colony. In setting this up he took the advice of an old Scottish gardener called William Wilson, who was one of the great-grandfathers of the now celebrated vigneron Owen Redman. In 1890 about a hundred 4-hectare allotments were offered for working men to grow fruit, at £100 each. The terra rosa soil was chosen for this subdivision. One of the reasons gardeners like terra rosa soil is that it has a naturally good tilth; this ease of working would have been even more important a century ago.

The scheme collapsed with the bank crashes of the early 1890s. Despite this, Riddoch pressed ahead with plantings of vines and fruit trees. Indeed, by the end of the century over 100 hectares had been planted, of which about half was Shiraz, one-third Cabernet Sauvignon and less than 10 per cent Pinot Noir. The first winemaker was Ewen McBain, a Roseworthy gold medallist.

Initially, fruit prices were high: Cabernet Sauvignon was bought by the winery for £7 10s a tonne, but within a few years, as Riddoch was unable to sell the wine, its price had dropped to £5 a tonne and the more prolific, lower-quality Grenache only £2 a tonne. This was in 1903, two years after John Riddoch's death. Some of Riddoch's descendants still graze sheep in the area, and make wine as Rymill (Old Penola Estate).

The family of Redman, the name most characteristic of Coonawarra, came to the area just after Federation. They worked in the vineyards and on the land during the long era when first all the fine red wines that had been stored in the shearing shed on the Katnook Station were distilled, and then later any young wines made each year were also distilled. First, Château Tanunda, later part of Seppelt, bought the winery as a distillery, and later another South Australian distiller, Milne, notable more for its Australian whisky, ran the vineyards until 1946.

When Bill Redman bought 40 acres, some of it planted to vines, in 1908, he had worked in the winery for six years. He knew he could make good wine but not sell it, so he offered it to Douglas A. Tolley of Hope Valley. For several years this was a satisfactory market, until Tolley found that English buyers would not take his wine when they had tasted Redman's. However, Redman was able to sell his wine to Colonel David Fulton, who owned Woodley Wines, and Fulton persuaded Redman to start making light, relatively low-alcohol but high-acid wines, to aim at a true Claret style rather than the rich, strong wine which was taken for granted as the normal product of the Australian industry. Such wines would also avoid the cooked fruit flavour so often found in Australian wines.

During the 1920s and 1930s other attempts were made to start wineries at Coonawarra, but they all ended in failure. Despite this the Redmans were able to sell their wines successfully through Woodley throughout the 1930s. Buyers did not know that they were getting Coonawarra wine, but everyone was happy.

After the Second World War a dramatic change overtook Coonawarra, though nobody noticed at first. Indeed, prospects initially seemed so poor that the Milne brandy and whisky firm wanted either to sell out to Redman or to buy Redman out; but Woodley, led by Tony Nelson, knew the secret of its success and urged the Redmans to stay out of any deal.

In the event, S. Wynn and Company, which had appeared likely to buy Château Comaum, as Riddoch's property was now called, did not do so, and Woodley, now controlled by Tony Nelson, took over Riddoch's winery.

Soon afterwards, problems arose between the Redmans and Woodley, and the Redmans went their own way. This time, S. Wynn and Company did buy Coonawarra. It was the time of the Korean War wool boom, when good grazing land reached extraordinary prices, so it was a courageous step to buy a vineyard to enlarge and improve it. The decision was made by Samuel Wynn with strong encouragement from his son David, and though it was the Redman family that had continued to make good wine throughout the bad times, it could be said that it was David Wynn who brought about the revivification of Coonawarra. He named the Riddoch winery Wynn's Coonawarra Estate, promoted the area, and brought in Ian Hickinbotham, Coonawarra's first qualified wine-maker and the son of Alan Hickinbotham who had initiated the oenology course at Roseworthy.

The Wynns had well-established vineyards at Modbury, not far north of Adelaide, and sparkling wine cellars at Magill, so Coonawarra was a major change, far-sighted and characteristic of the family.

Samuel Wynn, born Solomon Weintraub in part of what is now the USSR, came to Australia in 1913. As his name implies, he had grown up in a wine-making family, but the persecution of Jews in the Russian empire of the time meant that when young Wynn and his new wife arrived in Melbourne, their financial resources were tiny. What Wynn had in abundance was business skill: insight, energy and foresight. Towards the end of the Great War, when he had saved a little over £100, he bought his first property, a small wine shop in Bourke Street. Within two years he was able to buy a restaurant to which he had been supplying wine. Soon afterwards he expanded to become a wine merchant on a large scale, participating in the fortified wine export trade in the late 1920s. At about the same time, he changed the name of his restaurant to the Café Florentino, and as an Italian restaurant it expanded and became more successful.

On his buying trips to South Australia, Wynn had become interested in the affairs of Roseworthy Agricultural College, buying its wine in bulk and selling it in Melbourne. Thus, when the first wine students of the College went on a tour of the eastern states in 1938, the Café Florentino was a highlight of the trip, and, if they had taken it to heart, the advice he gave them would certainly have helped them to sell wine:

Firstly, the wine-maker must carefully consider the tastes of the consumer. Secondly, the wine must be attractively bottled and neatly labelled – not over colourful. Thirdly, the wine must be well balanced and palatable. Fourthly, the wine must be crystal clear, and in this respect it is preferable to run the wine through a polishing filter prior to bottling.

Wynn's Coonawarra reds were quite outstanding in the 1950s and early 1960s, then as production rose and as much Coonawarra wine could be sold as was made, quality seemed to suffer. Happily, recent vintages have been better than those made around 1970, though less austere and restrained than the established style. The currently drinkable wines are good without being outstanding, the 1979 Cabernet Sauvignon, for example, being a deep-coloured, rich-flavoured wine with enough of everything to improve for many years from a good starting point. Compared over dinner with 'Château La Tonnelle' 1977, a minor Bordeaux wine from a poor year, the Wynn wine showed much more fruit, a little of the minty character typical of Coonawarra's best, and rather less balance than the Claret. From 1986 there seem to have been steady increases in price and quality of Wynn's top Cabernet, now called 'John

Riddoch'. Indeed, the 1986 version is outstanding, truly blending the area's character with Penfold's way of making wine.

The temptation to produce a great deal of tolerable wine rather than restrict fruit production and improve wine quality is ever present at Coonawarra. Everyone seeks to plant on the productive terra rosa. Indeed, so firmly is terra rosa established in the public mind as something to be sought after that there was a racehorse with this name running in 1983 in South Australia. Not everyone has been able to find terra rosa at Coonawarra. In 1972 John Greenshields and Sue Andrews bought a small isolated patch of terra rosa north-east of Coonawarra, after they had been unsuccessful in a twelve-month hunt for terra rosa in the Coonawarra region itself. Like many other vignerons in the area, they had their vineyards planted under contract by the Coonawarra Machinery Company, normally called 'Katnook', but more unusually they did so because they were working in Papua New Guinea.

Planting, like so many others in the area, Cabernet Sauvignon, Cabernet Franc, Merlot and Riesling, they have already begun to make wines of the same character as the general Coonawarra style. In terms of wine, the partners, who are a neuro-physiologist and an architect, are working well in the regional tradition, aided by the skills of the Oenotec consultancy. Even though they are a little isolated from Coonawarra, the area is so large now that they may be regarded as part of it.

In essence, the Coonawarra growers would join W. H. Auden 'In Praise of Limestone':

If it form the one landscape that we the inconstant ones
    Are constantly homesick for, this is chiefly
Because it dissolves in water. Mark these rounded slopes
    With their surface fragrance of thyme and beneath
A secret system of caves and conduits . . .
. . . what I hear is the murmur
    Of underground streams, what I see is a limestone landscape.

It is hard to know where the search for terra rosa will travel next. Kangaroo Island, close to the South Australian coast and less than 100 kilometres from Adelaide, has a maritime climate, cool autumn, 600 to 750 millimetres of rain a year falling mainly in the winter and early spring, and quite large areas of terra rosa soil. Perhaps it is a candidate for the seekers of good red earth. In 1984 the only licensed maker of alcoholic beverages on the island was making mead at the north-eastern corner, diagonally opposite the most suitable vineyard country, but later closed in financial difficulty.

In the 50-tonne class are Bowen Estate (1972), Hollick Estate (1983), Penowarra (1978) and Zema Estate (1982), and Leconfield (1975) is only slightly larger, but most of the vineyards at Coonawarra have taken advantage of the abundant underground water to grow as much fruit as possible on the limited area of terra rosa. Hollick won the Jimmy Watson in 1985, only the second vintage from the label, which has continued to deliver very good wines.

Bowen is probably the best of the small Coonawarra growers, making a particularly fine Shiraz. The 1985 had distinct Hermitage character, though not the length of life of the Rhône wine.

Leconfield was started by Sydney Hamilton when he was in his late seventies, as he had become bored with limited vintage advisory work after his retirement from the long-established family firm in 1955. He had talked to Bill Redman about soils and sites, and bought a derelict farm at Penola on a spot where Redman had told him 'you couldn't go wrong'. All Hamilton was worried about after this was sufficient underground water, and when a boy found a cave in the limestone on one corner of the property, he knew it was hardly worth testing, since there must be plenty of water there. After this, he indeed did not go wrong. His Riesling has not been universally liked, as he gave it almost as long in new wood as his Cabernet Sauvignon, which broadens the flavour and removes some of the fresh fruit character. I find it quite attractive in its full-bodied way. The Cabernet, however, has been very successful, less austere and more fruity than the area style established by Redman. In 1981 Sydney Hamilton's surgeon nephew Richard took over, ending Sydney's wine-making career after sixty-two vintages.

Crushing between 100 and 500 tonnes are Brand's Laira (1966), Redman (1966) and Terra Rosa (1970). Owen Redman started his Redbank winery after he had sold the family winery, Rouge Homme, to Lindeman in 1965, and he retired in 1982, his sons taking over. At Redbank he continued to make the same relatively light, firm, graceful Shiraz and Cabernet Sauvignon that he had followed his father in making after 1946, when Bill Redman retired. The Shiraz, which is labelled Claret, is a spicy wine dominated by its firm acid finish, and is probably a better wine, in terms of what can be done with the grape, than the Cabernet; many, indeed, would compare

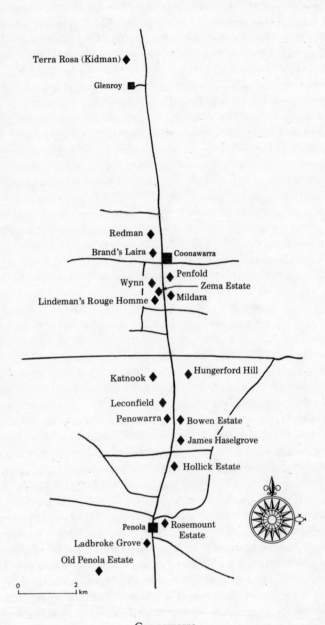

Terra Rosa (Kidman) ◆

Glenroy ■

Redman ◆

Brand's Laira ◆   ■ Coonawarra

Penfold ◆

Wynn ◆   Zema Estate

Lindeman's Rouge Homme ◆   ◆ Mildara

Katnook ◆   ◆ Hungerford Hill

Leconfield ◆

Penowarra ◆   ◆ Bowen Estate

◆ James Haselgrove

◆ Hollick Estate

Penola ◆ Rosemount Estate

Ladbroke Grove ◆

Old Penola Estate ◆

0   2
|————————| km

Coonawarra

118

the Shiraz to Bordeaux rather than to the Rhône. They are both very good, however. Redman has always used more art and less science than most of the other makers, so quality has varied from bottling to bottling, in vintages as distant in time as 1966 and 1981. However, his remain distinctive, reasonably priced wines.

Brand makes rather similar wine at Laira close by, as befits a Redman son-in-law. In addition, there is a clean, fresh, acid rosé using some Grenache, which reminds one that this difficult style can be very successful in sympathetic, careful hands.

Penfold, as distinct from the Penfold-owned Wynn, crushes between 500 and 1,000 tonnes, mostly Riesling and Shiraz to go into its 'Bin 231' and '128' – reliable, widely available wines of the type the big companies must supply. Light and unforthcoming in Australia, the 1978 'Bin 128' tasted quite berry-like in England in 1984, compared with many Crozes-Hermitages – an example of the fact that fruit flavour is the great strength of Australian wines, although taken for granted in Australia. Penfold began planting in about 1960, as did Hardy and Seppelt at Keppoch not many kilometres north.

There are five firms crushing between 1,000 and 5,000 tonnes a year: Hardy, Hungerford Hill (1971), Katnook Estate (1975), Mildara (1955) and Seppelt. Hungerford Hill, which also has vineyards in the Hunter, was a public company which was taken over in 1983 by a combination of Melbourne and Sydney interests, the former, associated with Katnook Estate, presumably wanting the Coonawarra part, the latter the Hunter. Because it has been thus divided, Hungerford Hill's true potential at Coonawarra may never become clear, but it had in fact failed to establish itself in the top rank in the public mind, so its best wines were bargains. Indeed, its Cabernet Sauvignon wines from 1978 to 1982 may stay in this category, where they are to be found, for they are all good examples of the firm yet fruity Coonawarra style usually associated with Mildara.

Mildara had its origins at Mildura on the River Murray in Victoria, to be discussed in the next chapter. It came to Coonawarra in 1955, through its management's recognition that elegance in table wines was not to be found along the River. The wines from Coonawarra are well made, softer and richer than those of Wynn, Rouge Homme or Redman. They have won the Jimmy Watson Trophy twice, in 1982 and 1989, the latter with the 1988 'Jamieson's Run' blend.

Katnook sells small quantities only under its own label, crushing fruit and making wine for many others as well as developing their own vineyards. What is labelled Katnook is therefore outstanding, especially the whites: Chardonnay, Sauvignon Blanc, Riesling and Traminer are all very good, the Chardonnay exceptional in its depth of flavour. The 1986 Cabernet blend won the Jimmy Watson Trophy in 1987, yet another Coonawarra wine of great staying power yet attractive when little more than a year old.

Lindeman has expanded Rouge Homme greatly since buying it in 1965. Indeed, Lindeman is now probably the largest producer in the Coonawarra–Keppoch area, having over 1,000 hectares of vines. In order to ensure high quality from this area, Lindeman has identified individual vineyards, some of which lie along the road from Coonawarra to Adelaide, such as Limestone Ridge (and the slopes of any such should be good for grapes, of course), Pyrus, which won the Jimmy Watson Trophy in 1986 (for the 1985 wine), St Cedd's, after the small, pink-washed Anglican church of the area. The wines are very well made, and recently graduated agricultural scientists find Rouge Homme a good place to work because things are done so carefully. The Pinot Noir from the area is a good example of the result: attractive, cough-elixir nose, clean varietal palate, soft finish, but with none of the depth of flavour or promise of development of, say, the best Victorian Pinot wines.

THE RIVERLAND

The big wineries, Penfold–Seppelt, Orlando and Yalumba especially, take fruit from the Riverland, from both their own vineyards and those of others, and buy wine from the river co-operatives, but for the most part their wine-making operations on the river are small.

Irrigated grape-growing looks easy when one walks through, or rather under, the huge canopies weighed down by tonnes of swollen berries, but it is not. Penfold, for example, determined in the late 1960s to develop a large vineyard near Morgan. It bought a large tract of elevated land, to avoid frost, and noted later with some pleasure that it had very little sandy soil, so that nematodes would not be a problem. However, the vines had to be planted into what was nearly solid rock, and every summer there has been a struggle to keep the water up to them, as they do not have normal root

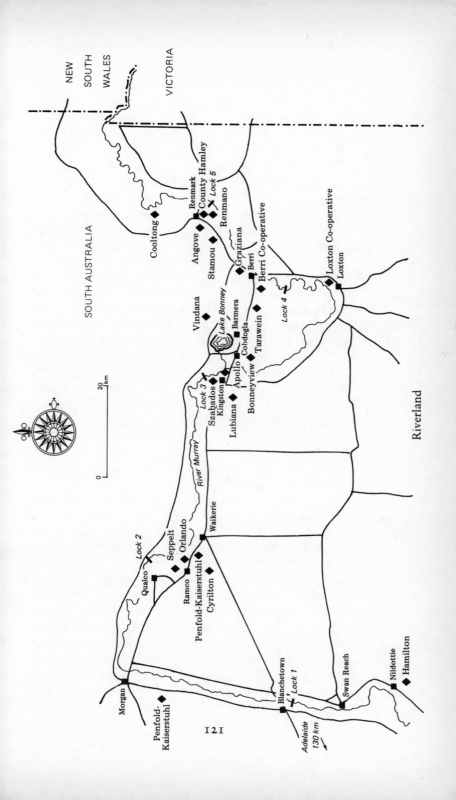

systems. Further, they must be given nutrients with the water, since so much of the nutrients becomes rapidly unavailable on entering the soil. In the early 1980s the vineyards were drastically reduced to the least troublesome few hundred hectares, and the enterprise is now reliable and productive, a tribute to Dianne Davidson, Penfold's first vineyard manager, originally an academic plant physiologist, appointed after the company was 120 years old.

When the first irrigation settlements were established around the turn of the century, the sandy alluvial flats and related higher ground were chosen, and it is from such flood- or spray-irrigated vineyards rather than the trickle-irrigated modern vineyards that the bulk of the area's more than 100,000 tonnes of fruit comes.

Along the river in South Australia are no more than a dozen independent wineries, ranging from small to vast.

There are two very small ones. County Hamley (1974) is unusual in that it takes its 100 tonnes of fruit from the Adelaide Hills and the Southern Vales rather than from close at hand, and makes a wine called 'Semichon' by putting fresh grapes into the previous year's wine and fermenting the result to dryness. Bonneyview (1975), which has a view of the brackish Lake Bonney, crushes a little over 100 tonnes and makes a number of very reasonable fortified wines, especially from Shiraz.

Lubiana (1959) crushes over 1,000 tonnes and makes a wide range of table and fortified wines.

All the other Riverland wineries crush more than 10,000 tonnes.

Angove is unusual in growing one-third of its 15,000 tonnes. Much of this has always gone towards its highly successful 'St Agnes' brandy. However, after the tax advantage which brandy had over other spirits was removed in the early 1970s, Angove was forced to move more towards table wines, as well as its popular 'Marko' vermouth, a consistent prize-winner in the flavoured fortified wine classes.

Renmano (1918), now part of the Berri–Renmano co-operative empire, is about the same size as Angove and is successful in the very large 'bag in a box' market which I shall discuss later. In 1989 many amazed wine-lovers recognized in its 1988 'Chairman's Selection' Chardonnay a truly outstanding wine rich in lemon, peach and smoke, altogether delicious and about one-third of the price of the 'Eileen Hardy' 1987 which I have mentioned earlier with great pleasure. (The only false note is the ugly label, recalling earlier chairmen of the co-operative who thought 'wood' meant a good mahogany-coloured Scotch and soda.) In the early 1990s there will be more than 60,000 tonnes of Chardonnay crushed annually in Australia, and if the large users of irrigated fruit can continue Renmano's success there will be great pressure on producers in other areas. Renmano's other wines include a Cabernet–Shiraz blend called 'Paringa Hill', almost completely innocuous apart from the alcohol.

The Barossa–Waikerie Co-operative (1953), also about the same size as Angove, is now part of Penfold–Kaiser Stuhl and supplies much of the latter's bulk wine needs.

The Loxton Co-operative crushes over 20,000 tonnes and sells over 15 million litres. It has been quite active in introducing new technology to the Riverland, such as the brimstone process. This is the addition of a large quantity of sulphur dioxide to grape juice so that it can be economically stored until six or eight weeks before wine is needed in the marketplace. At this time, the sulphur dioxide is stripped out of the grape juice with hot nitrogen, yeast is added, a controlled fermentation is carried out, and the wine is racked, stabilized, polished, packed, shipped and sold. It is a masterpiece of delay, allowing fermentation facilities to be economically used throughout the year.

The Loxton Co-operative also makes quite small quantities of wine of some interest. I have, for example, tasted a clean, fresh, yet tanic dry red made from Saint Macaire, a minor Bordeaux variety, which suggests that Riverland grape-growers should be looking further afield for different varieties and not simply growing the same as have proved suitable for the cooler areas of Australia.

The Berri Co-operative (1918), its marketing associated with Renmano for some years followed by a full merger in 1984, has the largest single winery in South Australia, but it may be that Lindeman's Karadoc in northern Victoria, taking irrigated fruit from much further up the Murray, is now the biggest in Australia. Whatever the case, Berri–Renmano will crush about 50,000 tonnes each vintage. Before the merger Berri made some excellent early-maturing red wines, even some which have won trophies at the major shows, an example being the 1974 Cabernet Sauvignon which, though perceptibly thinned, was clean and drinkable in 1984. The fresh, lively, fruity whites are meant to be drunk young, whether made from Trebbiano, Riesling, Chenin Blanc or Muscat Gordo Blanco.

4
Victoria

Although there was a vigneron among the Tasmanian businessmen who were so important in the establishment of the colony at Melbourne, he does not seem to have promoted the vine there. Perhaps this was simply because his Tasmanian vineyards were sufficient to occupy him. In any case, others soon recognized that the climate was ideal for good wine-growing. All around Melbourne vineyards were planted.

As settlers spread out, so they took vines with them, and wines were made experimentally in many places, successfully in most, profitably in quite a few. This is hardly surprising as Victoria, the most southerly of the mainland states and the best watered, has few areas where fruit cannot be grown. Initially, of course, many vineyards were planted that were rendered unproductive by frosts, because there were no climatic records to guide the growers. Later, the American fungal diseases, for which no effective treatments were known, became important, and finally phylloxera arrived, fresh from its European triumphs. During the first half-century, however, outstanding wines were made, wines good enough to arouse the French to accusations of cheating (French wine in colonial bottles) when the newcomers won prizes at many of the mid-Victorian expositions.

THE YARRA VALLEY: HISTORY REVIVED

The first vineyard in Victoria seems to have been planted by Donald and William Ryrie in 1838, at their station (large grazing property), Yering on the Yarra. They were followed by others soon afterwards and the surrounding area, called Lilydale, had 40 hectares under vines by 1848, 3,000 by 1870. In 1873 Trollope wrote:

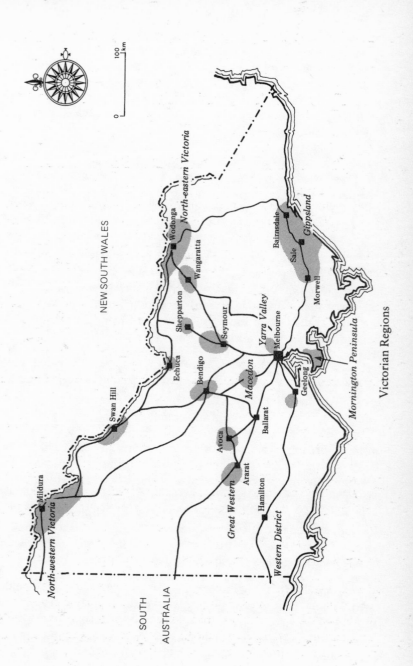

Victorian Regions

There is now on sale in Melbourne, at the price of, I think, three pence a glass, – the glass containing about half a pint, – the best *vin-ordinaire* that I ever drank. It is a white wine made at Yering, a vineyard on the Upper Yarra, and is both wholesome and nutritive. Nevertheless, the workmen of Melbourne, when they drink, prefer to swallow the most horrible poison which the skill of man ever concocted.

Trollope's 'poison' was cheap brandy, not the local beer. It is not clear with which Yering he was so pleased, for in addition to Ryrie's Yering wines there were also those of Paul de Castella's Château Yering and Baron de Pury's Yeringberg, but the variety was probably Marsanne.

The de Castella brothers, Charles Hubert and Paul Frederick, were born two years apart in the 1820s at Neuchâtel in Switzerland. Hubert was an architect, and also spent five years in the French army. Paul, on the other hand, worked in a bank for four years, and then went to England to learn English and English business ways.

Paul was the first to come to Australia, in 1849. The following year, he bought Yering station from Donald and William Ryrie. The most important part of its 12,000 hectares was a ten-year-old 4-hectare vineyard planted by the Ryries. Over the next few years he relinquished most of the property to the government but increased the vineyard to 40 hectares. Despite his lack of direct training in viticulture, he was successful in winning prizes at many of the Victorian exhibitions, as was his brother Hubert, who had arrived in Melbourne in 1854 and worked in partnership with Guillaume de Pury. After various false starts, Hubert, like his brother, bought a part of Yering station and called it St Hubert's, eventually establishing over 100 hectares of vines there.

A thoughtful man with a great fondness for Australia, he lauded his adopted country in his two books about Australian wines and vineyards, *Notes d'un vigneron australien* and *John Bull's Vineyard*: 'a free and prosperous country, where every man gets his share of what makes life happy – his share of family joys – his share of work and his share of hope'. When he returned to Switzerland in 1886 he left his oldest son, François, in charge. François was destined to have a great influence on the Australian wine industry for, as chief viticulturalist to the Victorian government, he was most effective in overcoming the problem of phylloxera, though he saw his own vineyard dwindle and disappear like the other Yarra vineyards. Although there is a hamlet called Castella on the map, north of Lilydale, most Australians today know the name because of the success of the marathon runner Robert de Castella who is a grandson of François.

Most writers of the time, and judges at exhibitions in Europe, agreed that this area produced the closest Antipodean approximations to the wines of Bordeaux. It was therefore disastrous that phylloxera, frost and competition from the more productive South Australian vineyards destroyed this area as a vignoble in the succeeding fifty years. Yeringberg's last vintage was 1924, after which the area fell into desuetude.

Happily, in the 1960s, when table wine consumption began to increase dramatically, and when improved wine-making really began to make its presence felt, a number of small wineries were established, or in one case re-established. The de Pury family had kept Yeringberg and replanted it with the best varieties, Pinot Noir and Cabernet Sauvignon. By the mid 1970s they were making light, elegant wines with great finesse. The 1975 Pinot, for example, consumed when eight years old, had a quite remarkable amount of Pinot character and an elegant, developed nose, yet was merely pink in colour; a deeper colour might have been expected. The Cabernets of the same year and the ones immediately preceding and following it were firmer wines, with more complexity, but still with the same remarkable delicacy.

A New Zealander, Bailey Carrodus, who had trained at Roseworthy after learning about wine-making in his native country, began Yarra Yering in the later 1960s. Returning from Europe, he found Australian wines unsatisfactory, lacking 'complexity of flavour, continuous flavour right through the palate, an aftertaste which stays in the mouth', and decided to make wines which would match this standard. He chose land which had never grown vines but which had an appropriate northern slope, and which was unlikely to suffer the severe frosts which have troubled the area throughout its cultivation. Calling his wines simply, 'Number 1', which is Cabernet Sauvignon based, and 'Number 2', which is Shiraz based, he set out to make wines of the complexity and length that he recalled. Extreme volatility was a problem for a number of years but in more recent times he has achieved his aims. A firm believer in the French tradition that the best fruit will make the best

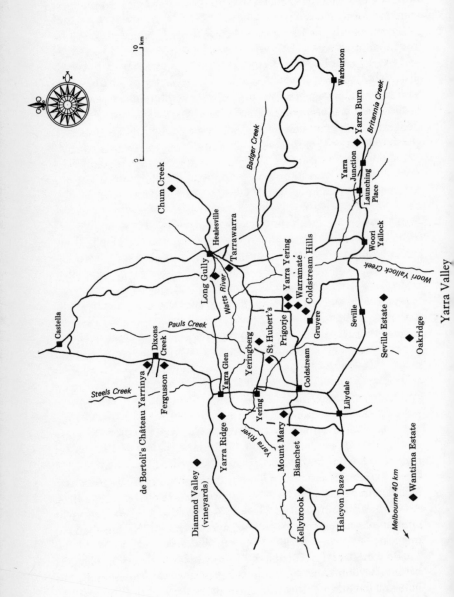

Yarra Valley

wine, and that high technology will never substitute for good fruit, he has been quietly influential in setting the styles of the best southern Victorian wines.

More recently, he has made Chardonnay and Pinot Noir. These are superlative wines. I tasted the 1982 Chardonnay with smoked eel in late 1983, and it was full of rich fruit and powerful acid, yet disciplined, so that it will open out and improve for many years. The 1981 Pinot Noir, tasted blind with a respectable 1978 'Nuits-St-Georges', was recognizably in the same class; I was surprised and delighted. Later vintages have been even better, his 1988 Underhill (formerly Prigorje) Shiraz and 1988 Pinot Noir quite outstanding.

Land values in the Yarra Valley took a long time to soar after the revival of the wine industry there. Standing at the top of the Middletons' vines at Mount Mary, one can see why: there seem to be so few vineyards and so much good land. The broad valley is lush, rich pasture in all directions, the townships of Coldstream and Yarra Glen almost completely invisible, with wooded hills in a big circle from south-west to south-east, and clouds hiding Mount Donna Buang to the north-east. Aberdeen Angus cattle munch their way slowly along, up to the clod or at least the silverside in the ryegrass, phalaris, fescue and cocksfoot. No other vineyard is visible. Certainly a north-eastern slope is best in this cold area, but the nineteenth-century vineyards were on hillocks and outcrops above the river and the streams, between 10 and 50 metres in altitude above them, and were over 800 hectares in extent. John Middleton will point out where they were. Now there are 800 hectares again and in 1990 bare land fetched $25,000 a hectare.

Middleton's site is perfect and on the gentle grey-black sloping soil – cultivated rather than sprayed because of the near-certainty of build-up of even the most reliable herbicide – he has over 8 hectares of Chardonnay, Sémillon, Sauvignon Blanc, Muscadelle, Pinot Noir, Cabernet Sauvignon, Cabernet Franc, Merlot and Malbec. These last four varieties go into what he calls his Cabernets. An enthusiast's enthusiast, he is concerned with every aspect of vineyard management and winery practice from the technical to the magical.

The wines are a tribute to this informed enthusiasm. If there is a better Chardonnay in Australia, it has escaped my attention. Full of honeyed flavour, peaches and citrus perceptible to nose and palate, solid to the finish, attractive, young yet durable, wines such as this best of Australian Chardonnays are largely more obvious, open wines than white Burgundies at this stage of their development. Wines such as the 1984 and 1987 have been criticized for lacking finesse but given time this can develop; tasting them, or more enjoyably drinking them, in comparison with Burgundies can be most misleading. For example, I recall enjoying both the 1984 Mount Mary and a 1971 Montrachet (bottled by Avery) with Moreton Bay bugs, and the comparison was most unfair to the Mount Mary, yet it was evidently an excellent food wine, full of flavour with, rich, toasty overtones. The Pinot Noir is equally outstanding in the eyes of most judges. The 'Cabernets' is exceptional. The proprietor admonished me for my South Australian palate when I expressed almost unmodified rapture over the 1981 version. 'All those great strong phenolics hiding the fruit; you South Australians are only impressed by excess.'

'But it will be such a fine wine in a decade.'

'Yes, but the usual Mount Mary has better balance, the fruit isn't hidden, and the development is equally good.'

'How are the real Clarets usually when they are two years old?'

Wines like these would have everyone beating a path to his door, so John Middleton does not have cellar-door sales: 'Then I can enjoy the visitors.'

Diamond Valley has been a marginal constituency for some time in Federal politics, but it is also the name of a good small winery in the Yarra Valley. It has vineyards at both St Andrew's, in the Diamond Valley, and near Seville, in the Yarra. It is also a rare example of the brewing industry having a benign influence on the wine industry, since it was set up by three men who had worked together as research scientists with the Carlton & United Brewery in the 1960s and who aimed to use their technological skills to make fine wines. They began planting in 1976 at both locations, and now have about 12 hectares growing virtually all the high-quality varieties: Cabernet Sauvignon, Merlot, Cabernet Franc, Malbec, Chardonnay, Traminer, Riesling, Pinot Noir, they are all there. The wines are exceptionally good, and becoming less hard to find. While the Pinot Noir is outstanding in almost any company, an oddity worthy of singling out is 'White Diamond', made from 1986 onwards. It is a blend of Müller-Thurgau, Sylvaner, Gewürztraminer and Chasselas. The wordy label does not explain why such a blend is made, but when two years old these wines are fresh, fruity and floral, and modest in alcohol, unlike a Moselle yet perhaps made with that target in mind.

Crushing less than 25 tonnes are Bianchet (1979), Kellybrook (1966), Chum Creek (1985), Wantirna Estate (1963), Warramate (1977) and Yeringberg (1862–1924, 1969). Kellybrook also makes as much cider as wine, indeed began as a cider-maker. Its success in this endeavour is a further indication, if such were needed, of the cool climate of the Yarra Valley.

In the 25–50 tonne class are Mount Mary (1971), Oakridge (1982), Seville Estate (1971), Yarra Burn (1976) and Yarra Ridge. Seville Estate is owned by John Middleton's former partner in medical practice, but its wines are not of the exceptional quality of Mount Mary's, though very good. Yarra Ridge makes a wonderful young Pinot Noir, the 1989 rich, cherry coloured and flavoured, so good that one defies an abstemious couple, hoping to work in the evening, to reinsert the cork before finishing the first bottle. Very few will have the patience to keep such delicious wine for the years that would undoubtedly benefit it.

The 50–100-tonne class was for some years the largest in the Yarra, containing Château Yarrinya (1971), Diamond Valley (1976), Fergusson (1968), St Hubert's (1838–1920, 1968) and Yarra Yering (1969). St Hubert's is no longer a family concern, and the wines can be rather variable, but at their best are very good. It has a second label, Andrew Rowan, called after a partner of Hubert de Castella, which disguises quite a drinkable Pinot Noir, so cheap that one can hardly believe that it is all made of Yarra Valley fruit. Yarrinya achieved rapid success in the late 1970s when it became the first Victorian wine to win the Jimmy Watson Trophy for the best one-year-old red wine at the Melbourne Show, a prize hitherto the exclusive preserve of South Australian makers. Yarrinya's wines are well made, and though in my view not by any means the best the Yarra has to offer, they are still good, especially the Pinot Noir, and quite good value. The winery is an unsuccessful evocation of a Norman keep and lacks charm.

Fergusson is a successful business, having a large restaurant with the ability to cater for coaches and parties. For this reason, and also because he makes wine from irrigated fruit from north-western Victoria, the founder, Peter Fergusson, has come in for much criticism. This seems unreasonable as he has attracted both custom and publicity to the area. Furthermore, his Yarra wines, which are clearly indicated to be such on the label, are good, though they need rather more breathing than most of the others from the Yarra.

Largest at the moment is Coldstream Hills, established in a rush in the mid 1980s by James Halliday, a noted Australian wine writer (and solicitor) who was one of the original partners in Brokenwood in the Hunter, with the assistance of Tony Jordan, who has since moved on to organize Moët et Chandon's Australian venture, also in the Yarra. Coldstream Hills is designed to crush several hundred tonnes of fruit, about half its own, the other half from several small growers in the area. The wines are all well made, French in style (whether the style is Burgundian or Bordelais), and some are outstanding. One coup was the purchase of Miller's Pinot Noir in 1986 when he decided to move out of wine-making; the result was as good as Yarra Yering's, whereas the 'Young Pinot' tends to be just that.

With the arrival of Moët et Chandon, not to mention de Bortoli of Griffith, the Yarra must change, no doubt to the disappointment of many, and become completely professional rather than merely enjoyable or profitable.

GIPPSLAND

Australia's first successful cheeses of the Camembert type came from Moe in Gippsland. In fact, much of Gippsland is good dairying country, the rain spread somewhat more evenly through the year than in most of southern Australia. The pattern of the winds is different also, south-westerlies less dominant, and the result is quite high relative humidity during the summer as the grapes swell and ripen. This should lead to better fruit, as should the cool, late vintage.

Because the climate seemed so propitious, a small number of intrepid growers began planting in the 1970s. Gippsland had never seen extensive vineyards in the past, those planted in the middle of last century not enduring long, but de Castella wrote at the time that 'many Australians will be surprised to be told that Gippsland is a country propitious to the growing of grapes'. So far, there are few wines available to assess how right de Castella and the recent planters were. Golvinda (1971) was one of the first to be established and is the only grower to crush a significant quantity, around

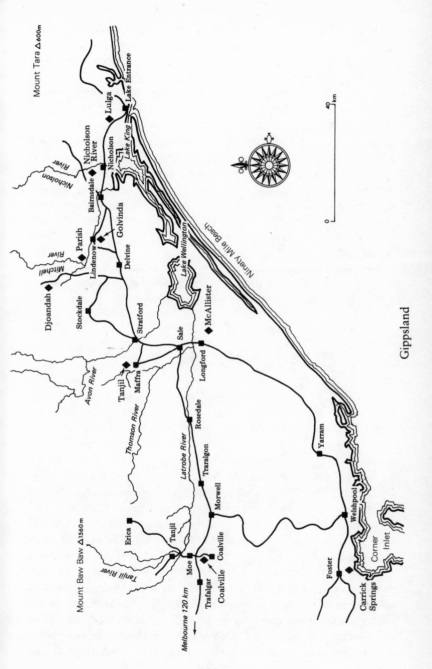

Mount Tara △600m

Nicholson
River

Nicholson River

Lulga

Lake Entrance

Bairnsdale

Nicholson

Lake King

Mitchell River

Parish

Lindenow

Golvinda

Djoandah

Stockdale

Delvine

Ninety Mile Beach

Lake Wellington

Avon River

Stratford

Sale

McAllister

Maffra

Tanjil

Longford

Thomson River

Rosedale

Yarram

Latrobe River

Traralgon

Mount Baw Baw △1560m

Erica

Tanjil

Morwell

Welshpool

Tanjil River

Moe

Coalville

Corner Inlet

Foster

Melbourne 120 km

Trafalgar

Coalville

Carrick Springs

Gippsland

0   40 km

133

50 tonnes from 10 hectares of mainly white varieties. The wines are variable.

The others all crush less than 25 tonnes: Carrick Springs (1978), Coalville (1978), Djoandah (1980), Lulga (1970), The McAllister (1975), Nicholson River (1978), Parish (1975) and Tanjil (1975). Most have planted Bordeaux varieties but Parish has only Chardonnay and Pinot Noir, having planned to make sparkling wines but selling still wines made from each under the label Brigalong Estate. They may be best drunk young.

North of all of the East Gippsland vineyards, near Mansfield at quite a high altitude, is Delatite (1968), where Rosalind Ritchie is making some very elegant cool-climate wines. Initially the wine-making was guided by the then Croser–Jordan company Oenotec, so faultlessness can be the wines' most striking characteristic. Gewürztraminer, however, benefits from such attention to detail more than most varieties, and Delatite's is one of the best available.

At an even higher altitude, on the edge of the Australian Alps at Bright, is Boynton (1986). The wines are promising.

GEELONG

Near the You Yangs, odd little hills which leap out of the plain north-west of Geelong, is Mount Anakie. The winery was begun by the Maltby family, but for various reasons it was for a time leased and run by the Hickinbotham family. It is now run by the Zambellis. The Hickinbothams are eclectic wine-makers of great experience and competence; following the death in an air crash of Stephen, they relocated to the Mornington Peninsula on the other side of Corio Bay from Geelong and continue to make very fine wines there, but their influence on the industry relates to their time at Anakie, so I describe it here. (I have tried only one Maltby wine, a 1972 Cabernet Sauvignon, Shiraz and Mataro blend that in 1990 was tired, brown, muddy and hinting at cooked fruit, so cannot comment fairly on the earlier incarnation.)

The Anakie vineyard itself, found by following the Fairy Park signs to a Jack-and-the-Beanstalk castle on top of a rock and going straight past it, is a well-laid-out vineyard more than 100 metres above sea level on a north slope. The Cabernet Sauvignon has been outstanding, as one might expect from the man who made so many well-regarded Coonawarra wines for Woodley Wines in the 1950s.

Tasting the 1982 early, I could not detect any botrytis character, despite being advised in advance of its presence. Most makers would probably have despaired of making tolerable red wine from mould-affected grapes; the Hickinbothams made a very good one. Later vintages have been even better. The Chardonnay is also very fine, in the same class as the best from the Yarra Valley: intense fruit character, despite its youth, so that the figs, peaches and other strange characters mix well with the lemony oak. Tasted much too young, the 1981 and 1982 examples were obviously fine wines of the future; in 1989 they were living up to this promise, with smooth, buttery development supporting the still rich fruit. The 1988 wine, from the Coghill Vineyard, seemed dry by comparison but with as much promise of development as the earlier wines.

Carbonic maceration, the ancient technique whereby grapes are fermented whole under pressure, then allowed to expand, so that the crush is self-generated and pigment extraction is very gentle, is a process that the Hickinbothams have made their own. It produces extraordinarily fruity yet well-balanced wines which are true to variety but charming as a class. A 1976 Saltram Cabernet Sauvignon from the Barossa, for example, was at six or seven years old as clean and fruity as a year-old River Cabernet Sauvignon, yet with depth and balance. The Hickinbothams' wines are even better: the 1984, made from Cabernet Sauvignon, Shiraz and Grenache, slipped down easily, the 1983, made from Tarrango, was similar to Brown Brothers' Tarrango but cleaner and fresher, and the earlier years, made from more durable and interesting varieties such as Shiraz, are similarly easy to enjoy in hot weather yet possess some staying power.

Lightness is not all, however. Hickinbothams' Tasmanian Riesling, from Meadowbank near Hobart, has great depth and complexity of flavour, just like a mouthful of melon. Consumed with lasagne, the 1982 Riesling had at both two and four years sufficient flavour to demand attention, unlike a 1982 Plantagenet Riesling from another new area, Mount Barker in south-western Australia, which was an elegant, slightly floral Riesling with plenty of staying power (a wine, moreover, as the label advises, picked as late as 3 May 1982 at 31.1° Baumé, pH 3.08, and total acids of 8.3 gm per litre). The Hickinbotham wine, despite the crush being almost two days after picking, is deep, round and durable, almost raisiny in its Riesling intensity, thick with a hint of quinces, a fifteen-year wine.

Other wines from the same team have as much interest. Their early Elgee Park Cabernet Sauvignons, made from the Myer retailing family's grapes, grown on the Mornington Peninsula, were simpler wines than their Anakies, yet firm and long-lasting, similar in style. The Anakie Shiraz has a regional herbal character, claimed by many to be that of the bay tree. The post-Hickinbotham Chardonnay is fresh and grassy when young, the Dolcetto uninteresting, the Cabernet Sauvignon dense like many a central Victorian red.

Yet a doubt remains: wine-makers are indulging themselves in making superb wines from outstanding fruit. Can an industry be based on such activities? Are there long-term prospects, despite the exceptional merits of the makers and the wines? In describing an industry, one is hard put to make any reasonable predictions.

When Idyll Wines was established in 1966 it was the first new vineyard in the Geelong area since the nineteenth century. This meant that the owners, the Seftons, a vet and a social worker, had to learn for themselves. Most Australian viticultural and wine-making expertise relates to hot or moderate areas, and Geelong is very cold, harvest often finishing in May. Fortunately, as every visitor to the winery finds, the Seftons are people of almost overwhelming enthusiasm and resource, and though there are now about ten wineries in the Geelong area, Idyll is still the first winery most visitors to Geelong would think of visiting.

It is situated close to the main Ballarat railway, and as one enters the property one passes an old stone station-master's house, which belongs to the winery. The winery itself, however, is not made of the local black basalt but of the much more traditional galvanized iron over a steel frame. This was all built by the wine-maker, just as he made his own bottling and labelling line.

There are 20 hectares of vines, about 70 per cent planted to Cabernet Sauvignon and Shiraz. The red wines from these are firm, long-lasting wines typical of the colder areas of Victoria. The Traminer, of which as many as three vintages may be available at any one time, is an exceptionally clean and elegant wine for this variety.

Prince Albert Vineyard was established in 1857 and was successful until about 1885, when it was one of around fifty vineyards destroyed by phylloxera, temperance and competition. Replanted

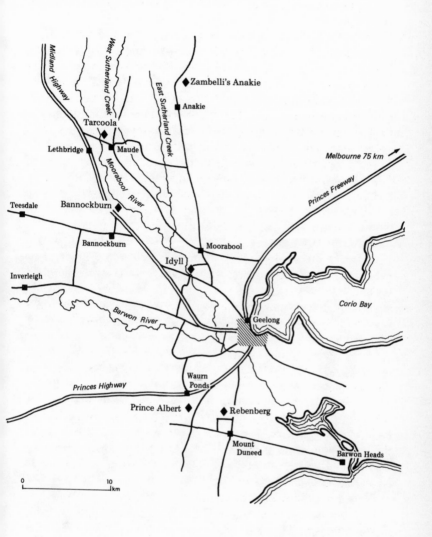

Geelong

with Pinot Noir in 1975, it is now only 2 hectares in extent but yields good wine, as would be expected from the area's high reputation when it was a virtual Swiss colony a century ago.

Rebenberg (1970) is also very small, and sometimes makes very good botrytis-affected Sémillon and Sauvignon Blanc.

In the 25–50-tonne category are Bannockburn (1973) and Tarcoola (1972). Bannockburn's Pinot Noir is even better than Prince Albert's. Its Chardonnay, whether sold as Bannockburn or Clyde Park, is also worth chasing. Slightly larger is Anakie, and Idyll is the largest in the area, crushing a little over 100 tonnes (and exporting red wines to Switzerland and Germany).

It is surprising, given the outstanding quality of the Anakie wines and the best of the Idyll wines, that Geelong attracted so few hopeful vignerons during the wine boom of the 1960s and 1970s compared with the other lost vignobles. Surprising, that is, until one has felt the bitterness of winter and the frosts of spring, a dismal climate compared with most of Australia's grape-growing regions. Yet, when one widens the comparison, the air nimbly and sweetly recommends itself.

On the other side of the bay lies the Mornington Peninsula, where Elgee Park (1972), already mentioned as having supplied fruit to the Hickinbothams, now has its own wine-maker, who has also made wines for Stonier's Merricks Vineyard (1978). Carmody, the wine-maker of Craiglee near Sunbury (near Melbourne's main airport), makes the wine for Warren (1980). Another small apparently distinct maker is Schinus Molle (the Linnaean name of the Chilean pepper tree, traditionally to be found in backyards from Perth to Sydney). The wines are not yet as good as the name, but the Pinot Noir shows promise. Karina Vineyard (1984) has made a very good Riesling, durable though low in alcohol, a style to be encouraged since more can be enjoyed for the same intake of alcohol. Main Ridge, Moorooduc Estate and Merricks Estate also show promise.

The area has expanded so fast that it is hard to do more than list all of the new vineyards: Allen's (1986), Balnarring, Coolart Valley, Cotton Springs (1990 but grapes from a vineyard established in the 1970s), Craig Avon (1990), Darling Park, Erinacea, Hoffert Balnaring Estate (1990), R. R. Hollick (1990), King's Creek, Massoni Main Creek, Mornington, Paringa Estate, Peninsula Estate, Peninsula Hills (1987), Shoreham Vale, St Neot's Estate, Tanglewood Downs, Teurong Estate, Vintina Estate. Most have less than 5 hectares of vines, and all are aiming at high quality and price, so none should crush as much as 50 tonnes. Many have their wine made by Hickinbotham or Peninsula Estate, thereby ensuring good making.

Among this new area's best wines are those from Dromana Estate (proprietor of Schinus Molle), especially the Chardonnay and Pinot Noir. Perhaps this area will be Australia's Burgundy. It is certainly too small to meet the likely demand.

THE WESTERN DISTRICT

Grapes will grow everywhere in Victoria and many of the best regions were discovered and developed in the nineteenth century, but new ones are still being established. In the early 1960s, in search of more fruit for its bottle-fermented sparkling wine, Seppelt began to plant a large number of different varieties at Drumborg, some 180 kilometres south-west of Great Western. A vineyard had been planted nearby in the 1930s, but Seppelt was using agricultural and climatic data to make its choice. The volcanic soils are very fertile, and rainfall and temperature patterns are not unlike those of Champagne. Many of the varieties tried have not ripened satisfactorily, but a range of cold-climate varieties such as Pinot Noir, Sylvaner, Müller-Thurgau, Riesling and Chardonnay are producing good wine. Drumborg Cabernet Sauvignon has stood comparison with most southern Victorian examples, suggesting that the other varieties mentioned are the ones with which to persist at this locality. The quality of the two sparkling wine varieties has meant that Ondenc has largely disappeared from Seppelt's repertoire, a pity given the special Australian sparkling style which Seppelt developed to use it. These wines are made at Great Western, so Seppelt's move to the district did not immediately initiate a new wine area.

Since then, however, two wineries have been established: Crawford River near Condah, and Cherritta near Branxholme.

Crawford River is about 40 kilometres north of Drumborg, in a slightly drier area with less problems of fungal diseases but a similarly cool climate. Indeed, very severe frosts are the main problem and can coincide with drought, as in 1982–83. John Thomson, the proprietor, established the vineyard in 1975, much encouraged by the success of Drumborg. With relatively high yields from his

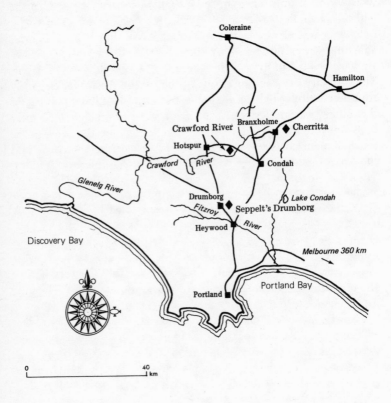

Western District

3 hectares of Riesling, 3 of Cabernet Sauvignon and 1 of Merlot, he is in the fortunate position of so many of the small Victorian wineries of selling out mainly by mail order very soon after he makes his wines available each year. His Cabernet is surprisingly rich for a wine from such a cool area, his Riesling much lighter, apart from a truly outstanding botrytis-affected wine made in 1982 – a wine to be kept for grandchildren, however little they deserve it. The ordinary dry Riesling is one of the best in Australia, elegantly fruity, beautifully balanced, supple and durable. Like a number of the south-western Western Australian wineries discussed in Chapter 6, Crawford River is part of an enterprise, not the whole; the establishment costs were carried by the rest of the enterprise and the development costs are still being met in the same way. As John Thomson put it: 'If I were solely a vigneron and waiting for my first feed, I would be losing weight.'

Making wines of similar character to those of the Geelong area and Drumborg, these new vineyards have little to fear unless fashion changes and austere, elegant, lively table wines are no longer sought after. Phylloxera remains the more obvious threat. Almost all the vines have been established on their own roots, though Crawford River will have an 'insurance block' on hybrid rootstocks once its existing plantings are completely established.

Cherritta is of similar size and makes wine of variable quality, reflecting the problem of establishing a new area. At their best the wines show considerable promise, reflecting the area's climate and Roseworthy-guided care in wine-making. Established in 1969 by the Sobey family on a farming property, Cherritta's vineyard now consists of a little less than 10 hectares of vines, mainly Shiraz and Riesling, with Cabernet Sauvignon and Chardonnay just beginning to bear.

GREAT WESTERN

Great Western, between Ararat and Stawell, was first planted by two French brothers-in-law, Jean-Pierre Trouette and Emile Blampied. With cuttings from Geelong they began St Peter's near Ararat in the late 1950s. This vineyard prospered for some twenty years, its wines being exhibited successfully in Europe, but did not survive the century.

Joseph Best began the vineyards which have persisted until today.

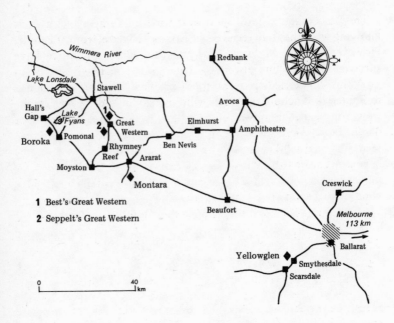

1 Best's Great Western
2 Seppelt's Great Western

Great Western

He and his brother Henry had made money out of supplying the gold miners, and Joseph was able to start planting his vineyard, at Great Western in 1865. Henry planted on the Concongella Creek a year later. Joseph's vineyard was a great success, and when he died unmarried in Queen Victoria's golden jubilee year, 1887, Hans Irvine bought it for £12,000.

The Bests made wines from a wide variety of grapes, not always knowing what they had received as 'Mixed Trouette' from St Peter's. However, Shiraz, Malbeck (Dolcetto) and Pinot Meunière have survived to make fine distinctive wines. After Henry Best died in 1913, his son carried on only until 1920, when he sold Concongella to Frederick Pinchon Thomson, who owned St Andrew's and Fairview vineyards. Thomson paid £10,000 for the vineyard and the name 'Best's Great Western Wines'. Through many vicissitudes, including near bankruptcy at the beginning of the Depression, they have continued to make wine at Great Western. They have also made products such as 'Best's Baby Bubblie', carbonated party wines with a sound base and a rapid fizz.

Irvine would not have approved of Baby Bubblie. As he wrote:

> Notwithstanding expressed opinions to the contrary, I am confident that in several districts of Australia champagne wines can be produced that will compare favourably with the best champagne wines in the world.

He brought out Charles Pierlot and others from Europe to make sparkling wines from Pinot Blanc and from a grape which for a long time was known simply as 'Irvine's White' but which is now known to be Ondenc. The gold miners had shown how easy it was to make drives through the soft rock of the area, and such tunnels were used for Champagne manufacture, providing ideal conditions for maturation: constant humidity and almost constant temperature. When Irvine's first sparkling wines were deemed acceptable by the future first governor general of the Commonwealth of Australia, it was a triumph of vision and pertinacity.

Irvine himself stayed in Australia until 1918 when he sold his Great Western to his old friend Benno Seppelt and retired, having no child to succeed him. For the next forty years, despite the decline in the Victorian wine industry, Seppelt's Great Western was relatively prosperous on account of its position in the sparkling wine trade, and because of the influence of the notable wine-maker and manager Colin Preece. In the 1930s Preece made very fine wines which wine-makers of today such as John Middleton of Mount Mary recall with pleasure, and in the 1950s, as table wines began to become popular, he developed Chalambar Burgundy, Moyston Claret and Rhymney Chablis as house styles. Initially these were premium wines, made mainly from Great Western fruit, but now, with fruit from everywhere, they are simply reliable.

Today, Seppelt's Great Western is very similar to Seppelt's Seppeltsfield. It is huge; it is geared for coaches; it makes, very competently, enormous quantities of acceptable wine; equally, it is not a place everyone would like to visit. The drives through the soft granite are still there – indeed, have been extended – and are still very important in making the Seppelt sparkling wines. However, the fact that Great Western is close to the heart of the pleasure-seeking area means that Seppelt has had to cater for the mass market. A few wines, some of them called 'Old Shaft House' wines, are sold at Great Western only, but the special sparkling wines are very similar to the ordinary Great Western sparkling wines. A Chasselas sold only at Great Western is not as attractive as Best's Chasselas, and the 'Old Shaft House' port is no better than many of Seppelt's north-east Victorian wines. Many outstanding red wines have been made by Seppelt from local fruit, the 1962 Cabernet Sauvignon an outstanding example, firm, elegant and distinctive. Quantities were always small, and the area's excellent reputation grew from the assiduity of Great Western's discriminating admirers.

Many of the newer Victorian wineries illustrate the difficulty of making white wine of merit in small quantities, yet produce exceptionally good red wines. Near Ararat, on the slopes of Mount Chalambar, Macrae's Montara is such a winery. The 1979 Shiraz, consumed with cevapcici, reminded one of six tasters of peanut butter, but no one else admitted to remembering what this smelt like. Others noted the peppery nose, the berry flavour and the splendid balanced finish. The 1980 Pinot Noir was even better. A Tulloch 1978 'Valley-Selected' Shiraz was flabby and over-oaked by comparison.

Boroka (1969) is the smallest winery in the area, crushing less than 50 tonnes. Montara (1970) crushes between 50 and 100 tonnes. Best crushes a little over 100 tonnes of its own Great Western fruit, most of its production coming from north-western Victoria. Seppelt's Great Western processes local fruit, its own and others', and fruit from Drumborg, about 60 per cent of its 5,000-tonne crush being bought in.

BENDIGO AND CENTRAL VICTORIA

Australia does not have a very violent history. The Aborigines were for the most part neither inclined appropriately nor numerous enough to provoke major battles as they were slowly dispossessed of the better lands and broken by disease, cheap grog and Christianity. The last organized 'punitive expedition' or lynch-mob murder of Aborigines took place only sixty years ago in central Australia but, like most of its antecedents, it was a low-key affair. For this reason, the few recorded outbreaks of organized violence have a great symbolic role in our history. One of these was the Eureka Stockade. This took place at the Ballarat gold-fields, but the trouble which caused Eureka was common to all the gold-fields.

Gold was discovered at Bendigo in October 1851, and by December a correspondent in Geelong wrote to the *Argus* in Melbourne: 'If the women and children would only go to the diggings we might placard Geelong with "this town to let".'

In 1851 over 200,000 ounces of gold were mined, in 1852 476,000 and in 1858 662,000. Returns were so great that many initially ignored Governor La Trobe's proclamation of 16 August 1851 that the Crown had the right to all the gold in Victoria, and a miner's licence to 'dig, search for, and remove gold' would cost £1 10s per month, the price of half an ounce of gold in Melbourne. Some remembered, however, including some republicans. On 8 December 1851 over 14,000 miners assembled to hear Captain John Harrison, a noted 'red republican', denounce La Trobe and the charges. The licence fee was to have been increased, but the meeting prevented this.

In fact, the government was hardly profiting by the licence fees; it had spent £600,000 to administer the gold-fields, and the licence brought in only £474,000. Despite this, agitation continued, as yields fell off at the fringes of the greatly expanded diggings. Revolution seemed to be near in the winter of 1853, but it did not come. The licence fee was reduced, and all seemed calm as a new enemy appeared: the industrious Chinese.

The mood of insurrection was stronger near Ballarat, and it was here, on 3 December 1854, that the Eureka Stockade was set up, by what was originally the Ballarat Reform League, essentially Chartist in tone. It was led by Peter Lalor, an Irish republican, and Raffaelo Carboni, an Italian opera-writer. Troops had been hunting unlicensed diggers near Lalor's Eureka shaft, where he was working 40 metres below ground, and Lalor proved himself a natural leader in the moment of crisis.

Twelve thousand diggers gathered under their blue and white Southern Cross flag on 30 November, and Lalor called on the men to arm to defend themselves: 'We swear by the Southern Cross to stand truly by each other to defend our rights and liberties.' Fifteen hundred diggers joined a day later in the defence of the Eureka digging, around which a stockade was thrown up. Over the next day miners drifted away, and when the troops and police attacked at 3 a.m. on 3 December they could kill only about thirty-six miners and capture a hundred.

Lalor was wounded and lost an arm, but he was not captured. Hidden at Geelong by his fiancée, he returned to Bendigo later in 1855, and was elected to the Assembly in November. He showed in parliament that the 'independence' he had sought in the stockade was freedom from oppression, and not from the British Crown as such; in fact, he became quite conservative and defended land-owners' rights.

Throughout the gold rush vineyards were growing near Bendigo, although they were not always well tended. Each time a new discovery was made, a new rush developed, and vineyards were neglected. Even the Germans, who developed most of the vineyards in the 1850s, would flee, against the urgings of the leader of their community; but despite this, the names of Bruhn, Kahland, Fuchs, Grosset, Pohl and Griefenhagen rapidly became notable in the area. These Germans, like those who established the Barossa Valley in South Australia, were sturdy Dissenters who had come to Australia because of the revolutionary ferment at home. They made good grape-growers, though they were rarely from wine-growing areas. By 1870, 270,000 litres a year were produced. As late as 1890, 700 tonnes of grapes for wine made 400,000 litres, though almost half the production of the 400 hectares was used for eating.

François de Castella's remarks on the Bendigo wine industry in 1890 are much as could have been written of the Australian industry in 1960, at the start of the wine boom.

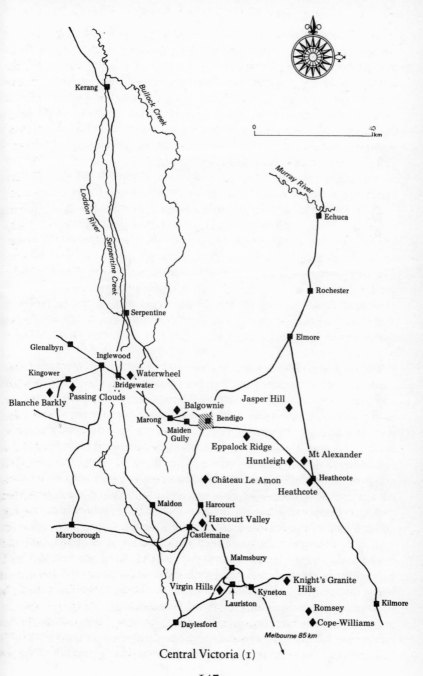

Central Victoria (1)

The climate of the Bendigo district is warm, but not excessively so, and is intermediate between that of the Yarra Valley and Rutherglen; it is, therefore, capable of producing lighter wines than the latter place, although, as a rule, the wines produced are not of a very light description. Some that I tasted were excellent, and were remarkable for their bouquet and freedom from what is known in France as *goût de terroir*; they are mellow, round, and possess good keeping qualities. The kinds grown are chiefly the Red Hermitage, Carbinet [*sic*], Sauvignon, Burgundy, Mataro, Grenache, Dolcetto, and one or two others, though to a limited extent, for red wines; whilst for white, the principal varieties are Riesling, Chasselas, Pedro Ximines [*sic*], Madeira, Verdeilho [*sic*], Gouais, White Hermitage, Frontignac, and many table varieties. Although the white varieties are, as a rule, suitable, this is not entirely the case with the red, the Shiraz or Red Hermitage meeting, in my opinion, with an undue amount of favour, and such varieties as the Mataro, Carignane, Dolcetto, etc., being more or less neglected. Were the latter cultivated to a greater extent, the resulting wines would be lighter and better suited for the European market.

Yet in late 1893 phylloxera was discovered at Emu Creek, near Bendigo, and since the only government-approved treatment was eradication, vines were torn up within a 2-mile radius. As the more productive South Australian vineyards gained access to the protected Victorian market after Federation in 1901, the industry collapsed. By the First World War, it was dead.

Its revival in the 1960s was inevitable given the quality of the previous century's wines. At Balgownie, near Bendigo, Stewart Anderson, a pharmacist who also played the bassoon in the Adelaide Symphony Orchestra, has made some of the best wine in Australia. Like so many others, he began planting Cabernet Sauvignon and Shiraz in the late 1960s, then later Pinot Noir and Chardonnay. Ever since the wines became available in the early 1970s, drinkers have been delighted with them, especially the Cabernet Sauvignon and, more recently, the Pinot. Wines from this area can have an unbalanced superabundance of fruit character, as compared with those of the more southerly vineyards, but Balgownie does not have this problem. The Cabernet is a very fine wine, even when only a few years old, with balance and soft, velvety fruit yet enough acid and tannin to improve for a decade. Having no successor, Anderson sold Balgownie to Mildara in the early 1980s. The wines from Anderson's 12 hectares have remained outstanding, but Mildara's introduction of a second label, 'Balgownie Premier Cuvée', for wines made from fruit grown elsewhere, has confused customers. This is despite the fact that some of the 'Cuvée' wines are very good, such as the 1984 Cabernet Shiraz, a leafy, oaky, smoky wine in its youth at five years old. But then, it was made partly from local fruit from Dalwhinnie, which makes good wines of its own, and partly from Mildara's Coonawarra material.

Located at Kyneton, not far from the state forest and only an hour's drive from the Yarra Valley, on rolling land which had never really been tested for vines, Virgin Hills was set up by a Melbourne restaurateur, Tom Lazar, who wanted, like many others, to make the best red wine in Australia. With the first two vintages in 1975 and 1976, he seemed well on the way towards the foothills surrounding his objective, with dense, powerful, purple wines combining Cabernet Sauvignon, Malbec and Shiraz to give an intense fruit palate with a long, strong finish. If later vintages had improved on this they would have been fine indeed, but the 1977 smelt and tasted like carbolic acid, and the 1979 had, when only four years old, something of the balance and feel, but not the strength, of an old Delaforce port. The vineyard has suffered from financial difficulties, but under new ownership it is beginning to strike its initial form again, and with mature vines the results are outstanding. Some would say that the 1988 vintage may be the best yet. In addition, for confirmed bottle-watchers it has one of the most attractive labels in Australia: 'Virgin Hills', the year, 'Produce of Australia', and not much else in a broad octagon.

Tasted from wood, Virgin Hills' wines can be remarkable, like trying Clarets *en primeur*. Both the 1983 and 1982 were deep crimson, with barely a hint of purple, and tremendous, aggressive tannin and acid but with sufficient fruit in the middle not to be overwhelmed but still clearly perceptible. These wines last well over a decade, after becoming drinkable at three or four years of age.

Even though Tom Lazar is no longer involved with what has become the Domain Gilbert, many of his ideas linger, quite apart from the fossilized hulk of his restaurant, lurking in the trees a little distance away from the winery. The maturation cellar is beautifully simple and works very well: a large excavation in the slope below the winery was roofed with rough timber, black plastic and galvanized iron, and covered with a few feet of earth. It maintains a uniform temperature, ideal for the wine and for cellar work in the height of summer.

The vineyard's location on a sandy loam hill overlying quartz, between a state forest and the defunct gold-mining town of Lauriston, was recommended to Tom Lazar by the Victorian Department of Agriculture, but while the wines are outstanding, in other ways this spot is a viticulturalist's nightmare. Yields have never reached 3 tonnes a hectare, and the wine-maker tells where the grapes are ripe by where the crows are attacking the fruit most fiercely.

Most of the vineyards in the heterogeneous region near Bendigo are very small, crushing much less than 25 tonnes: Blanche Barkly (1972), Château Dore (first established in 1866, then replanted in 1975 by descendants of the de Ravin family who began it), the Leamon family's Château Le Amon (1973), Cope-Williams (1980), Harcourt Valley Wines (1976), Heathcote (1978), Mill Vineyard (1980), Passing Clouds (1974) and Romsey (formerly Rocky Hills, 1977). Le Amon, close to Balgownie, is making good reds in similar mould in its concrete-block château, but like so many small makers has much work to do on the whites. Passing Clouds makes a Pinot Noir with the strong varietal attributes (although little resemblance to Burgundy) that characterize so many Australian Pinot Noir wines.

Slightly larger, crushing 25–50 tonnes, are Eppalock Ridge (formerly Romany Rye, 1978), Knight's Granite Hills (1976), Virgin Hills (1968) and Zuber (1972). Knight's wines are very good indeed but less distinctive than those of Virgin Hills, no doubt because a range of styles is attempted. I particularly like the Shiraz made from Harcourt Valley fruit, as it has something of the scented character of a true Hermitage. The Riesling is the area's best. Remarkably, for a vineyard planted so recently and at 550 metres above sea level to obtain a cool micro-climate, Knight's plantings included Palomino and Crouchen.

Balgownie and Waterwheel both crush between 100 and 200 tonnes but are otherwise very different, Waterwheel wines having some of the characteristics of the better wines of north-eastern Victoria.

A flour milling company, Waterwheel, at Bridgewater on Loddon, has the small winery as one of several enterprises. The wines are erratic in quality, but at their best are very good. Taken at lunch, with a salad which included many radishes, their 1982 Cabernet Rosé was, when two years old, sweet with clean fruit but no nose, in contrast to a 1980 Grenache Rosé from Biltmore in the Granite Belt, which was ultra dry, clean, with a strong Grenache nose and a hard finish. The 1983 Chardonnay was lacking in fruit when compared with the Roseworthy 1982 Chardonnay enjoyed at the same time. The 1981 Cabernet Sauvignon, however, which required a great deal of breathing, was a wine with plenty of backbone as well as attractive stalky fruit.

The Pyrenees are attractive hills, mostly gently rolling country which was once thickly wooded. Now, most such timber is on or around the steeper hills and occasional cliffs which gave the area its name. Certainly the triangle between Avoca, Moonambel and Redbank, which contains most of the Pyrenees wineries, is not mountainous; there are signs pointing proudly to distinctive peaks a few hundred metres above sea level, the same height as the Great Dividing Range at its southern extremity not far away. The wines do not conform to Hilaire Belloc's prescription for true Pyrenean wine: none of them tastes of tar.

The first winery in the area was Château Remy, established by Remy Martin in 1963 with advice from Colin Preece, who had been responsible for so much of Seppelt's good wine from the 1930s to the 1950s. Originally the aim was to make good brandy, since at that time Australian brandy was protected against both imported brandy and locally made spirits other than brandy. When the rules were changed and the brandy glut began, Château Remy was redirected towards bottle-fermented sparkling wines. These are big wines, with some fruit flavour as well as much yeast, distinctive as well as enjoyable. Made initially from White Hermitage (Ugni Blanc) as well as Chardonnay, they rest for three years on the yeast, and the bead is very fine for an Australian sparkling wine. A vintage is declared only if the year promises exceptionally well; 1982 was such a year, and the wine was released as late as 1987. These wines are well worth seeking out.

The château, or *chai*, consists of an abruptly shaped building set among stringy barks, big cellars dug into the hillside behind. Inside the winery the tall still and its appurtenances stand covered with dust, illustrative of the state of the brandy industry.

Mount Avoca is a smaller winery nearby making deep-flavoured red wines of considerable merit, the ripe-fruit Shiraz representing value for money. The whites are less interesting. Mount Avoca has also made wines for Dalwhinnie (1980) of nearby Moonambel; Dalwhinnie Shiraz is perhaps the most stylish of the range.

Redbank is more a maker than a grower, taking fruit from some of the better growers nearby and making very fine wines. That made from Redbank's own fruit, 'Sally's Paddock', a blend of Cabernet Sauvignon, Malbec and Shiraz, is excellent. Like so many of the cool-area wines, these reds need time to show their outstanding quality but are so enjoyable young that few have the patience to keep them long enough.

Taltarni, which has one of the most distinctive labels in Australia – an exotic haloed figure on a buff background – also makes some of the best wine in Victoria. American-owned with a French winemaker, Dominic Portet, it generated much bemused discussion with its first few vintages, which were so thick and tannic that people responded as they had to 'Grange Hermitage' twenty-five years earlier: 'Can this man be serious?' But he was, and so are the wines. The Cabernet Sauvignon has quite remarkable depth of flavour, the 1976 and 1977 vintages slowly coming into balance by late 1983. The Malbec is much softer, the 1981 vintage drinkable in a tooth-blackening way at the same time.

Not content with these reds and some good still whites, Portet has also made some very good sparkling wines, the white 'Cuvée Daly's' and pink 'Taché Brut' widely available and both good and good value for money.

Summerfields (1974) crushes less than 25 tonnes a year, Redbank (1973) between 25 and 50 tonnes, of which about 10 are grown on the property. Warrenmang (1974) crushes an amount similar to Redbank but grows most of its own fruit, the Cabernet in particular being very good. Dalwhinnie (1973) is about the same size and makes a rich Chardonnay with something of the character of an 'Apricot Nectar' rose. Mount Avoca (1970) crushes about 100 tonnes. Château Remy (1963) and Taltarni (1972) both crush about 500 tonnes. Not far to the south is Ballarat, near which there are a few small wineries. St Anne's (1970) crushes less than 25 tonnes, Home and Landrigan's Yellowglen between 50 and 100 tonnes.

Yellowglen, which merged into Mildara in 1984, has made some of the best sparkling wines in Australia. At a site some 450 metres above sea level it grows a range of varieties, from Sylvaner to Shiraz, but its future probably lies with Chardonnay and Pinot Noir, for

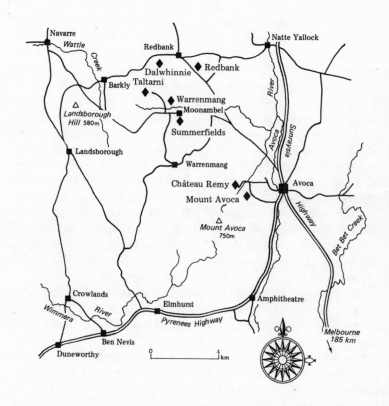

Central Victoria (2)

the sparkling wines it has made, using irrigated Chardonnay from
the Murray and varieties such as Chenin Blanc from the Pyrenees,
have been very good. Some were made by Neil Robb of Redbank,
but Landrigan, who first came to Australia from France to work at
Seppelt's Great Western, has been the main wine-maker although
he has now moved on to his own winery. The best Yellowglen
wines, when relatively young, show a good pale-straw colour, a fine
bead and a good deal of yeast.

NORTH-EASTERN VICTORIA

In the late 1880s the Victorian government decided to encourage
the wine industry. In 1889 there were less than 5,000 hectares under
vine, but, as a result of a bonus of £5 per acre to anyone who would
plant and cultivate vines, by 1985 there were over 12,000 hectares,
most of the increase being in the north, particularly around Rutherglen. Additional encouragement to growers was provided by P. B.
Burgoyne, an English wine merchant who made a fortune out of
'Burgoyne's Big Tree Burgundy' and other similar products.

In the Australian Depression of the 1890s, new wineries had
difficulty enough, but when phylloxera struck the area in 1899 it
was the crowning blow. Furthermore, after Federation fashion
changed, and the heavy red wines of the area were no longer in such
demand. However, other heavy wines came into favour: sweet
fortified wines.

Cheap fortified wines sold well on the domestic market, and wine-
makers began to build up stocks. Over time, as they blended to a
style, they realized just how exceptional these fortified wines were,
particularly the whites. Whether labelled Frontignac, Muscat, or
Tokay, the well-made ones are almost always outstanding.

The young wines have strong fruit character, a marked raisiny
flavour, but as they age, particularly in old wood, they become
much more intense, with an extraordinarily lingering richness and
astringency. Bailey, Campbell, Lindeman, Morris, Chambers – they
are all fine wines. Stanton & Killeen is one of the few wineries of
the area which has produced a vintage Muscat, a wine of much
greater freshness than most of the blended ones, but it is not clear,
because of the rarity of such wines, that there is a place for vintage
Muscats as with vintage ports. Seppelt, with its enormous stocks, is

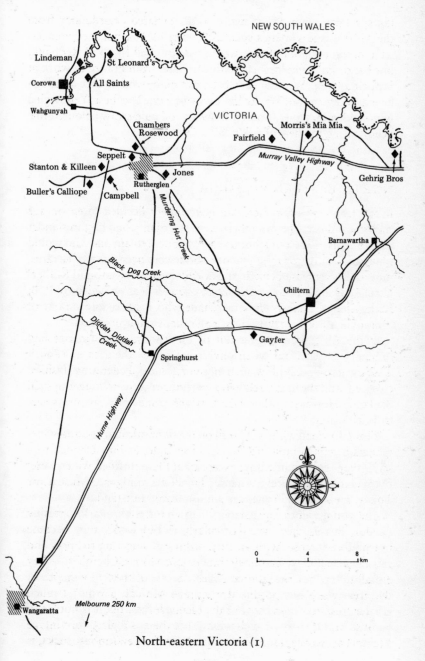

NEW SOUTH WALES

Lindeman
St Leonard's
Corowa
All Saints
Wahgunyah
VICTORIA
Chambers
Rosewood
Fairfield
Morris's Mia Mia
Seppelt
Stanton & Killeen
Jones
Gehrig Bros
Buller's Calliope
Campbell
Rutherglen
Murray Valley Highway

Murdering Hut Creek

Barnawartha

Black Dog Creek

Chiltern

Diddah Diddah Creek

Gayfer

Springhurst

Hume Highway

0   4   8 km

Melbourne 250 km

Wangaratta

North-eastern Victoria (1)

155

another company which makes, at the top of its range, a fresh Muscat despite it being a blend of many years' wines.

The combination of the Australian wine consumer's rejection of fortified wine, the loss of the Imperial Preference, the movement away from sweet wines, and the briefly imposed tax on fortifying spirit at the time it is added to wine which may be a decade old before it is sold, may damage the Victorian Muscat industry irreparably, to the discredit of all concerned. These wines are worth seeking out, as something Australia has made which, like Phar Lap or Don Bradman, is the best of its kind in the world.

The classic table wines of the area echo the fortified wines' attributes: they have vast body and fruit flavour. They develop very slowly but, at their best, very gradually exchange subtlety for immensity. In recent years lighter styles have been aimed at, such as Campbell's 'Rutherglen Red', but they do not match the lighter wine of Bendigo or the Pyrenees and certainly do not approach the lighter Rhône wines, as one might have hoped.

The road from Wodonga to Rutherglen runs through rich pastoral and cropping country. In late winter it is a flat, bright green. Every flooded creek or river swirls round huge river red gums, the water a muddy grey. Every soggy paddock is full of ibises, straw-necked or white.

The first winery to which one comes is Gehrig's, an unspoilt agglomeration of tin sheds and beautiful old golden brick buildings, old machinery surrounding trees near the buildings.

Next comes Morris's, on Mia Mia Road, a neater collection of buildings but still with galvanized iron as the predominant structural material.

On Highway 16 itself is 'historic' Fairfield House, with its rather Mediterranean-looking winery. Fairfield House itself is a fine example of late-Victorian country architecture, such as can been seen around Melbourne and Adelaide. On a gentle slope on the opposite side of the Highway is a fine stone building looking rather like a monastery. The locked gates and unused drive suggest that it is no longer a thriving community.

Closer to Rutherglen there is a turn-off to Mount Pryor, and in the opposite direction the Jones winery, a collection of sheds in green-painted crumbling brick and galvanized iron, from which surprisingly fine Shiraz wines sometimes come.

In Rutherglen itself, on a quite different scale, is Seppelt's tank farm, its Clydeside winery. This is large-scale professional wine-making. From the old buildings backed by so much stainless steel have come many very fine fortified wines, a distinctive lighter dessert wine called 'Barooga Sauternes', made from Ondenc (Irvine's white), and many fine regional Shirazes, even a few Pinots with intense rich fruit and no Burgundy feel to them at all. In 1984 Clydeside was closed by Seppelt for economic reasons; sentiment perhaps prevailed when Clydeside was bought and reopened by Jolimont, to go on making the same kinds of wine.

Continuing on to Echuca, almost opposite each other are Campbell's 'Bobbie Burns' Winery and Stanton & Killeen. Campbell's is a curious mixture of new facade, old, well-kept tin sheds and stainless steel carefully set well back from the other buildings. Like all the other wineries in the area, it has much small wood and large wood, much of it close to the roof, for this is the source of the superb Muscats of the north-east with the hot-summer, cold-winter treatment. Old equipment, like a disused polished copper-pot still, is laid about carefully to give the impression of continuity and tradition, but this is a winery which has had a fair amount of capital expenditure in the recent past. The atmosphere is friendly: one is pressed to try everything, even wines that are unavailable for purchase but of which a few bottles remain.

Further on, on the road to Echuca, a turn-off leads to the fortress-like All Saints Winery, its rear rather like the front of Fairfield.

Because of the extremely rapid expansion of the Victorian wine industry after 1850, as compared with the much longer, slower development of the New South Wales and South Australia wine industries, as well as its subsequent collapse, the vegetation of the little surviving islands of wine in Victoria carries far more strange relics than are to be found in the industries which survived in better shape. Thus, at All Saints there is a strange grape called 'Rutherglen Pedro Ximines', now known to be Dourado, and what is called a Chablis is made from this. The 1982 wine shows none of the fatty, rich, coarse fruit of Pedro as one finds it in South Australia. Indeed, the wine has a clean, hard finish, like licking a carving knife, a finish which characterized the 'Riesling Hocks' of the South Australian Southern Vales in the 1950s and 1960s.

Further on still, one comes to the Goulburn River and can follow this to Château Tahbilk.

Continuing still further towards Swan Hill and Ouyen, one passes

Mystic Park and Lake Boga, irrigated vineyards supplying Brown Brothers at Milawa and Best's at Great Western with reliable fruit in substantial quantity.

But one should have made a detour to Château Tahbilk.

R. H. 'Orion' Horne was of the type who came to Australia to make his fortune. As he wrote,

A sultry haze broods o'er the silent bush,
And horse and ox move slow through steaming dust;
In each man's face is seen the feverish flush
Of hope, or of success; the ceaseless thirst
For gold

urged him too, but prospecting was one of the few enterprises he did not try. He acted, he stood for parliament, he wrote, he tried to promote companies, and he saw that viticulture was important. The Goulburn Vineyard Proprietary Company was to be formed to grow vines and make wine on the banks of the Goulburn River, on the Noorilim run; Horne was honorary secretary from 16 March 1860. He also wrote the prospectus for the public issue of shares: 'The Wines of the Rhine and the Moselle can certainly be equalled, but in some instances will be surpassed, by vintages of the Goulburn, the Loddon, the Campaspe . . .' Three months later, following the unexplained death of one of the promoters, Horne was promoting the Tahbilk Vineyard Proprietary Company, Tahbilk being the run adjacent to Noorilim. J. P. Bear, one of the other promoters, recommended advertising for 1,000,000 cuttings.

Twenty-five men were needed to work the square mile of the Tahbilk run, and less than six months later 60 hectares were cleared and 25 planted. Horne himself planted the first vines, but his connection with Tahbilk lasted less than two years. As he put in another poem, he vanished 'in the yellow Wog-Wog', but within a decade the company, now the family firm of the Bears, was producing and shipping as much as 225,000 litres a year, with 450,000 in storage. Advanced plant and French wine-makers ensured quality, though a vast range of wines was attempted: Riesling, Verdelho, Pedro, Muscat, Shiraz, Cabernet, 'Burgundy', Gouais and 'Aucerot', and a sweet white wine called 'Pascorata'.

Thomas Hardy visited in 1881 and advised wider planting of the vines for ease of working, the South Australian practice. Irrigation

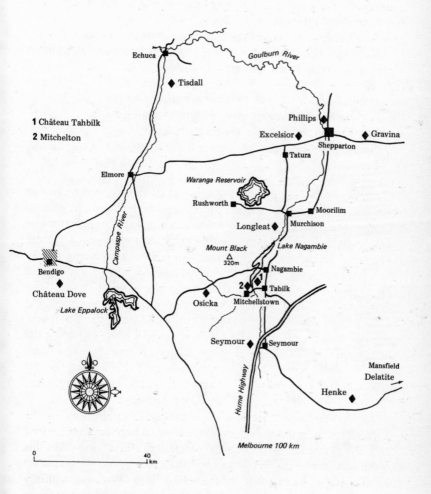

1 Château Tahbilk
2 Mitchelton

Echuca
Tisdall
Goulburn River

Phillips
Excelsior
Shepparton
Gravina
Tatura
Elmore

Campaspe River

Waranga Reservoir
Rushworth
Moorilim
Longleat
Murchison

Mount Black
△
320m
Lake Nagambie

Nagambie
Bendigo
2 1
Château Dove
Tabilk
Osicka
Mitchellstown
Lake Eppalock

Seymour
Seymour

Mansfield
Delatite
Henke

Hume Highway

Melbourne 100 km

0   40
└─────────────────┘ km

North-central Victoria

159

also was sought by François de Coueslat, the wine-maker, but was not available.

The name Château Tahbilk was adopted in the late 1870s, and as such it has continued, though declining towards the end of its first half-century through the same problem as affected a number of other Australian agricultural properties: an absentee landlord. When the Purbrick family bought it in 1929, Tahbilk had less than 50 hectares of vines of which 30 were old. Marsanne, now one of its notable wines, was part of the new planting. Phylloxera had affected the vineyard but it had survived, a rarity in Victoria.

Despite the Depression, Eric Purbrick reconstructed much of the winery and out-buildings, replanted the vineyards, then went off to the Second World War. Afterwards, wine sealed into the wall of the old winery by Bear in 1876 was taken out and tasted; the red was drinkable, the white not. Wine of the 1960 vintage was sealed into the wall by the prime minister of the day (and other days), R. G. Menzies; one suspects that the 1960 white will last better than the 1876.

Tahbilk is a Victorian institution, a major tourist attraction, and a maker of very fine wines. It has made exceptional wines, at different times, from Riesling, Shiraz and Cabernet Sauvignon. The Cabernet, at its best (which is quite often), is a big wine, ruby in colour, with strong berry fruit and a firm finish, yet with elegance as well as power. The Marsanne is usually delicious. Early in changing from European names to grape names for wines, the proprietors have seen fashion follow them.

Near Château Tahbilk are Osicka and Mitchelton. Not far north is Tisdall; to the south is Seymour.

Tisdall has two vineyards, one irrigated near Echuca and another, Mount Helen, at about 500 metres above sea level. Wines from Mount Helen are usually very good.

Mitchelton was established as a fun parlour as well as a winery, with a tower, to be seen on its labels, which is a kind of parody of Tahbilk's Australian vernacular (i.e. corrugated iron) pagoda. It had trouble with flooding from the Goulburn River soon after its establishment and more recently has had a severe outbreak of phylloxera, endemic in the area. Despite all this, it makes good wines, segregating them from its bulk wines by calling the latter 'Thomas Mitchell'. Rescued from financial difficulties in the early

1980s by the Valmorbida family, it still makes too many different wines and handicaps some with 'artistic' labels.

Osicka (1955) crushes less than 100 tonnes, Seymour (1968) between 100 and 500, Mitchelton (1969) and Tahbilk (1860) between 500 and 1,000, and Tisdall (1975) over 1,000 tonnes.

From Rutherglen one could instead have gone south to Glenrowan. Glenrowan is part of Australian history, and also part of Australian myth, for it was here at about 5.00 a.m. on Monday 29 June 1880 that Ned Kelly, Australia's most famous bushranger and bank-robber, was captured, wearing 40 kilos of armour made from plough mouldboards. Opinion is sharply divided as to whether he was a typical Irish victim of British injustice or, as the Australian historian M. H. Ellis said, 'One of the most cold-blooded, egotistical, and utterly self-centred criminals who ever decorated the end of a rope in an Australian gaol'; either way, he is part of popular lore, so it is only appropriate that the winery associated with Glenrowan – Bailey's – should itself be legendary.

Cooled to −271°C, liquid helium climbs out of a glass and down the outside. At room temperature, Bailey's Shiraz wines leap out of the glass and take the drinker by the throat. They are quite exceptional in flavour and very high in alcohol, usually over 13 per cent. Unlike most Shiraz wines from warm areas, however, but similar to the ones from Clare, they are very clean; it is just the immense body of blackberry fruit that makes the tongue furry and sticks the teeth together. Diacetyl, which gives hot-area wines their buttery smell, is a substance which is more often found in wines after the malolactic fermentation than before it. Very small quantities (two to four parts per million) enhance flavour, while amounts much greater than this detract from it; Bailey's wines rarely show this trait. In this they may be contrasted with similar wines from Bungawarra in Queensland's Granite Belt. The standard 1980 Shirazes from both vineyards were enjoyed with pizza, and the Bungawarra definitely showed some diacetyl, whereas the Bailey simply showed the enormous body of bramble fruit.

Bailey's is a very old established winery; it was ten years old when Ned Kelly was captured, and some of the alcohol under the influence of which Ned and his gang were when arrested may well have come from Bailey's wines. During the wine boom of the late 1960s the winery was taken over by Davis Consolidated, a maker of gelatine, which in turn was taken over by a maker of starch and related

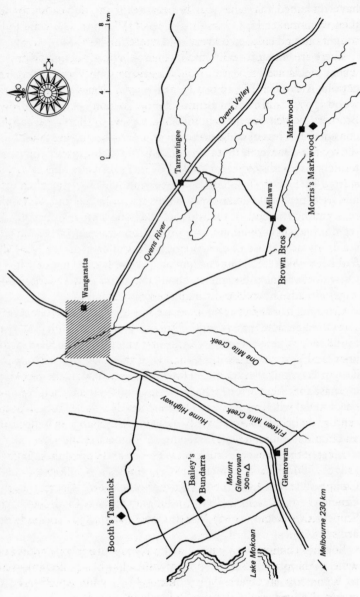

North-eastern Victoria (2)

products, Goodman Fielder Wattie. Since these changes the wines have remained the same, partly because of the dedication of the then wine-maker H. J. Tinson. Bailey's HJT Shiraz is a wine to be sought out and enjoyed on very cold winter nights.

There are very few really small wineries in north-eastern Victoria, where yields are high even from vineyards with very limited irrigation: Avalon, HJT (1979), Henke (1970), Jones (1888), Markwood (1970) and Mount Bruno (1970). Avalon is close to Brown Brothers' cooler vineyards in the King Valley, so should perhaps be considered as less of a hot-area maker, but its promising Pinot Noir shows the character that comes from not being afraid of a hot ferment, or perhaps warm fruit. HJT, as the name suggests, was started by Harry Tinson, the long-serving wine-maker of Bailey's, and as expected he makes very big wines, both red and white, the reds among the best of the style. Henke's reds are also true to the region: big, slightly jammy, long-lived, good value. Markwood was set up by a member of the Morris family after Morris's Mia Mia had been sold to Reckitt & Colman, whose former major winery, Orlando, was also bought at about the same time. Markwood's wines already show their distinguished provenance.

Crushing from 50 to 100 tonnes are Stanton & Killeen (Gracerray, 1925), Excelsior (1868), and Phillips' Goulburn Valley Winery (1908–66, 1978). Excelsior was the first vineyard in the Shepparton area, and has remained in the hands of the family of its founder, Trojan Darveniza, ever since. However, it seems that the best days are past for Shepparton, which awaits a revival, another François de Castella, who ran Château Dookie for a decade at the turn of the century on behalf of a creditor bank before the change in wine tastes and markets eliminated it, like so many Victorian wineries.

Most of the vineyards crush between 100 and 500 tonnes: Bailey's (1870), Booth's Taminick (1893), Buller's Calliope (1921), Campbell (1870), Chambers' Rosewood (1860), Gayfer (1913), Gravina (1972), Gehrig (1858), Jolimont (1886 as Clydeside, 1914 Seppelt), Monichio (1962) Morris's Mia Mia (1859) and St Leonard's (1860).

Booth's Taminick is a winery with very few products, and its best wine, perhaps, is its Shiraz, most of which has been sold in the past to Wynn for its 'Ovens Valley Burgundy', a wine which has also included some material from Bailey and elsewhere. It is a very reliable fruity wine which reminds one of hot summer afternoons without tasting cooked. It was not disgraced by a number of 1978 and 1979 Rhône wines when we tried the 1980 in England in 1984. However, it was being retailed there at a little over twice what it costs in bottle shops in Australia, a good illustration of the difficulty a high-cost country like Australia has in competing with lower-cost countries, a problem which would exist even without the EEC's discriminatory import rules and taxes. Comparing the Booth 1980 Shiraz with the Wynn version in Australia in 1983, the most obvious difference was that Wynn's was cleaner and less rich, with no sediment, clearly the result of adhering to Samuel Wynn's rule about taking the wine to the consumer only when it is brilliant to the eye.

Chambers' Rosewood is another old family winery which has continued to use odd grapes, for example Gouais, which is part of the blend in a firm white wine rather lacking in fruit but lasting very well.

Morris's Mia Mia makes, apart from its excellent fortified wines, a fine inky Durif with enough backbone and fruit to allow it to last a decade without tasting old.

The biggest wineries in the area, crushing between 1,000 and 5,000 tonnes, are All Saints (1864) and Brown Brothers (1889). Brown Brothers have been among the great successes of the industry in the last twenty-five years. I first recall noticing their blend of Cabernet Sauvignon, Shiraz and Mondeuse, a reliable, fruity wine of considerable complexity and a cleaner finish than many comparably priced wines from McLaren Vale or the Barossa. However, the Browns were among the earlier of the medium-sized established wineries to realize the possibilities of cold fermentation and related techniques for making good wines from fairly warm areas. They were also interested in trying different varieties and different styles, with the result that they make a bewildering number of different wines rather well. Their whites, made with everything from Riesling to Muscat, are fruity, attractive, well-balanced wines. Their reds include the blend I have already mentioned and small batches of everything from Tarrango to Barbera.

Of particular interest is their move to develop vineyards at higher altitudes, for cooler ripening. Koombahla, south of Milawa, is only a few hundred metres above sea level, but both the Cabernet Sauvignon and Chardonnay reflect the advantages of the area. The 1979 Cabernet, for example, is a big, rich wine with strong berry flavour but none of the earthiness which has characterized the wines from Milawa itself. Whitlands, nearby, is at about 800 metres altitude, and also suits early-ripening varieties like Pinot Noir and Chardonnay.

Seppelt made mainly wines for fortification and bulk sales in this area, but also produced very good dessert wines typical of the district and surprisingly good Pinot Noir in the late 1960s and early 1970s. Possibly a hotter fermentation was allowed, running up to the 30–40°C peak used in Burgundy, thereby producing wines of strong character and depth of fruit. I recall preferring both the 1969 and 1970 to Robert Mondavi's Napa Valley 1970 Pinot Noir in the winter of 1975. Jolimont has not yet had time to demonstrate whether this traditional style will be maintained.

THE MURRAY: NORTH-WESTERN VICTORIA

There are small wineries along the Murray, but the impression one retains is hugeness. Towering stainless steel tanks, vast concrete blockhouses, cavernous tin sheds supported by massive red gum beams: old like Mildara at Mildura, or relatively new like the Loxton Co-operative in South Australia, they verge on grossness. Tasting areas must have large capacity and remind one about the licensing laws, for the tourists are there for the river first, the wine later.

Mildara's tasting room has huge illustrations simulating the atmosphere of a winery of the 1880s; they do not match the present winery in anything but size. The wines do not match the room either; those from the river tend to have a little sweetness, but those from Coonawarra are elegant, restrained and firm, smooth though they are when young, compared with Redman's or Brand's. Mildara's skills have changed with the times, but those developed to make sherry and port when these were demanded have persisted: their 'George' and 'Supreme', bone dry and smoothly dry, both with some *flor* character, remain among the better Australian sherries. If the climate, physical, social and economic, changes so that sherry is once again drunk in large quantities, Mildara will still be there to benefit from it. Meanwhile, its extensive Coonawarra vineyards, its acquisition of Hamilton and its association with William Grant & Son Ltd, which owns 15 per cent of Mildara, give it an extraordinary range of products to meet changing tastes. Mildara is a survivor.

More than a survivor, in fact: it has risen from the dead twice.

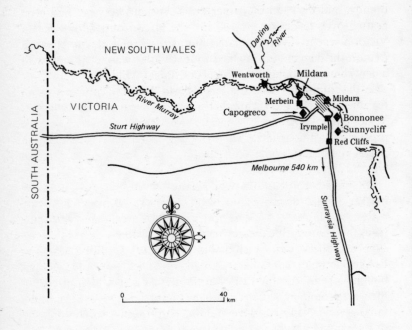

North-western Victoria (1)

Founded as Château Mildura in 1888 by the Chaffey brothers who pioneered large-scale irrigation in Australia, it was bankrupt within five years, and George Chaffey left the country, returning to North America. William Chaffey remained but could not sell his wine or brandy, and by 1908 the winery was shut and all vines had been grafted over to drying grapes, still the largest outlet for vines in Victoria seventy-five years later. But as the wine industry changed to meet the demand for fortified wine, Chaffey was ready and, with a new company, bought the assets of Château Mildura.

In the slump just after the First World War, the company again became insolvent and yet another company, this time called Mildura Wines but still chaired by Chaffey, took over the assets in 1922. It prospered in the artificial export boom of the later 1920s, and in the 1930s began, under Ron Haselgrove, to make good fortified wine as well as good brandy.

After the Second World War Haselgrove saw that a table wine market should develop, and began to move to meet it, buying material from many sources, principally McLaren Vale, with some from the Hunter. But the key move was to Coonawarra, to ensure supply, in the 1950s. Much had been bought from Bill Redman of Rouge Homme, but others wanted his wine. The land Mildara bought cost £3,500 for 12 hectares, in 1954 a very high price, but their first commercial Cabernet Sauvignon, made in 1963, is still a famous wine. Nicknamed 'Peppermint Patty' because of the intensity of its minty fruit character, at twenty years of age it tasted like a good five- or six-year-old wine. The company has yet to repeat this success, but its wines are always very good.

Mildara crushes over 15,000 tonnes of grapes a year, but little more than 5 per cent comes from its slowly and carefully acquired 200 hectares at Coonawarra and 25 hectares at Eden Valley.

Mildara's net profit after tax was for some years only about 2 to 5 per cent of its sales of $20 million a year, 2.5 to 5 per cent of shareholders' funds, despite its premium wines, its efficient management and its range of agencies, such as Pommery & Greno, which are far less capital-demanding. This illustrates again the problems of the industry.

Recognizing that its Sauvignon Blanc, its Cabernet Sauvignon from Coonawarra, and its skill in handling enormous quantities of good fruit would not alone make it financially secure, Mildara set out on the path of expansion, and its sales have more than doubled in five years through increased sales of its own wines as well as from the acquisition of Krondorf, Balgownie, Yellowglen and Hamilton's Ewell. Profits have increased more than commensurately. It is to be hoped that this success, which has been accompanied by a proliferation of initially meaningless brand names such as 'Alexander's Cabernet Sauvignon', 'Jamieson's Run' and 'Balgownie Cuvée', as well as by some rather confusing labels, will be followed by the stability necessary for new names to be trusted.

There are very few small wineries along the Murray in the area also called north-western Victoria. The smallest is Capogreco (1976), which crushes less than 100 tonnes, and the next smallest is Robinvale (1976), which crushes between 100 and 500 tonnes, about half of it bought in, to make wines with a Grecian model, for the proprietors are of Greek origin. In passing, quite a few Australian wineries have tried fermenting wine in pine to make Retsina, and the results certainly taste of pine, but somehow under Australian skies as blue as those above the Mediterranean, these wines seem tainted rather than enjoyable. Chatterton in the Barossa makes a wine called 'Obliqua', a kind of white port stored in casks made of messmate (*Eucalyptus obliqua*), a native hardwood, but the result is interesting rather than a portent of things to come. Sunnycliff (1973) at Iraak, about 40 kilometres south-east of Mildura, makes a Chardonnay that is almost a burlesque of the rich Australian style but which is well made as well as delicious.

Best of Great Western established a vineyard, St Andrew's, at Lake Boga in 1930 to supply fruit more economically than it could be grown at Great Western. It now takes almost 1,000 tonnes from the area, about half from St Andrew's.

Crushing between 1,000 and 5,000 tonnes are Bonnonee (1974), Buller's Beverford (1952) and Fairefield (1968). Beverford was established by Buller's in the same way as Best's St Andrew's. Fairefield is a co-operative.

Mildara (1888), the giant of the region, crushes over 18,000 tonnes.

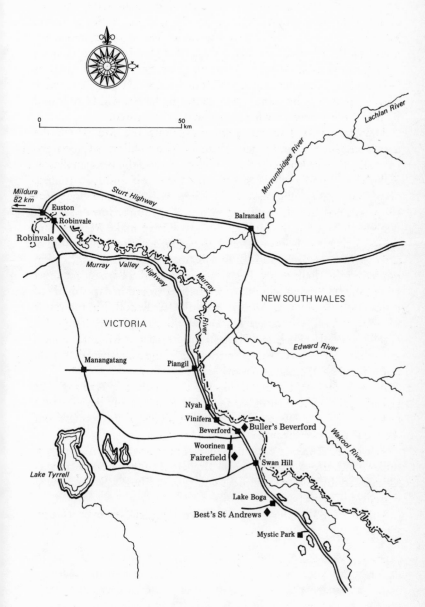

North-western Victoria (2)

5
New South Wales

The early history of wine-growing in New South Wales is the early history of Australian wine-growing, discussed in Chapter 1. Despite this early start, New South Wales was never the dominant wine-producer. While its range of climates includes some adverse enough to produce good wine, like that of the Hunter Valley, the problems of disease from summer rainfall and poor fruit set in a dry spring meant that the first colony became a large-scale producer when it was no longer a colony, after Federation, through development of the irrigation areas on the Murrumbidgee and Murray Rivers after Victoria and South Australia had established large areas of both dryland and irrigated vineyards.

The Riverina College of Advanced Education at Wagga Wagga set up an oenology course some forty years after Roseworthy, well after the revival of the Hunter Valley and Mudgee and the establishment of the Upper Hunter. Even then, the problems of fine wine-growing in summer rainfall country have hardly been the main priority, given that students come from all over Australia, as they do to Roseworthy.

Looking ahead, wine-growing seems unlikely to expand in New South Wales, as against Victoria, Tasmania and Western Australia, despite the attraction of the nation's largest market, Sydney.

THE SYDNEY AREA

Captain William Minchin, an Irish army officer, first set out for New South Wales in March 1797, but the prisoners in the female convict transport *Lady Shore*, in which Minchin was in command of the troops, mutinied, and Minchin, his wife and others were cast adrift off the coast of Brazil. When he returned to Britain he was

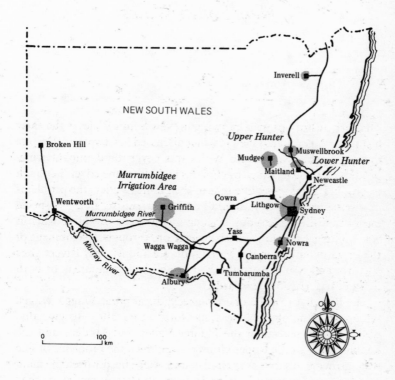

NEW SOUTH WALES

Broken Hill

Murrumbidgee Irrigation Area

Wentworth

Murrumbidgee River Griffith

Cowra

Lithgow

Inverell

Upper Hunter

Mudgee Muswellbrook

Maitland *Lower Hunter*

Newcastle

Sydney

Yass

Wagga Wagga

Nowra

Canberra

Murray River

Tumbarumba

Albury

0   100
km

New South Wales

able to explain the problem away and once more set out for New South Wales, arriving the following year.

Despite sharing the experience of a mutiny with Governor Bligh, Minchin was one of the officers who took a prominent role in the rebellion in Sydney in January 1808, though his true part in this unpleasant episode has never been satisfactorily clarified. Remaining in the army, Minchin saw service in the American War of 1812–15, although not with much distinction. When he retired in 1817 he returned to New South Wales with his family, and he received a land grant of 400 hectares in 1819. This he named Minchinbury, but he did not live long enough to enjoy it. After his death in 1821, wines were made from vines which were planted by his wife and daughter, and extensive vineyards were planted and cellars built.

Expansion continued until phylloxera struck at the end of the century, and in 1899 the vineyard was destroyed. Before this, Leo Buring had made the first sparkling wine there, and he stayed on until 1920, so he was manager for the first eight years for which Penfold owned the property. Buring was followed by a French Champagne maker, and it was over the forty years that Penfold had vines on the property that Minchinbury became a major Australian name for sparkling wine fermented in the bottle. In fact, Minchinbury was the first Australian winery to use the transfer method, which is to say that after the secondary fermentation of about fifteen months, the wine is disgorged into stainless steel, filtered, liqueured and rebottled.

Although the last vintage was as recent as 1980, from the 1950s onwards the vineyards were gradually running down, and the sale of the vineyards for building blocks marked the rule of the accountants, following the takeover of Penfold by Tooth & Co. In recent years the old cellars have been a dismal sight, despite the developers' assurance of their 'preservation as an historical asset' at the time of the first subdivision of the land. Perhaps it is just as well that they burnt down in 1988, thereby relieving the developers of the onerous obligation of keeping their word.

There are still three small vineyards and wineries within what to the visitor seems the never-ending sprawl that is Sydney: Cogno Brothers (1964), Richmond Estate (1967), crushing a little more than 50 tonnes, and Camden Bridge (1974), crushing a little less than 100 tonnes. Camden Bridge is of particular interest because it is on the Nepean River just opposite the Macarthurs' Camden Park, where much early vineyard experimentation went on with some success. A range of wines has been made from most of the major varieties, and the early vintages showed considerable promise, though the area cannot become a major source of good wine, given its proximity to Sydney and the consequent high value of the land for residential purposes. Cogno Brothers is north of Camden and makes, among other wines, a Barbera. As I have mentioned, it is surprising how rarely Australia's Italian wine-makers use this variety. I do not think that Cogno's version provides a guide for others. At Bringelly, Vicary (1923) crushes over 100 tonnes and makes a surprisingly good sweet Traminer.

THE HUNTER VALLEY

The Hunter has a big-city offshoot's feel about it. The restaurants are not simply good (where they *are* good), they are smart. Less than two and a half hours by road from Sydney – not so close as Clare to Adelaide, let alone the Swan to Perth or Lilydale to Melbourne – it seems part of Australia's only metropolis. Hungerford Hill, Arrowfield and some of the other larger wineries have taken advantage of this to add touches of big-city boutiquery to their grounds, so that one can do more than merely taste wine, talk or wander around looking at things. Hungerford Hill has what it calls a 'Wine Village', in fact, where one can spend a fortune without buying any wine or leaving the premises.

Although the normal approach to the Hunter is from Cessnock, it would be much better to arrive from somewhere else, as Cessnock looks like what it has always been: a decaying coal town. Driving north out of it towards Rothbury, one passes, without necessarily noticing them but just absorbing the ambience, the sewage works, the corrective centre and a large wrecking yard. After this anything would seem attractive, but the valley proper is beautiful in usual vineyard country style – gentle slopes, small, well-kept buildings, tall, wooded hills behind.

Charles King founded Mount Pleasant in about 1875, and it was already well established when his sons sold it to the New South Wales Wine Company soon after the company was founded in 1896. The NSW Wine Company was John Augustus O'Shea, an Irishman with a French wife; it was formed in an era when titles of this kind were coming into fashion: United States Steel, Standard

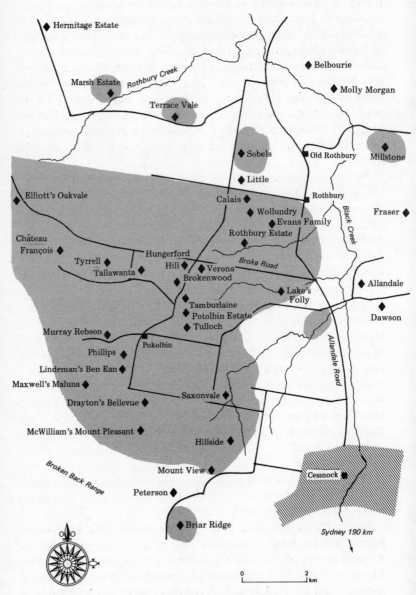

Hermitage Estate

Belbourie

Molly Morgan

Marsh Estate

Rothbury Creek

Terrace Vale

Sobels

Old Rothbury

Millstone

Little

Elliott's Oakvale

Calais

Rothbury

Wollundry

Evans Family

Fraser

Château François

Rothbury Estate

Black Creek

Hungerford

Broke Road

Tyrrell

Hill

Tallawanta

Verona

Brokenwood

Allandale

Lake's Folly

Tamburlaine

Dawson

Potolbin Estate

Murray Robson

Tulloch

Pokolbin

Allandale Road

Phillips

Lindeman's Ben Ean

Maxwell's Maluna

Drayton's Bellevue

Saxonvale

McWilliam's Mount Pleasant

Hillside

Broken Back Range

Mount View

Cessnock

Peterson

Sydney 190 km

Briar Ridge

0   2
|_____|
km

Hunter Valley (lower Hunter)

Oil, Patrick Auld's Australian Wine Company in London. However, John O'Shea was setting up a wine business for his sons.

One son, Jack, went to war and never really became involved in what was only large enough to support one man. The other son, Maurice O'Shea, completed his education in France after leaving school in Sydney, and returned to Mount Pleasant, where more land was bought just after the war. There he became a legend, for his sense of humour, his cooking, his kindness, but above all for his wine. He was exceptional in Australia in using very small batches of grapes from particular small blocks in the vineyard, so that he knew just how the fruit would finish and how the wine must be made.

He would take fruit from Tyrrell, Elliott and some smaller growers, as well as his different blocks at Mount Pleasant, and make wines with Christian names – 'Philip', 'Elizabeth' and others – blending carefully and usually successfully, whether red or white. After the McWilliam Brothers bought him out, they allowed him to continue in this way, and some of the names are still used, though O'Shea died in 1956. The quality is not the same; the wines are representative Hunter wines, no more.

O'Shea's was the French approach, but he did not have the immense backing of local knowledge that centuries of wine-growing leave, so he was really experimenting. At their best his were wines of exceptional elegance for Australia and yet they had great staying power, similar in style but not flavour to the best Burgundies. They occasionally surface at auctions and fetch very high prices, for they are still reminders of a remarkable wine-maker. As the late Sydney Hamilton told me, 'The Hunter isn't any place for good wine. Only three people made good wine there – that French chap, Lindeman's and one I forget.'

'French chap?'

'Yes. O'Shea. And how he did it in a tin shed with a dirt floor and a roof even I' – he was a very small man, physically – '– could touch, I'll never know. But he did.'

Mount Pleasant is still a beautiful spot, with gentle slopes down to the winery, small reasonably neat winery buildings and the wooded curves of the hills beyond, but it has changed a lot since Maurice O'Shea died. He had used close planting in the European manner, and McWilliam pulled out every second row, giving it a more orthodox Australian appearance, especially as further vines were planted and a new winery built of the giant shed kind, replacing O'Shea's small shed, 'L'Hermitage'. Total plantings are now well over 100 hectares, and the crush is about 1,500 tonnes, divided equally between red and white.

One of the reasons why the styles have changed is that McWilliam, like every other big company, likes to be able to offer a continuous service. That is, rather than release a dozen quite different wines over the course of a year, it would rather offer two or three throughout the year. It therefore offers the 'Philip Hermitage' every year, even in outstandingly bad years like 1971, whereas others, such as 'Charles', 'Robert', 'Frederick', or 'O.P.,' are made or sold only occasionally. The 'Philip Hermitage' is said to have the largest sale of any Hunter red wine, so magic has given way to reliability. McWilliam has made some exceptionally good wines from the Pinot Noir which O'Shea planted in the 1930s, blended with Shiraz: its 'Pinot Hermitage'. The elegance of the Pinot Noir is particularly evident in the 1978 wine, but over the years the combination of the two varieties has made for balance, depth of flavour, cleanness, and lightness of finish. The 1979 did not have the vitality of a 1986 'Irancy' (André Melou) over a scotch fillet in 1990, but was still sound.

Ben Ean is Lindeman's winery in the Hunter Valley, but it is also the name of its 'Moselle', a wine which, while it has lost its pre-eminence, was for many years the wine which sold more bottles than any other in Australia. A clean, smooth, fruity, sweet white wine, it is made at Karadoc near Mildura in north-eastern Victoria. The predominant grape is Sultana, but others such as Muscat and Trebbiano contribute to the fruit flavour.

It was introduced by Lindeman in the mid 1950s when Ray Kidd, who was given a centenary award of achievement by Roseworthy Agricultural College in 1983, realized that Hamilton's 'Ewell Moselle', with a simple label and the same attributes of clean fruity flavour and some residual sweetness, was a wine which people were starting to buy in increasing quantities. For a decade, sales of 'Ben Ean' rose at about 50 per cent a year, a rate which could not continue indefinitely, of course, but which was succeeded by more steady growth. In marketing parlance, 'Ben Ean' is now a mature product, and in recent years has been overtaken by Orlando's 'Jacob's Creek' as well as several of the sparkling wines of the Penfold–Kaiser Stuhl combine as the biggest-selling bottled brand name. It introduced an extraordinary number of people to wine, and was one of the attractions to Philip Morris, the American tobacco company, when it took over Lindeman during the great Ben Ean growth phase.

Lindeman has traditionally used other old local names for well-made brand-named wines. Coolalta is a Shiraz-based wine of light fruit character which is given considerable oak treatment yet retains balance and flavour for about a decade, the 1965 and 1966 for example drinkable in the mid 1970s. Porphyry is the name for two levels of dessert wine made predominantly from Sémillon. The ordinary 'Bin 36' has been a useful wine, at its best when about five years old, whereas the four-digit bin-numbered Porphyries have been among the best Australian dessert wines. Four digits signify high price and, usually, exceptionally high quality. This applies to dry wines, old Hunter Shirazes and Sémillons, as well.

If the Hunter sometimes seems much closer to Sydney than it really is, this is because of its Sydney orientation. When Murray Robson set up the Robson Vineyard in 1973, he called it the Squire Vineyard after the Squire shop which he had had in Sydney. He saw that the Hunter Valley was the 'number one wine retailing area in Sydney' as he put it, and made fine wines of distinctive character. He saw further that with large numbers of visitors he could develop a reliable mailing list, and that if he made only very high-quality wines in very small quantities he could carve out a market niche for himself.

All this planning, of course, would not have achieved success unless the wines had been very good. This they were, and indeed are. In 1986, noting in Robson's list that the 1979 Pinot Noir should be drunk now, we compared it with a 1976 Echézeaux from Prosper Maufoux. An unfair comparison, some would say, but on the other hand the best Hunter wines are quite often claimed to be the equal of the best Burgundies. The two wines were indeed in the same style, but there was more complexity in the Echézeaux, and more integration of the different attributes. None the less, the Hunter wine was a fine Pinot, true to variety and showing scarcely a trace of the traditional Hunter earthiness.

The Robson Vineyard was like something out of Beatrix Potter. 'You will not find a faded leaf or blighted blossom there,' at least in a good season. The crush of 100 tonnes represents an investment of about $1,000,000 at 1984 values. This covered everything from elegant labels on the ends of the rows, through cool storage for customers' wine, to a little holiday house, Squire Cottage, set among trees in the middle of the vineyard. Customers of the vineyard were welcome to rent it, but it was no threat to the local motel industry.

Robson's Cabernet Merlot is a most unHunter-like wine, of great elegance and depth of flavour, yet his Hermitage, though cleaner than most, is a true Hunter Shiraz wine, brick-red, complex and soft. His Sémillon, at its best, is quite hard when young, but softens and develops the overtones of honey and gum blossom which so distinguish the best old Hunter whites. His Chardonnay is even better, but with much more striking varietal characteristics.

Unfortunately all of this attention to detail came to naught in the late 1980s, when the receivers and managers of Robson Services Pty Ltd offered 'for sale as a going concern the assets and business undertakings at Mount View Road, Mount View via Cessnock'. The new owners are trading as Briar Ridge and their wines are similarly fine.

Murray Robson himself is back in business as Murray Robson Wines at the location of the old Audrey Wilkinson winery, and one hopes that the wines will be as good in the future as in the past.

The Rothbury Estate was launched with considerable fanfare in 1968, as a new kind of winery. Not only was the building a complex and attractive assemblage of shapes built for its purpose, rather than a collection of tin sheds or one giant shed, but also the winery was aimed at involving wine-buyers as members of the Rothbury Society. The aim of this Society was to educate its members in wine, as well as simply to have them buy it and drink it. Len Evans, an ebullient Welsh publicist who had been a very successful wine writer for the Sydney weekly *The Bulletin*, and a number of colleagues had seen the possibilities of the wine boom then gathering pace, and determined not only to share in it but to shape it.

Initially the vineyard was planted with Sémillon and Shiraz, the traditional Hunter varieties, in equal quantities, and from the start exceptionally good Hunter Sémillons were made, 1972 and 1974 being outstanding. Not all members of the Society realized this, however, since these wines were not very attractive when young and were at their best a decade old, by which time many members had consumed them at barbecues or given them away at successive Christmases. The reds were less good, the 1972 Hermitage (Shiraz) being unstable, the 1973 slowly improving over about eight years but thinning as it softened.

In the mid 1970s Rothbury was crushing as much as 3,000 tonnes from over 300 hectares, but later cut back, accepting the fact that the red wine boom was over almost before it had begun. The carbonic maceration technique is now used by Rothbury to make its red wines available earlier. Of those tried recently, the most impressive has been the 1988 Herlstone Vineyard Pinot Noir. Bought at the Sydney Fish Market in mid 1990 'on special', for well under $10, it held its own with blackfish cooked with coriander followed by Gippsland Blue cheese with home-made rye-bread, having a definite Burgundian feel, clear, dense and fragrant; surprising, really. Rothbury's Sémillons remain good examples of the Hunter style.

The best Hunter white wines are indisputably very fine, with a honeyed nose, a deep flavour and a lingering aftertaste, developing much complexity with age. They are difficult to describe more precisely than this. For example, in a book published in 1964 the surgeon, wine writer and wine-maker Max Lake described how 'the soft delight of the nose of the gracefully aged Hunter white more than favourably compared to the Montrachets of Burgundy. Those prepared to dispute this had better make the comparison first, as I have.' It has been said of George Eliot that while one can compare her to Tolstoy, one would never compare Tolstoy to George Eliot. As a matter of some interest, I conducted a masked tasting of Lake's kind in late 1983. The wines chosen were the 1971 and 1973 Aucerot Sémillon blend from Tulloch, 1967 and 1970 Sémillons from Lindeman, a 1973 Pinot Blanc Sémillon from Penfold, as the Hunter wines, and a 1969 Puligny – Montrachet Les Pucelles (Sichel) and a 1971 Chassagne-Montrachet (A. Lichine). All the wines except the Puligny-Montrachet had been in my cellar for at least five years, and in addition an Orlando 1968 Chenin Blanc–Madeira blend from the Barossa and a 1976 Crozes-Hermitage from Berry Brothers were included because they happened to be in the cellar.

Twelve interested people tasted these wines, and in virtually every case were able to distinguish the French wines from the Australian. Obviously this would not be a difficult exercise for any expert, but the group had been deliberately chosen to include some who, while knowing a considerable amount about Australian wine, knew much less about French wine, and their grounds for distinguishing the

French wines were not just that these were unfamiliar but that they had much greater intensity and depth of flavour, even though they were well below the level of 'Le Montrachet', by which, of course, all white Burgundies are judged.

None of these Hunter wines contained Chardonnay. The best Hunter Chardonnays would undoubtedly have made the exercise more difficult, but then so would the best Chardonnays from elsewhere. For example, the 1981 and 1982 Mount Mary and 1982 Yarra Yering Chardonnays will certainly be quite exceptional wines in a decade, and I would happily consent to be tricked at a masked tasting of these wines and some Montrachets in the early 1990s. The best old Hunter Sémillons have their own style, and are best compared with each other. They are one of Australia's two or three genuinely significant contributions to the wines of the world.

When Max Lake made those comments, he was just establishing Lake's Folly, the first new vineyard in the Lower Hunter for some forty years. No Chardonnay was grown in the Hunter at that time and almost no Cabernet Sauvignon. It was the influence of the forceful, confident surgeon Lake as much as any other person which has led to the upsurge of experimentation in the Hunter. In fact, Lake's wines and views have been widely influential, for he is a vivid writer and his wines are indeed good. At their best they have been compared cheerfully to very fine French wines: Lake has listed for me his 1969 Cabernet Sauvignon compared in 1976 to the best Pauillac by Harry Waugh, the 1968 to the best St Julien by Ian Hickinbotham, among others, and to very good Pomerol by Robin Bradley. The Chardonnay is said by Lake to stand 'well between Puligny and Corton Charlemagne, depending on the year's influence on wine size'.

Besides Lake's, the other major recent influence on Hunter wines and wine-making has been that of Murray Tyrrell, who succeeded Dan Tyrrell, a man who had seen more vintages than even Sydney Hamilton, in the late 1950s. The Tyrrell family had settled at Rothbury on reddish volcanic soil about 1860, one family member marrying a McDonald, then of Ben Ean. Dan Tyrrell began his wine-making at the end of the century and used very traditional methods, but very carefully, until his retirement, so that little sulphur was needed, and the wines were no more earthy than the grapes allowed. He was also a firm believer in the proper use of oak for maturation of all wines, so that what Murray Tyrrell brought to the enterprise were some newer methods, some different varieties and considerable marketing flair. His Chardonnay and Pinot Noir perhaps did even more than the Lake's Folly wines to alert the Hunter wine-makers and their customers to the Burgundian possibilities of an area which had always made soft wines, big when the summer did not have too much rain, the spring too many storms. Tyrrell is an outspoken wine-maker who has always bought in much fruit and some wine, and made no pretence to do otherwise. His true Hunter wines are outstanding examples of the area's possibilities. The whites turn gold and soften in only a few years, whether Chardonnay or Sémillon, and then for years are big, fleshy wines which somehow also possess balance and restraint. The 1973 'Vat 47' Chardonnay was very fine and if I had any left would be magnificent as I write. The 'Vat 1' Sémillon is also one of the best of its kind, as is the Pinot Noir, and all these are still made fairly traditionally. The big, open, concrete fermenters are traps for young players, and a former student who worked a vintage there described to me how it was almost obligatory for new chums to be assisted to fall in, a long, thin friend of hers having emerged from fermenting Shiraz looking like a new-born foal.

In late 1988 Tyrrell had its export licence suspended for a time because sorbitol, a natural sugar found in, for example, apple juice, but not grape juice, was detected in some of Tyrrell's wines. Bruce Tyrrell said that the family had been using sorbitol for twenty-five years. It has been used in a similar way in Chile but is not a permitted additive in wine in either Australia or the EEC. Concern was expressed on all sides that such outstanding wine-makers as the Tyrrell family should be ignorant of the rules. The then Federal Minister for Primary Industry and Energy, John Kerin, said that the loss of Australia's 'enviable reputation . . . for quality value-for-money wine' could place in jeopardy exports of more than $125 million in 1989 terms.

While drinkers of Tyrrell's wines for a time made jokes about tasting 'that sorbitol smoothness', the Tyrrell numbered bin wines represent the best range of well-made traditional Hunter styles. Even the Cabernet, which many feel, despite the best efforts of Max Lake, is not the right grape for the Hunter, has a traditional air about it. The 1984 Cabernet Sauvignon ('Vat 70'), for example, smells like a pigeon loft when opened, but given a chance opens out with elegant fruit and a firm finish.

Crushing less than 25 tonnes are Château François (1970), Millstone (1973), Mount View (1970), Tamburlaine (1966) and Wintertree (1985). Mount View is run by a Tulloch, so that even though the long-established Tulloch name is owned by Gilbey and SA Brewery, Tullochs are still making their own wine.

Crushing between 25 and 50 tonnes are Brokenwood (1970), Château Pato (whose proprietors are called Paterson), Dawson, Honeytree (1973), Horseshoe, Lake's Folly (1963) and Murray Robson (formerly Oakdale, 1866).

Horseshoe is one of many small makers which produce reasonable 'nouveau style' wine from Shiraz, usually by carbonic maceration. One wishes they would try Gamay.

Brokenwood is owned by a small group which used to include James Halliday, a lawyer who is also Australia's most industrious and prolific wine writer. He has written valuable guides to almost every Australian wine-growing area, and is indefatigable in his pursuit of even the smallest, most recent grower for information. Brokenwood in a sense reflects this wide-ranging search, since it makes blends of Cabernet Sauvignon and Shiraz from its Brokenwood vineyard and its vineyard at Coonawarra. They are wines of good flavour and balance with, at their best, almost unlimited cellaring potential. I look forward, for example, to drinking the 1981s between now and 2001. Given that they are blends, these wines are hard to identify, but can be worth seeking out.

Oakdale is one of a number of vineyards owned by the Stephen family last century. It came later into the hands of the Wilkinsons, and virtually went out of production about 1960 in the hands of a man called Audrey Wilkinson, a sad figure in the long decline of the Hunter. Revived, it makes traditional soft Hunter wines. In the hands of Murray Robson it will make excellent wines, though more expensively than before.

In the 50–100-tonne class are Allandale (1977), Belbourie (1964), Elliot's Belford (1893), Marsh Estate (1971), Mistletoe (1967), Briar Ridge (formerly Robson, 1972) and Wollundry (1971). Allandale's Ed Jouault was one of the few small makers growing almost none of their crush. Jouault bought in all his fruit from a small number of growers, their names to be found on his labels. Particularly good have been the Leonard Sémillon and Cabernet Sauvignon, the former fresher and crisper than the traditional Hunter style, the latter clean and firm, almost stalky like a cool area-Cabernet. Under different management the company still makes very good but perhaps less distinctive wines, crushing a little more than 100 tonnes in most years.

The Elliotts were among the makers who kept going through all the vicissitudes the Hunter suffered, making good Shiraz and Sémillon wines and selling them identifiably in bottle rather than in bulk. They expanded as others contracted and owned several good vineyards, Oakvale the first, Belford having been acquired when the firm was almost forty years old. Their Hunter Sémillons typified the traditional style when old, being almost luscious, despite being bone dry and hard when young. The 1965 was outstanding. Their Shiraz wines are also of the traditional form, earthy, soft and rich when young, but as they age becoming brick-red and gaining in delicacy. One should drink them when one finds them. The name is now owned by Wyndham Estate, and at the time of writing the wines offer reasonable value for money, at least for the Hunter.

In the 100–500-tonne class are Maxwell's Maluna (1971) and Terrace Vale. Terrace Vale was the name of a successful vineyard in the middle of last century, and has not been disgraced in its new incarnation, for both its Chardonnay and its Sémillon are among the best the Hunter has to offer.

Crushing between 500 and 1,000 tonnes are Drayton's Bellevue (1860), McPherson (1968), Tulloch (1893) and Tyrrell (1858).

Bellevue was first planted at the foot of the Brokenback Range, near Mount View, just north of Mount Pleasant. The Draytons thus chose some of the best possible vineyard land in the Hunter, and the wines reflect this happy choice, though between the two world wars the enterprise was divided up for financial reasons, one branch of the family taking Bellevue, the other the Happy Valley property. At Bellevue the extensive range includes a modestly priced, earthy Pinot Noir with distinct Hunter character.

Tulloch was established somewhat later, buying Glen Elgin from a member of the Hungerford family in the 1890s, and stayed in the family for almost seventy years, gradually growing through purchase to over 100 hectares of mainly alluvial soil suitable for whites. These were rather hard wines which repaid a great deal of patience when eventually they softened.The Aucerot Rieslings already mentioned have taken a good four years to become drinkable after their purchase when a year old, for example. After the takeover by Reed, the paper company, the style did not alter, but Reed was followed by Gilbey, and much wine was bought in for sale, so that, for example, a Tulloch 'Valley Selection' Shiraz 1978 did not say on the label whence it came but did not taste of the Hunter, lacking earthiness and a firm finish to complement the softness on the palate. The wines clearly stating their Hunter origin have remained good. The marketing side of Tulloch was bought in 1983 by Allied Vintners, then a Castlemaine Toohey subsidiary, which owns Seaview and Wynn and which now belongs to Penfold–Kaiser Stuhl. Tulloch's Hunter wines have since then been made by Patrick Auld, and they are not all 'drink now' products, the 1988 Shiraz, like the Lindeman four-digit bin wines of the same year, needing a decade to reach its peak, a very good buy in 1990. Auld is now also maker for Lindeman, the long-serving and highly respected Gerry Sissingh having retired when Penfold acquired Lindeman.

Crushing between 1,000 and 5,000 tonnes are Hungerford Hill (1967), Lindeman (1870), McWilliam (1880), Rothbury (1968) and Saxonvale (1971). Hermitage Estate (1967) was also in this category, but in the late 1970s financial difficulties led to its fragmentation and acquisition of the largest fragment by Wyndham Estate. Mistletoe vineyard, originally in production in the early part of this century, was also part of Hermitage Estate.

Hungerford Hill has also been taken over, most recently by South Australian Brewing, proprietor of Seppelt, so its future is uncertain. Its lack of clear market image has made its Hunter wines relatively cheap for their reliably high quality, as I have already mentioned for its Coonawarra wines. The Hunter Chardonnay is typical: big, rich, tasty, only two-thirds the price of the competition.

Saxonvale was established very rapidly, with black grapes at Pokolbin and white at Fordwich, and its production surged rapidly to 4,000 tonnes a year. In consequence, it made and sold some dreadful wines, the 1975 Cabernet Sauvignon, for example, being unattractive when young and undrinkable by 1983. Saxonvale was also involved in the financial difficulties of a large trading company which took it over, and this did not help the manager's struggle to improve quality. Now, however, it has improved, and vintages since about 1980 have been clean and well made.

Saxonvale is now part of Wyndham Estate, which can claim to have been established as early as 1828 because it is Penfold's Dalwood, previously Wyndham's Dalwood, established by the Hunter pioneer George Wyndham and sold by Penfold when it made its ill-judged move to Wybong in the Upper Hunter in the 1960s. Penfold kept the name Dalwood for its line of reliable, undefined area house-style branded wines, so that a new name was necessary. With backing from Anglo-Thai of the UK and a finance company belonging to what used to be the Bank of New South Wales, together with the skills of the wine-maker and part-owner Brian McGuigan, Wyndham Estate came to make a range of very sound wines, the reds usually better than the whites. It expanded very fast in the 1980s until it was crushing 40 per cent of the Hunter's fruit in its total of some 10,000 tonnes, but was acquired by Orlando in 1990 in a time of tight money and lost sympathy for entrepreneurs.

HUNTER VALLEY (UPPER HUNTER)

The upper Hunter area is very new, but this does not mean that it has no history: like many other currently successful areas, it had an era in the nineteenth century when it made fine wines. More than a century ago, Rosemount, the vineyard of a German, Carl Brecht, was producing good red wine.

The recent development of the upper Hunter followed Penfold. Their old vineyard, Dalwood, first planted by George Wyndham more than a century earlier, was one of the last lower Hunter vineyards left on the river flats, for floods and erosion had destroyed many of the others over the years, particularly when the cost of labour and loss of markets made vineyard management an expensive luxury. The alluvial soils along the Hunter, Patterson and William rivers had made the name of the Hunter in the middle of the nineteenth century, but in the late 1950s Penfold found they were no longer profitable.

Accordingly, after an extensive search Penfold planted over 200 hectares at Wybong Park, their new 'Dalwood Estate'. The move was not a success. On the lighter soils of the higher slopes, some of the plantings of Sémillon, Blanquette, Chardonnay and Traminer were suitable for the better Penfold whites, but few of the Wybong Park reds were successful. Many, in fact, began dirty and stayed dirty, the 1968 to 1971 Shirazes and Cabernets remaining in the memory for this reason.

It was an imaginative move for Penfold, the kind of move that was likely for a family-run company in that they could take a very

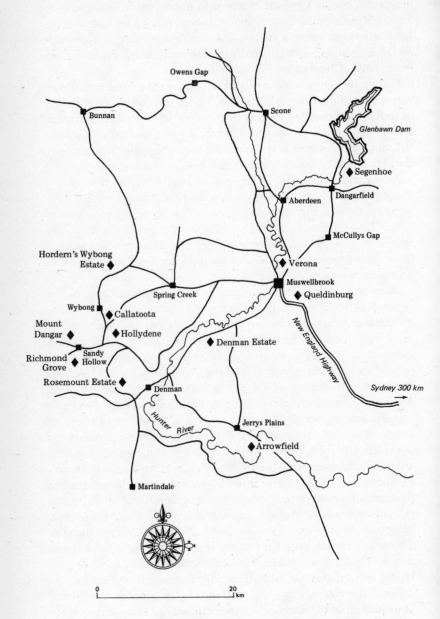

Hunter Valley (upper Hunter)

long view, but in 1976 the family sold out to the Sydney brewers Tooth & Company, and Wybong Park was sold to Rosemount. Rosemount is making a success of these Penfold vineyards, just as the McGuigan family has made a success of the old Dalwood in the lower Hunter, now called Wyndham Estate.

During the white wine boom of the mid 1970s, Rosemount was very successful, and later expanded, buying part of Denman Estate as well as Wybong Park. Other relatively large wineries of the area, such as Richmond Grove and Arrowfield, have had varied success, but currently it seems that by staying with the white wines which the area certainly makes very well, both will be successful.

Arrowfield, established by the Pacific Island trading firm W. R. Carpenter, which now belongs to a Western Australian coal-mining company (such is the instability in Australian company life), almost collapsed soon after its first sales began, some six years after it was started in 1969; but by concentrating on white grapes the winery has to some extent re-established itself. What the coal miners will do with it remains to be seen.

Mount Dangar Vineyards was one of the first vineyards in the upper Hunter to be set up with the aim of having complete supplementary irrigation. In this, as in other ways, it suffered for pioneering the area. In the 1960s, when the Adelaide Steamship Company was seeking to diversify away from its historic involvement with shipping, a former lord mayor of Adelaide, Jim Bowen, and Robert Hamilton of Hamilton's Ewell Vineyards approached Adelaide Steamship with the proposal that they jointly develop a 200-hectare vineyard at Sandy Hollow. It was established in 1967–68, initially with underground piping wherever possible for the irrigation. This proved unsatisfactory because the pipes were always blocking, so the irrigation had to be redone above ground. In addition, the property suffered from early frosts, damaging the flowers and diminishing fruit set, from rain at harvest, from lack of rain, and from bird damage – not unexpectedly, as there were few other vineyards nearby. However, very good fruit was produced in a number of years, even from quite young vines. The vineyard was very fortunate in its manager, Richard Hilder, a nephew of J. J. Hilder, the noted Australian artist of the turn of the century.

When the vineyard was planted, the red wine boom was almost at its peak, and the 200 hectares were about equally given to black and white grapes, Cabernet Sauvignon, Shiraz, Sémillon, Traminer and Chardonnay being the main varieties. Since then, after a reappraisal, the vineyard has been reduced to less than 80 hectares, mostly made up of white varieties.

Initially it seemed that the white wines were much better than the reds; the 1974 Cabernet Sauvignon, for example, was most unattractive when young, a thick, acid wine, but it softened into a drinkable, slightly porty wine over about eight years, Cabernet character never having appeared at any stage. In fact, when a trial parcel of wine was sent to England, the red proved more popular than the white. However, of recent vintages the whites, many of them made by Rosemount, have been typical of the area, fairly light and relatively attractive when young, unlike the earlier Sémillons which took four or five years to open out, like many lower Hunter wines.

The Adelaide Steamship Company divested itself of this small operation which, while it had never been an 'unmitigated disaster' like its Shark Bay salt venture (to quote one of the directors), had required an inordinate amount of managerial attention for a very modest return. Mount Dangar now belongs to Rosemount, further evidence of the remarkable success of Bob Oatley, who also owns Wybong Park which originally belonged to Penfold.

The upper Hunter is mainly the preserve of medium to large companies, and so the wineries are relatively large. Queldinburg (1972), Reynolds (formerly Hordern's Wybong Estate, 1965) and Verona (1971) all crush between 100 and 500 tonnes. Queldinburg was established by Kevin Sobels of the family which founded Quelltaler in the Clare area. Buying in virtually all his fruit, he made some very good wines from the start. The 1974 Sémillon was a fine example of the aged Hunter style in 1983, golden in colour, soft on the palate with a dusty, honeyed finish. When young it had been very fruity, yet with sufficient hidden acid to survive.

Verona has planted Valdepeñas as well as all the expected white varieties – Chardonnay, Riesling, Sémillon and Traminer. It will be of great interest to see whether such an unusual cultivar has a future.

Six wineries crush between 1,000 and 5,000 tonnes a year: Arrowfield (1969), Denman Estate (1969), Hollydene (1967), Mount Dangar (1968), Richmond Grove (1977), Rosemount Estate (1969) and Segenhoe (1970). As I have already described, some of these are connected with each other or with other groups, so that they are effectively parts of larger organizations, which should make for more consistency than some upper Hunter makers have achieved in the past, though perhaps for less distinctiveness. Segenhoe was begun as a kind of consumers' co-operative but is now run by Tyrrell from the Hunter proper. Richmond Grove was associated through the wine merchant Rhinecastle Wines of Sydney with Thomas Hardy, which gave it a national presence which even its original labels (such as 'Hunter River White Bordeaux') would not otherwise have achieved. It is now part of Wyndham Estate and has a current premium brand name of 'Brandon Manor', but Orlando may change this.

MUDGEE

Mudgee was first settled in 1822. At an altitude of almost 500 metres, it lies in the valley of a tributary of the Macquarie River, a little more than 250 kilometres north-west of Sydney. The name is an Aboriginal word for 'nest in the hills', and that is how the town sits. Vines were planted very early and one of the wineries, Craigmoor, was established in 1858; none of the others of the time has survived. The altitude makes the nights cool, and vintage is a month later than in the Hunter, which helps wine quality.

Most of the early viticulturalists were Germans, brought out because the mainly British settlers knew so little about vines. During the First World War, when many of the sons and grandsons of the German settlers were being killed fighting for English King and British Empire at Gallipoli and elsewhere, anti-German feeling resulted in one of the more notable German vineyards, Fredericksberg, being renamed Westcourt after the winner of the 1917 Melbourne Cup. This vineyard no longer exists, so one does not know whether the name would have been changed back, as has rightly happened with many of the place names which were xenophobically changed.

The appropriately named Dr Thomas Henry Fiaschi established a winery somewhat later than the Germans, and it lasted almost until the Second World War, by which time the only survivor was Craigmoor, which had once been named Rothview by the Roth family who had established it.

Learning of Botobolar's existence from a student daughter of the proprietors, Gil and Vincie Wahlquist, I was not surprised by the intelligent yet unconventional atmosphere of the winery and its remarkable publicity vehicle, the *Botobolar Bugle*, published from the vineyard to advertise both it and the Mudgee area. It is quite different from most wine journals. The lead story may tell how Botobolar in 1983 harvested 10 tonnes instead of the normal 120, on account of the drought, or it may simply announce new wines, but inside, the *Bugle* can tell you how to run an ecologically sound vineyard, where the native birds keep out introduced pests like starlings and keep down insect pests as well, and the sheep keep the weeds down in winter, how to prune and what the cost should be (24 cents a vine in 1982), or how to build a stone-walled winery with none of the stonemason's art.

The wines are equally individual, apart from the Shiraz, which can be surprisingly thin from such a 'big' area. A straight Mataro of limited charm has sensibly been eliminated from the range, yet was a very durable wine, the first vintage (1974) being still drinkable in 1988. The Cabernet Sauvignon is extremely fruity when new, and quite forward, yet ages very gracefully. But the oddities are the most interesting. 'Vincentia' was named after one of the proprietors and was a successful full-bodied dry white, yet in 1981 it was changed to a dessert wine aimed at the Sauternes style, very high in alcohol, flavour and sugars. 'Budgee Budgee', called after a township near Mudgee, is a pink wine made from Muscat and Shiraz, low in alcohol, high in acid and sugar. Add to these the first Marsanne in the Mudgee area and a surprisingly intense and yet well-balance Riesling, and one can see why so few Australian vignerons are certain what to make: they can enjoy making so many different wines.

In the Mudgee district proper, the wineries crushing less than 50 tonnes are Bramhall (1981), Hill of Gold (1974) and Mudgee Wines. Mudgee Wines suitably carries the name of the area, since it was set up in 1964 by Alf Kurtz, a descendant of Andreas Kurtz, one of the area's first wine-makers.

There is also a very small winery, Glenfinlass, which crushes less than 25 tonnes at Wellington near Mudgee, and another, Markita, at Neurea near Wellington.

There is just one winery which crushes between 50 and 100 tonnes: Burnbrae (1971). Most crush between 100 and 500 tonnes: Amberton (1975), Augustine (Dr Fiaschi's winery, established in 1918 and re-established in the 1960s after a lapse of some twenty years), Botobolar (1970), de Windmolen (1979), Huntington Estate

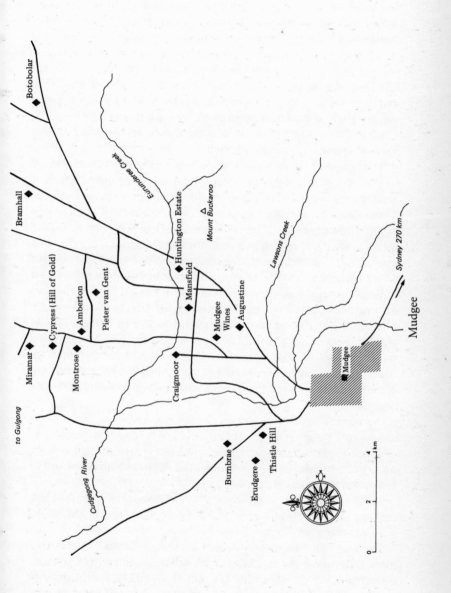

(1969), Mansfield (1975, also established by a member of the Kurtz family), Miramar (1977), Montrose (1974) and Thistle Hill (1984).

Amberton, now part of Wyndham Estate, has made many good, full-bodied whites, including a blend of Sémillon, Chardonnay and Sauvignon Blanc. The first vintage dry red, from 1976, was still drinkable, with a little fruit and a barely bitter finish, in 1989, but in general the reds are not among the area's longer-lasting wines. Amberton's Dutch wine-maker Pieter van Gent now has his own winery, de Windmolen; the wines are sold as Pieter van Gent.

While a number of wineries, such as Botobolar, Huntington Estate, Montrose and Craigmoor, make good wines, usually better whites than reds, probably the best whites have come from Miramar. The wine-maker, Ian Macrae, who taught at Roseworthy as well as taking the course there, has wide experience of wine-making and also winery design and made exceptional wines at Mudgee before actually having his own winery. His Chardonnay has been particularly good, his rosé one of the best in the country. Huntington's reds are very good, the 1977 Shiraz Cabernet a classical warm-area wine at twelve years old, full of the scent of bees on hot days. Thistle Hill makes perhaps the best Cabernet of the area.

Craigmoor (1858) is the largest and oldest winery in Mudgee, crushing over 500 tonnes. Its Shiraz, a rich, earthy wine, is usually good value for money. It develops rather fast, so that it is best drunk fairly young. The 1980s were disappointing years for Craigmoor, so its very recent acquisition by Wyndham Estate, which bought Montrose at the same time, will probably aid in yet another restoration of this very old winery.

THE MURRUMBIDGEE IRRIGATION AREA

The Murrumbidgee Irrigation Area (MIA) was established in the first decade of this century, following the earlier ones on the Murray. The McWilliam brothers arrived at Hanwood in 1912, built their first winery there during the First World War and expanded to Yenda just after the war, as soldier–settlers took up irrigation blocks and needed an outlet for their fruit. Italian wine-makers followed, and this area is still the major one in which Italian names predominate, though there are many families of Italian settlers along the river in South Australia and at Stanthorpe in Queensland.

Griffith has the reputation of being the marijuana capital of

Australia, though much of the production is said to be subcontracted to growers in South Australia. This recent perception of the region's character has not aided in the national acceptance of its wines.

McWilliam has overcome the problems of production essentially based on low-quality irrigated fruit, first by its identification with the Hunter through its Mount Pleasant vineyard, secondly by marketing skill, and thirdly by great attention to prevention of faults in its wines from Hanwood and elsewhere. Other Griffith wine-makers have not been so successful. San Bernadino Wines, a winery which on the basis of its 1981 crush of 18,000 tonnes is as large as Hardy or Mildara, does not have national marketing arrangements, nor identification as a high-quality producer. The wines are generally clean and fresh but I can recall a 1977 Traminer which, though true to variety on the nose, had a taste reminiscent of mixed essential oils. Although it traded out of its 1980s difficulties, San Bernadino is the kind of medium-sized winery which will be in increasing difficulty as the wine glut fluctuates.

Whatever its financial past – and in trading out of receivership it performed a feat that fewer than one in a thousand such enterprises achieves – San Bernadino has certainly shared in the training of one of the best Griffith wine-makers, John Swanston of Jolimont. At Jolimont light, fresh, fruity wines were made, of great charm and immediate appeal. Furthermore, the wine-maker, in his Cabernet–Merlot, overcame the problem of using lightweight fruit of good variety to produce balanced wine. Available for drinking within six months of vintage, this Cabernet–Merlot has been a bright red wine showing strong Cabernet character and delicious fruit on the palate. It was the kind of wine for which one hopes from the irrigated areas, but so rarely finds. I am not sure what Jolimont's move to Rutherglen means for these wines.

De Bortoli bought Seppelt's vineyard when Seppelt withdrew from the area, and has itself expanded elsewhere, as mentioned in Chapter 4. It has moved away from being solely a mass-producer of sparkling and fortified wines, to make botrytis-affected white wines of surprising complexity and balance. These are not wines that replace the 40 per cent of sales which came from fortified wines, sales which were severely affected by the fortifying spirit tax briefly imposed in 1983. They are simply very good. Tasted in 1984, the 1983 Sémillon showed considerable development, bright gold in colour, the varietal character almost swamped by the botrytis smell,

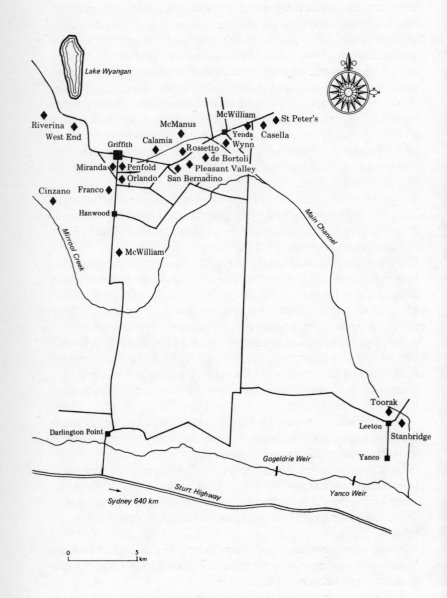

Lake Wyangan

Riverina
West End
Griffith
Miranda
Penfold
Orlando
Franco
Cinzano
Hanwood
McWilliam
Calamia
McManus
Rossetto
San Bernadino
de Bortoli
Pleasant Valley
Wynn
McWilliam
Yenda
Casella
St Peter's

Mirrool Creek
Main Channel

Toorak
Leeton
Stanbridge
Darlington Point
Yanco
Gogeldrie Weir
Yanco Weir
Sturt Highway
Sydney 640 km

0   5
|————————|
km

Murrumbidgee Irrigation Area

194

the palate broad and creamy with vegetable overtones. Five years later, consumed with rambutans, it was almost as tropical but much more complex. Carrying 12.5 per cent alcohol and a great deal of residual sugar, the 1984 wine held not quite enough acid to be outstanding in a few years' time, unlike the older Sémillon. The 1982 Pedro, tasted with the Sémillons in 1984 and 1985, was a much more grapey wine of rather less interest. Tasted in 1990 side by side with a 1988 New Zealand botrytis-affected Riesling from Ngatarawa over a Tasmanian True Blue cheese, it was still grapey and jovial, hardly grown up at all. The New Zealand wine, much better balanced, seemed almost thin by comparison. Subsequent vintages of Sémillon have been almost as good as the 1983, perhaps as good but lacking the elements of surprise and delight.

For any winery's first attempts at a style, these wines are remarkable. The problem will be to continue to justify making them. De Bortoli has only 60 hectares of its own grapes, on account of the restrictions of ownership in the irrigation area. If therefore it has to buy botrytis-affected fruit, it must pay growers not to spray with fungicides and to deliver 1 to 2 tonnes of grey, crumpled berries per hectare rather than 15 tonnes of gleaming, bulging bunches. That is, the fruit is twelve times the usual irrigated price. With so many makers producing these rich wines, the market may be over-supplied even without the import competition which I mentioned in connection with Primo Estate. As already stated, de Bortoli has bought land and a winery in the Yarra and is developing a substantial vineyard, so is serious about finding a place in the high-quality market.

There are two very small wineries in the MIA, each crushing less than 50 tonnes: McManus (1969) and Stanbridge (1977). Despite their size, both make a large range of wines from most of the high-quality varieties – one of the advantages of buying in one's crush from a large number of growers.

At Trentham Cliffs, a place small enough to have no postcode, Trentham Estate makes a creditable Merlot in the 'drink now' fashion.

In the 100–500-tonne class there is only the West End Winery (1948), despite its name run by a family hailing from Italy. Its port is most enjoyable when young.

In the 500–1,000-tonne class is St Peter's Distillery (1978), which was established very courageously, given the glut of brandy that followed the removal of its tax advantage in about 1970. It is not clear what the future of such a distillery can be, unless it can achieve a large share of the market for fortifying spirit, which seems unlikely.

In the 1,000–5,000-tonne class are Franco's (1959), Sergi (1971) and Toorak (1963). Franco's, like many more recently established wineries elsewhere in the country, began on a well-established farm which the family had taken up in the 1930s. Its reds are surprisingly drinkable, with only a little of the hot-fruit taste one expects.

Crushing between 5,000 and 10,000 tonnes a year are Wynn, which came to the area in 1930, Miranda (1939) and de Bortoli (1923). Miranda is notable for having had as its wine-maker Ron Potter, inventor of one of the more successful cold fermenters; Potter now has his own manufacturing company, and Miranda has a wine-maker who previously worked for Christian Brothers in the Napa Valley. Wynn's Yenda operation is not one of its more widely publicized activities but provides fruit for its bulk and soft-packed wines.

San Bernadino (1973) crushers between 10,000 and 20,000 tonnes a year, and McWilliam dwarfs the others with its crush of more than 30,000 tonnes. McWilliam's Hanwood wines are extremely well made, and the Cabernet Sauvignon and Chardonnay frequently belie their irrigated origin in their balance and depth of flavour. The Cabernet can be most enjoyable when a decade or more old, despite having gained a slightly cooked flavour during this time in bottle.

THE AUSTRALIAN CAPITAL TERRITORY

Grapes grow satisfactorily in the Australian Capital Territory but the vineyards, as yet, have not established themselves other than in their captive market, the out-of-this-world world that is Canberra. Visitors gawp at the War Museum, the National Library, the National Gallery or the High Court, but they are unlikely to drive out to the north past Hall and sample the local product, from the Murrumbateman Winery. Customers are mainly local, as they are for the other, smaller, less actively promoted wines, such as Helm's (1974). There are other signs of the wine industry, however: the Embassy Hotel, for example, was owned by Denman Estate wines, an upper Hunter winery, and these one could buy in the dining room.

Near Lake George are a number of small wineries, such as Lake George Winery (1971) which crushes about 10 tonnes of most of the fine varieties. Doonkuna Estate (1973) crushes about 15 tonnes, and the wines continue to improve. Lark Hill makes a drinkable Chardonnay, extremely light by comparison with most Australian Chardonnays. These wineries have yet to make much of a mark but are close to a wealthy, almost inflation-proofed market, the Commonwealth public (i.e. government) service.

OTHER MINOR AREAS

George Wyndham was a well-educated, well-travelled Englishman of the gentleman farmer type. He came to Australia in 1827, when almost twenty-seven, and at his property, Dalwood near Branxton, he tried growing almost everything. What throve best was the grape wine. However, although it was a very successful property during the mid-nineteenth century, Wyndham himself had to leave the Hunter during the rural depression of the 1840s, so he moved north to Inverell, establishing vines there also. Today there is only one commercial vineyard, Gilgai, at Inverell, but should the current wine industry depression pass, it is one of the many areas in Australia which holds promise for the future.

Three hundred kilometres north of upper Hunter, at Manilla, is Dutton's New England Meadery (1969), making 'man's oldest drink dating back to 12000 BC' according to the labels. Muscat, Chardonnay and mulberries go into the honey-based beverages, which are sold very young.

A number of other areas have single pioneering vineyards. For example, near Shoalhaven, inland from the heavy industrial city of Wollongong, is Jasper Valley Wines (1976). Although it is over 100 kilometres from Sydney, in the opposite direction to the Hunter and Mudgee, it has every chance of success because of its proximity to the Wollongong centre of population, not to mention tourist resorts like Ulladulla and Mollymook. With a wine-maker trained at Roseworthy and a climate not unlike Mudgee's, its early vintages were well received in the local market (and unobtainable elsewhere). The wines are now made by Platt of Mudgee, rich reds and soft whites sold without pretension. ('That bloke bought $150.00 worth, Mother. Must be doing something right.') Much further south, at Bega, is Grevillea Estate (1985), crushing about 20 tonnes.

Other such wineries are mostly very small also. Barwang (1974), near Young (now owned by McWilliam and making good Shiraz and Sémillon), and Chislett's Wines near Forbes in the Lachlan Valley both grew and crush less than 50 tonnes, for example. These areas may be successful, but given the increases in production from established and successful areas one must predict little market impact in the near future.

At Tumbarumba in the Australian Alps the very small Tumbarumba Champagne Estates made a promising sparkling wine, Beaumont Brut, by the *méthode champenoise* from Chardonnay and Crouchen. It does not yet have the small bead of a good champagne or the strong fruit character of the best from Château Remy or Croser, but is good enough to be a wine to watch; I have not seen it on sale for some time.

An exception to the rule that unrecognized areas will have small wineries is Cubbaroo Wines (1970), which crushes over 500 tonnes from 20 hectares of vines in the Namoi Valley, Australia's main cotton-growing area. Despite the unpropitious climate and the irrigated vines, this hot-area vineyard produces quite drinkable red wines, though of the thick, inky type which is not to everyone's taste. Much of the credit for the wines' quality must go Brian McGuigan of Wyndham Estate in the Hunter, who has made them.

At Port Macquarie, north of the Hunter, Cassegrain Wines (1980) is one of many enterprises associated with a successful business family of the area. It produces a range of wines, some from its own fruit, some from Hunter fruit, and is becoming quite well regarded. However, although the area had many small wineries a century ago, few have followed Cassegrain's recent lead.

6

Western Australia

Grape growing in Western Australia began almost as early as in Tasmania, and earlier than in Victoria or South Australia. The cool wet winters and long dry summers made for reliable high yields and few disease problems. Only much later was it realized that these same advantages made fine wines harder to achieve, and by then the Swan Valley was established as the centre of the industry.

Change has come recently but rapidly, just as it has come to other aspects of Western Australian life, so that this very separate part of Australia, which voted to secede from the Commonwealth in 1933, is now richer and growing in population faster than many other parts of Australia, rather like California in the United States a generation ago.

THE SWAN VALLEY

The most notable of all the Western Australian wineries is Houghton, established quite early on. The name came from Colonel Houghton, one of three proprietors who jointly planted vines on the Swan, but it was a Scottish medical man, John Ferguson, who established the vineyard properly after buying it in 1859.

His son, Charles Ferguson, who was born in Perth in 1847 and died there in 1940, was the first cellar-hand, writing of the first vintage of 100 litres in 1859: 'It was my job to drop in more pebbles as evaporation went on, until fermentation ceased. This was tested by a match at the bung hole and when half a dozen burned one's finger before going out, fermentation was deemed to have run its course.' Despite being associated with wine for most of his very long life, Charles Ferguson went pearling in the north-west of Western Australia in the 1870s, and before this he had caught a

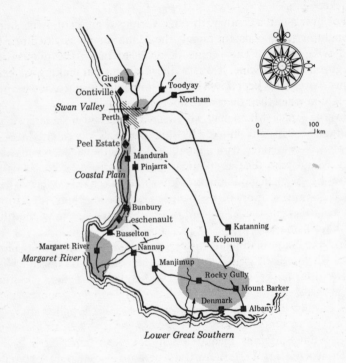

Gingin
Contiville
Toodyay
Northam
Swan Valley
Perth

Peel Estate
Mandurah
Pinjarra
Coastal Plain

Bunbury
Leschenault
Busselton
Katanning
Kojonup
Margaret River
Nannup
Margaret River
Manjimup
Rocky Gully
Mount Barker
Denmark
Albany

Lower Great Southern

0   100
km

Western Australia regions

notorious bushranger, 'Moondyne Joe', in the Houghton cellars. By the time Ferguson retired in 1911 there were over 50 hectares of vines at the property on the middle Swan, together with a cricket pitch which was for many years the home ground of the Swan Cricket Club.

For over a half a century, through various changes of ownership, Houghton had a constant factor: the Mann family as viticulturists and wine-makers. They came in 1910 to make the pioneering Ferguson family's wine. It was a vineyard aimed at making the best wines, with yields kept down below 5 tonnes per hectare, and grapes bought in when their own were not good enough.

In 1922 Jack Mann had his first vintage, and he remained in charge through fifty more. His son, Dorham Mann, was also a leading wine-maker, with Houghton's and elsewhere, but it was Jack Mann who set the company on the path to success. In the 1930s he used Chenin Blanc to make what was called a 'Chablis', in small quantities, most of the fruit being used for sherry, for from Western Australia as elsewhere, sherry was what was wanted by the English market.

In 1937 Mann had made his first 'White Burgundy', also mainly from Chenin Blanc grapes but picked riper and left on the skins for twenty-four hours, with extra acid added if the wine was too soft. As a result, a wine of tremendous flavour yet with good balance was produced, quite different from the Hunter Sémillon and yet appealing to the same kind of drinker. For many Australians, in fact, 'White Burgundy' meant Houghton's, not Hunter Riesling.

The isolation of Western Australia perhaps also encouraged Mann to experiment in other ways, for example with a Verdelho and Tokay (Muscadelle) blend, sold simply as 'Verdell'. Another experiment was a red wine called 'Strelley', light in character but very similar to the Cabernet and Shiraz which were made at the same time. Typical hot-area wines with considerable amounts of butter (diacetyl) and burnt jam on both nose and palate, they were none the less cheap and enjoyable drinking in South Australia from the early 1960s to the early 1970s, remaining tolerable until a bitter finish began to develop. Changes in markets made them less cheap after this, and the acquisition of the company by Hardy led to changes in wine-making, so that they are now less distinctive but better wines.

Sandalford was another vineyard established very early in West-

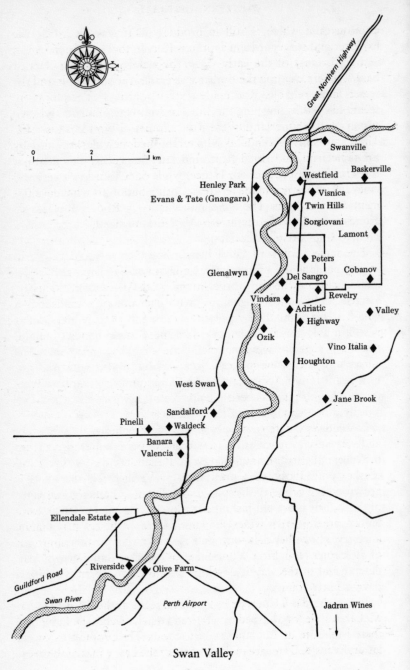

Swan Valley

ern Australia which is still in production. It was set up by the explorer and surveyor John Septimus Roe. It, too, was on the Swan – indeed, most of the early vineyards were on the river flats or banks, where clearing the timber was easier, the soil better and the water more reliable. Roe made sixteen journeys of exploration, seeing himself as finishing the work of Matthew Flinders and then surveying the hinterland of the new colonies in Western Australia. Thus, it was his descendants who established the vineyard, initially for table fruit and dried fruit, and later, especially this century, for wine-grape production. Hence, while Sandalford is a very old vineyard, it has not made as great a contribution to wine development as Houghton. The wine-maker is Tony Roe, a great-great-grandson of John Septimus Roe, but the managing director is a Frenchman, Christian Morlaes.

The same applies to Olive Farm, the other very old vineyard, indeed perhaps the oldest surviving in Australia. Thomas Waters, an Englishman who had worked in the South African wine industry, arrived, unlike most vignerons, with the aim of establishing a vineyard. He planted his vineyard in 1829 and 1830. Waters' cellar is still in use, though the vineyard has been in the hands of one of the many Yugoslav wine-making families for about fifty years. The current Yurisich wine-maker is Roseworthy-trained, however, not European-trained. Olive Farm's White Burgundy, similar in character to Houghton's, has been reliable for many years, always enjoyable by those who like their dry whites fruity.

Bassendean Estate is one of the best small wineries on the Swan, and very easy to reach as it is less than twenty minutes' drive from the centre of Perth. Established by an Italian family in 1951, it still crushes only about 50 tonnes a year, of which less than half is grown on the property. Despite its small size, it makes good wines of the slightly more old-fashioned style: the reds, mainly made from Shiraz, are soft, rich wines showing a little of their warm-climate ancestry, altogether delicious, and the Chenin Blanc is reminiscent of the earlier Houghton White Burgundies in its abundance of fruit flavour and in the way it develops an attractive, slightly oxidized flavour fairly young.

Just as there is a Côtes de la Vallée on some of the flattest land at McLaren Vale (established by a retired French teacher, D. L. Noon), there is a Côte de Boulanger in the Swan. The proprietors of the latter, Evans & Tate, are making some of the best wines of the area.

They seem to have done everything right since buying Gnangara Wines on the river. With the aid of refrigeration and air-conditioning they have been making elegant Swan wines, and from their property Redbrook at Willyabrup in the Margaret River region, they have been producing even better wines. In the future one feels that their Swan wines will become much less important since there are only 4 hectares at Gnangara and even less at Bakers Hill, a declining vineyard area where one of the proprietors has a farm. Accordingly, their wines should improve further, from a current high standard. But they are rather expensive.

In the smallest category, that is less than 25 tonnes, the wineries are all relatively new: Baskerville (1951), Lakeville (1978), Lamont (1978) and Vindara (1978). It is therefore pleasing to note that as well as aiming at the premium table-wine market, these vineyards are still growing varieties like Muscat to make rich dessert wines of the type which the area has always made so well, though in such small quantities that they are little known outside Perth. Baskerville is one of the few vineyards in the Swan Valley to plant Malbec, making a fine, rich, soft red of good, reliable quality. The proprietor of Lamont is the son-in-law of Jack Mann, formerly of Houghton, and the wines are as one would expect: made with great care and affection, and full of flavour. I like their light reds.

Crushing between 25 and 50 tonnes are Bassendean (1951), Henley Park (1935), Highway Wines (1953), Little River (formerly Glenalwyn, 1933), Revelry (1930), Riverside and Westfield (1922). Highway and Henley Park are among the many wineries in the Swan whose proprietors originate from Yugoslavia. Probably the most notable of these wineries is Westfield, which has a tiny vineyard of less than 2 hectares on which the aim is to limit production and raise quality, with modest quantities of very good fruit bought in to complement what is grown. The usual Swan full-bodied whites are made, from Verdelho, Sémillon and Chenin Blanc, but clean yet fruity reds are also made, from Cabernet Sauvignon, Shiraz and Malbec. Riverside is very close to Perth, opposite Olive Farm on the Swan, and its extremely unpretentious wines and buildings match.

There are only two wineries in the next largest category, 50–100 tonnes: Peters (1955) and Twin Hills (1937).

The 100–500-tonne class includes two already discussed, Olive Farm and Evans & Tate, notable for introducing modern wine-making techniques to the Swan. The wineries are Ellendale (formerly

Sveta Maria, 1904), Evans & Tate (1971), Jadran (1927), Olive Farm and Jane Brook Estate (formerly Vignacourt, 1955). Vignacourt used to make a good vintage port of the older style, much rich blackberry fruit and a rather soft finish; as Jane Brook the quality has improved, both for fortified and for table wines.

Crushing between 500 and 1,000 tonnes is Sandalford (1840). Valencia was once in this category, or larger, when it was part of Emu Wines of the United Kingdom, but now the name is no longer used by Hardy, the present proprietor, and the 20 hectares of black grapes which recently remained no longer have a separate identity.

Houghton crushes several thousand tonnes, much of it from Moondah Brook, over 100 kilometres to the north, and Frankland River Vineyard in the Mount Baker area of the far south. Thus, as at McLaren Vale and Clare, Hardy is the dominant producer.

About 30 kilometres south-east of Perth, at Bickley, is Woodhenge Wines (1975), where Brian Murphy, a jovial computer software entrepreneur, makes rich Cabernet–Shiraz wines with something of the Swan's character. The cooler climate may lead to even better things. In the hills at Darlington, where there were vineyards from 1880 to 1920, is Darlington Estate (1983) also taking fruit from Woodthorpe at Parkerville. There is a crush of about 100 tonnes of Cabernet Sauvignon, Chardonnay and the like, as one would expect, but perhaps of most interest for the future is a planting of Gamay in 1985. Current reds are rather big.

SOUTH-WESTERN WESTERN AUSTRALIA

In most cases, the surroundings of vineyards are boringly gentle slopes or even completely flat land susceptible to frosts, together with towns and villages, for vineyards are often planted on the land where life is less real and earnest than usual, and where people want to live as well. Only in a land of vast space, developed recently, are houses rare in vineyard land.

Travelling south from Kojonup towards Albany, one drops a few hundred metres in altitude gently over 200 kilometres, and though there is still considerable karri and jarrah forest remaining, it is for the most part relatively intensive mixed farming country, the houses closer together than in the sheep country further inland, as one nears Mount Barker much of it remaining relatively green all the year round. Western Australia is huge, but only a little of it is really suitable for vines: impose the 50 cm rainfall isohyet and the 18°C January mean temperature isotherm on the map, seek out suitable soils and the area is tiny.

However, around the farming towns of Mount Barker and Franklin River about twenty vineyards have been established, and a couple of hundred kilometres west around Margaret River there are rather more. They have all been established since the Western Australian Department of Agriculture, led by John Gladstones, identified in the early 1960s the combination of long, cool, dry summers, cool winters and adequate soils necessary for production of high-quality fruit.

Wine people are friendly everywhere, and Western Australians of all kinds are renowned throughout the Commonwealth for the warmth of their hospitality. Naturally the Western Australian wine districts are particularly friendly. When an elderly relation of mine was headed in that direction, I commented to her, regarding one vigneron, that I did not know him, though the name was familiar. As she is a little hard of hearing, when she and her sister arrived in the district, she said, 'These people are friends of Oliver's; we must visit them.' At the vineyard the proprietor was found to be away from home, the shop shut because the new season's wines were still in wood. However, armed with my name the intrepid ladies were welcomed in, shown the wines from the wood and the delightful holiday house and sped on their way much cheered. I have never had the courage to visit my unknown friends.

LOWER GREAT SOUTHERN AREA

There is a host of very small vineyards in the Mount Barker region, all crushing less than 25 tonnes: Castle Rock Estate (1986), Hay River (1974), Jingalla (1979), Mount Shadforth (1975), Narang (1979), Narrikup (1977), Perillup (1976), Porongorup, Redmond (1975), Tingle-Wood (1976), Waterman (1976) and Yannup (1980). Because they are so small, Narrikup and Perillup for example each crushing less than 5 tonnes, they can be eccentric, or at least different. Tingle-Wood is the only vineyard actually located in the karri forest, not quite like the witch's cottage in Hansel and Gretel, but with 50-metre-tall timber not far away, and it makes 'Red Tingle' and 'Yellow Tingle' from Cabernet Sauvignon, Shiraz and Riesling. The 1984 red did not match its name in 1989 but was a

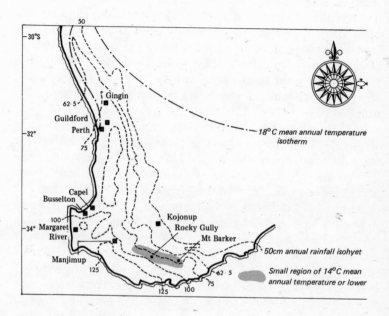

Western Australia climate

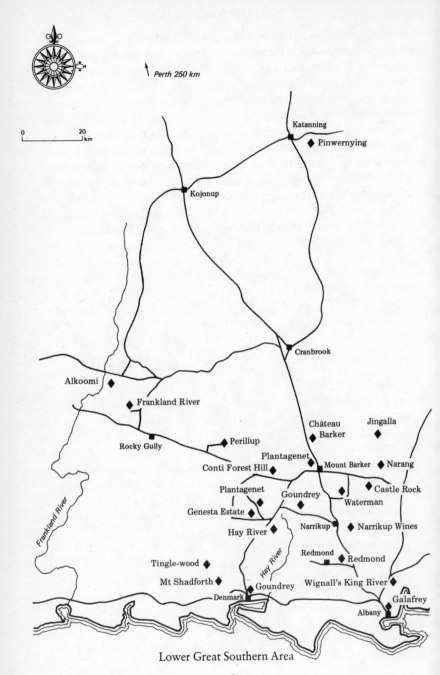

Lower Great Southern Area

firm, youthful wine full of fruit. Hay River, with a Roseworthy-trained wine-maker, planted only Cabernet Sauvignon, and Narri-kup only Riesling. Narang (1980), the only winery in the 25–50-tonne class, similarly planted nothing but Riesling, the resulting wine good rather than outstanding, but each vintage improving, season allowing. For small wineries like Narang, Narrikup, Porong-orup and Castle Rock that produce good but similar Rieslings, distribution and identification in large markets will remain a prob-lem; they are hard to find, and the more regional and varietal character they develop the harder will it be for the customer to distinguish them from each other.

Alkoomi (1971), Chatsfield (Waterman, 1976), Conti Forest Hill (1966), Galafrey (1975), Genesta (1975) and Goundrey (1971) crush between 50 and 100 tonnes. Alkoomi grows Merlot, Malbec, Sémillon and Sauvignon Blanc as well as the expected Cabernet Sauvignon, Shiraz and Riesling, and all are clean, fresh, fruity, well-balanced wines when young, suggesting that they will develop well. Conti Forest Hill, which had Dorham Mann as wine-maker initially, is in orchard country, for the Denmark–Mount Barker area has long been notable for the quality of its apples, codlin moth free, unlike the eastern states'. Goundrey has its winery in a former butter factory in the town of Denmark, like Grosset at Auburn in South Australia. The rise of the wine industry has helped to ease the decline of other primary industries in a number of high-rainfall areas of Australia, though wine remains relatively small as an industry.

Galafrey is one of the rare growers of the early-ripening Müller-Thurgau. I recall the 1986 blend with Riesling as being particularly inoffensive early in 1989, and the 1989 unblended wine as mild and slightly sweet (perhaps with a hint of a trans-linalool oxide, the main volatile terpene in the variety), hidden by a baked schnapper late in 1990. The 1987 Cabernet Sauvignon, on the other hand, is really big and will reward the patient cellarer.

Plantagenet began crushing what has now risen to more than 100 tonnes a year in a converted apple-packing shed in 1968, and its wine-makers have helped Goundrey, Narang, Waterman and others with their early vintages. As the largest local wine-maker, Plantag-enet has very happily determined much of the style of the area. Its Riesling is reliably good, its Shiraz much better. The Chardonnay, especially with fruit from Forrestville, is good, the style somehow neither in the more austere 'French' manner nor the rich Australian of such as Cullen.

Frankland River is, of course, much larger than Plantagenet, its 100 hectares of vines putting it into the 500–1,000-tonne class, but as the wines are made in the Swan by Houghton, its influence has not been as great as one might have expected from the fact that it has almost half of the vines in the area.

MARGARET RIVER

Most birds look awkward in palm trees, but it was not to keep them away that Seppelt planted its extraodinary avenues of palm trees half a century ago; it was to keep workers employed during the Depression. Bird damage is in any case a particular problem with small, isolated or fringe vineyards.

When Vasse Felix was established 8 kilometres west of the small town of Cowaramup in 1967, it had marri, *Eucalyptus calophylla*, very close to the vines, and virtually no other vineyards in the area. The marri is a handsome, slow-growing tree, similar in appearance to the red-flowering gum, *Eucalyptus ficifolia*, with pale, fissured, fibrous bark and gum-nuts about 3 cm in diameter. In January, when it flowers, large flocks of silver-eyes, *Zosterops lateralis*, congregate to feed on the nectar. For Vasse Felix the bird attacks on the small initial crops were disastrous, and could have been so for later, larger crops. Not only are berries eaten by birds, but damaged berries are splendid hosts for fungi of all kinds.

Vasse Felix's developer, medical practitioner Tom Cullity, tried everything possible, including the falcon which now decorates the label, but the only real solution to bird damage comes with much more extensive contiguous vineyards. Temporary aid has come from amplifying confusing sounds which interfere with the birds' contact calls, which they use in dense woodland to keep the flock together.

Fortunately, good wines have been made despite this problem. The reds tend to be lighter in style than others in the area, but clean, fruity and attractive, especially when young. The winery was subsequently purchased by a former 'richest man in Australia', the late M. R. A. Holmes à Court, but the style has not changed.

Margaret River has a maritime climate: the vineyards all lie on the coastal strip between Cape Leeuwin and Cape Naturaliste. Such a climate should protect against frosts, but in fact these have on

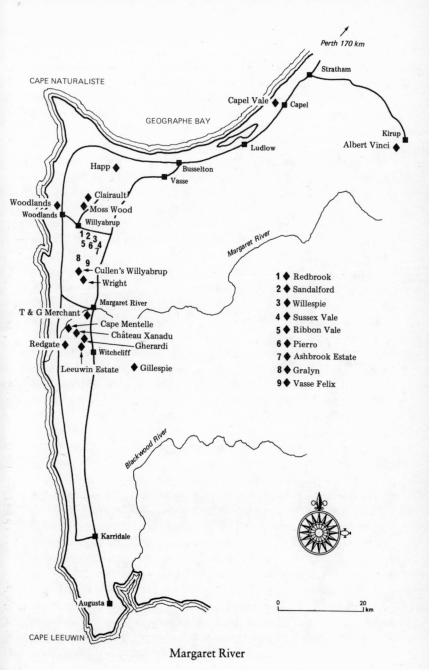

CAPE NATURALISTE

Perth 170 km

Stratham

GEOGRAPHE BAY

Capel Vale

Capel

Kirup

Ludlow

Albert Vinci

Happ

Busselton

Vasse

Clairault

Woodlands

Moss Wood

Woodlands

Willyabrup

1 2 3
5 6 4
   7
8 9

Margaret River

Cullen's Willyabrup

Wright

T & G Merchant

Margaret River

Cape Mentelle

Château Xanadu

Redgate

Gherardi

Witchcliff

Leeuwin Estate

Gillespie

1 ◆ Redbrook
2 ◆ Sandalford
3 ◆ Willespie
4 ◆ Sussex Vale
5 ◆ Ribbon Vale
6 ◆ Pierro
7 ◆ Ashbrook Estate
8 ◆ Gralyn
9 ◆ Vasse Felix

Blackwood River

Karridale

0   20
         km

Augusta

CAPE LEEUWIN

Margaret River

211

occasion been very severe. Moss Wood, for example, lost three of its first five possible Chardonnay crops to frost. For later flowering varieties, however, such as Cabernet Sauvignon, the very cold spring in years such as 1981 seems to have been helpful. In that year Moss Wood, Cullen's Willyabrup and Cape Mentelle all produced exceptionally fine Cabernet wines, deep reddish-purple, with strong berry overtones to smell and rich, strong, fruity taste. In 1983 Moss Wood produced an even better Cabernet. One remarkable characteristic which the red wines of this area seem to share is balance when young, so that even though the wines give promise of staying at their best for a decade or more, they are drinkable when only one, two or three years old. In this they differ from the colder-climate wines of Geelong or the Yarra Valley, and are closer to Coonawarra, though they are usually more intense than the Coonawarra wines.

A friend, who has some land in south-western Western Australia, gave us in the winter of 1982, for reasons best known to himself, a 1962 'Léoville Poyferré', a 1977 Vasse Felix Cabernet Sauvignon and a 1977 Moss Wood Cabernet Sauvignon. They were quite distinguishable. The French wine was in beautiful condition, light, soft, clean, balanced and elegant, with an indescribable nose and flavour. The Vasse Felix seemed to be nearing the end of its run, since it had a slightly bitter finish. The Moss Wood, on the other hand, was in splendid condition, showing fine chocolate caramel fruit and offering the possibility of further development. The comparison was most unfair; in twenty years' time some of the current wines from both Vasse Felix and Moss Wood should be compared with some of the current third- or fourth-growth Clarets, to the great satisfaction and edification of all. Just to confuse a little, one should add that Moss Wood's ridiculously strong Pinot Noir (the 1987, for example, was 14 per cent alcohol) is definitely Burgundian in character, and very fine indeed.

At Cape Mentelle, David Hohnen, who previously worked at Stonyfell in South Australia and Taltarni in Victoria, is making really big wines, influenced a little perhaps by the styles with which he has previously worked, but more by the remarkable fruit which Margaret River produces. The wines have richness and complexity in their fruit, great depth of tannin and strong acid, so that they can cope with quite a bit of oak treatment, yet they are enjoyable when only two or three years old, with the certainty of five or ten years' improvement ahead. Merlot is not needed to soften the Cabernet Sauvignon, but Hohnen uses it to add further complexity to his wines. He won the Jimmy Watson Trophy twice in succession (1983 and 1984), showing how the richness of his wines attracts when young. His whites may be even better than his reds. He handles Sauvignon Blanc particularly well, whether from Cape Mentelle or Cloudy Bay in New Zealand. Some 70 per cent of his company is now owned by Veuve Cliquot, which will help the wines' distribution but not their quality; that is established.

With about 90 hectares under vines, and a crush of up to 500 tonnes per annum, Leeuwin Estate is much larger than the other wineries in the Margaret River area. It is unusual in other ways, too: the proprietors have aimed very deliberately at the top end of the market, in quality and in price, the aim at one time, according to press reports, being to have 'the highest priced Chardonnay on the shelves of New York bottleshops in 1984' (*Australian Financial Review*, 8 July 1983).

The winery is also unusual in that it aims to make all of its grapes into first-grade wines, as do the French châteaux, but unlike, say, Château Lafite Rothschild, with its 80 hectares of three varieties yielding approximately 200,000 litres of one wine, Leeuwin Estate grows Cabernet Sauvignon, Chardonnay, Gewürztraminer, Riesling, Pinot Noir and Sauvignon Blanc.

The winery has simple, wooden-posted verandahs around a building where form suggests function, and function, as so often in Australia, suggests pressed sheet-metal. However, it is not the corrugated galvanized iron that is such an important part of the Australian landscape; at Leeuwin Estate the metal is Lysaght 'Colorbond' or some similar product in army green. Ducks flying by moonlight are most unlikely to plunge into the roof under the impression that it is a pond, as happens with new galvanized iron.

Whether the wines justify their remarkable prices is a matter for time and the market to tell, but the wines are still selling, are very fine when young and mature quite well. The Chardonnay smells of ripe peaches and tastes much better, and the Cabernet is intense and powerful, with very big berry fruit, a wine which will last for years and yet has some finesse.

Only two vineyards in the Margaret River area crush less than 25 tonnes: Redgate (1977) and Thomas (1976). Redgate has planted most of the Bordeaux varieties, black and white, and has made some very good Cabernets (e.g. 1984, 1985 and 1987), but Thomas grows only Pinot Noir, with most impressive results from young fruit already, soft wines with plenty of depth of flavour.

Most of the area's wineries crush between 25 and 50 tonnes: Ashbrook Estate (1976), Clairault (1976), Eagle Bay (1987), Gherardi (Freycinet, 1979), Gralyn (1975), Happ (1978), La Taj (1980), T & G Merchant (1982), Pierro (1980), Ribbon Vale (1978), Wignall's King River (1982), Willespie (1976), Woodlands (1974) and Wright (1974). Most have planted Bordeaux varieties, but too few vintages have passed for many to make a major impression, given the eagerness with which their wines are snapped up in Western Australia, a problem shared with the very small wineries of Tasmania. Eagle Bay makes a very useful, crisp Sémillon. Gralyn is notable for taking its name from the given names of its proprietors, Graham and Marilyn Hutton. They are primarily graziers, so that they have been able to experiment and make the area's first fortified sweet red wine from their Cabernet Sauvignon and Shiraz fruit. It is said to be a wine of considerable promise, though one feels that the strength of the region should lie in table wines. Happ's wines have bright young fruit and age well; Chatsfield's reds are thicker and may take longer to develop, in the Victorian manner rather than the regional. Wignall's Pinot Noir is regarded as the least Australian of the area, having balance and depth as well as the expected fruit.

It is in the next category, 50–100 tonnes crushed, that the rather older wineries have made a great contribution to Australian wine quality in the last decade. There are five: Château Xanadu (1979), Cullen's Willyabrup (1971), Gillespie (1976), Moss Wood (1969) and Vasse Felix (1967).

The three largest wineries have also established themselves in the same way, Cape Mentelle (1969) and Redbrook (established by Evans & Tate of Gnangara in the Swan in 1974) making 100–500 tonnes and Leeuwin Estate (1974) crushing almost 1,000 tonnes.

SOUTH-WEST COASTAL PLAIN

The coastal plain has a small number of vineyards stretched out over a long distance south from Perth. The Tuart sands, on which most of the vines are planted, are well-drained acid sands over limestone, the maritime climate providing adequate rainfall in many cases, though some have drip irrigation. Fanciful locals compare the combination of soil and climate with Bordeaux. Yields range from moderate to high, Capel Vale for example averaging over 9 tonnes a hectare. Some of the wineries are relatively long established. Luisini, for example, began in 1929 and uses relatively traditional methods to make big Chenin Blanc wines in the Houghton manner.

Contiville is one of the most interesting, since it also has vineyards in the Lower Great Southern area and at Yanchep to the north of Perth. It was established in 1948 and its expertise has helped others, such as Peel Es⁺ate.

Because these wineries are closer to Perth and longer established, they can more readily sell larger quantities of reasonable but unremarkable wine than can the more southerly areas. For the most part, their wines are less good than those of the more southerly areas.

Hartridge (1970) is the smallest in the area, crushing only about 20 tonnes a year. Capel Vale (1975) and Leschenault (1973) crush between 50 and 100 tonnes. Contiville and Luisini fall into the 100–500-tonne category.

Capel Vale makes, at its best, one of the State's finest Rieslings. Those of 1986 and 1988 are outstanding, tropical fruit for the nose, rich and full on the palate, generally delicious. The fleshy 1986 Cabernet is very slowly developing into an outstanding wine.

All of the wines from the south-west of the State show great promise, and they show it young. These wines may be distinguished from those of the colder parts of Victoria by their early attractiveness, the forwardness of their fruit. Yet many of them last and develop very well.

7

Tasmania, Queensland and the Northern Territory

Viticulture has been economically significant in only four states, those already considered, and only in South Australia has it been of real importance (see Appendix 5). In South Australia this has been largely because other industries have failed to develop. In the other states, wine has been of even less moment. Despite this, these smaller wine industries are of great interest, and Tasmania's at least will in due course be widely recognized for its outstanding wines.

Queensland and the Northern Territory are, by and large, too hot to make good wine, Tasmania too wet and cold to make it in any quantity. They represent the extremes offered by an island continent and its largest non-tropical offshore island. If the so-called 'enhanced greenhouse effect' becomes a reality, Tasmania may be the only satisfactory place to make good wine, the rest ranging from tolerable through too hot to impossible.

TASMANIA

Tasmania or Van Diemen's Land as it was known at the time, was the second British penal colony to be established in Australia, so it is not surprising that grapes were planted there more than a decade before the establishment of Victoria, Western Australia or South Australia. The first vineyard was planted by Bartholomew Broughton in the mid 1820s at Newtown, near Hobart (or Hobart Town as it was called then). However, he did not long survive and his vineyard was bought by Charles Swanston, a pensioned-off captain in the East India Company's army, who had arrived at Hobart Town early in 1829. Swanston had been a successful military paymaster for six years in India, so he was able to buy Fenton Forest, a property on the River Styx, other properties further from

Hobart, and Newtown Park at Newtown, which was Broughton's property. By the late 1840s vintage was almost 10,000 litres a year and plans were in hand for further expansion, but Swanston's Derwent Bank ran into great difficulty in the Depression of the 1840s and, when two major banks withdrew their support in 1849, Swanston was forced to resign, his creditors receiving ten shillings in the pound. On his return from a brief trip to America to raise funds, he died at sea in 1850.

While Swanston's vineyard was unsuccessful and his bank collapsed, he is remembered as being one of the two major supporters of John Batman's colonization of Port Phillip, which led to the establishment of Melbourne and the colony of Victoria.

Many attempts were made to grow wine grapes in Tasmania over the next hundred years, the obvious attraction being that the major European wine regions lie at latitudes more than 40° North, and none of the mainland of Australia is as much as 40° South, whereas the 41st parallel runs through the north of Tasmania, and Hobart lies almost at 43° South.

The map shows some of the places where grapes have been grown in the past or are being grown now, all in the eastern two-thirds of the island, for the western third is too wet.

It is hard for mainlanders to obtain Tasmanian wines, for the quantities produced are tiny. Indeed, at the moment less than 500 hectares are planted to vines in the entire island.

In the early 1950s a Frenchman, Jean Miguet, made wines at La Provence near Launceston from Cabernet Sauvignon, Pinot Noir, Gamay, Chardonnay and Grenache, and those who tasted them (myself not among them) have suggested that had Miguet stayed in Australia rather than returning to France in the mid 1970s, he might have made very fine wines indeed.

A little later, in 1958, Claudio Alcorso, an Italian-born businessman and opera patron, established a vineyard, Moorilla, at Berriedale just north of Hobart. Like most new vineyards it suffered great bird damage for the first few years, and the tiny vineyard, which grows Pinot Noir, Cabernet Sauvignon and a few other fine varieties, was entirely netted to keep the birds out. Both as a result of this kind of problem and because of the much colder climate, costs are extremely high, and so are prices. In Adelaide his 1981 Cabernet Sauvignon, when first on sale, was almost twice as expensive as the best of Balgownie, Brokenwood, Petaluma or Cape Mentelle. It is a

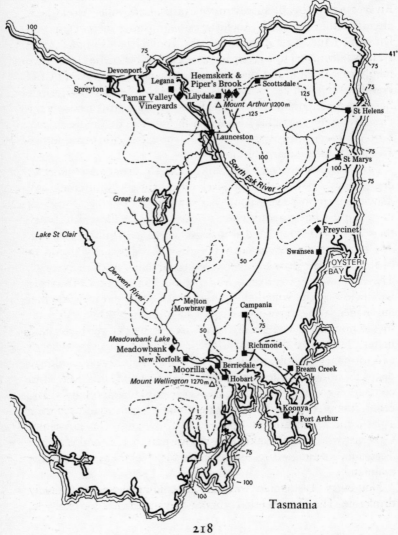

very firm, dark wine, with a strong herbaceous nose and an almost stalky palate, so strong is the tannin. While its quality is very high, it will not be sought out by everyone, simply on account of price.

To the north-east of Hobart, on the east coast near Marion Bay, Alcorso and a number of others, encouraged by the quality of the Moorilla wine, have established another vineyard, Bream Creek.

While the wines from the south of Tasmania are of great interest, not far inland from the north coast, at Piper's Brook on the Piper River, are two already successful vineyards. One, called Heemskerk after the ship in which Abel Janszoon Tasman discovered Van Diemen's Land, New Zealand and the Tonga Islands in 1642, was established in 1974 by a group involving a member of the Haselgrove family of Mildara, and the Sydney wine and spirit merchant Bill Fesq. To the south are mountains 1,000 metres high, to the north is Bass Strait, and on the far slope is Piper's Brook, established by the Pirie family in 1973. Like Petaluma in the Adelaide Hills, Piper's Brook has very closely spaced vines, and the wines from this vineyard are also of quite remarkable quality.

Piper's Brook vineyard has almost exactly the same number of degree days – essentially fruit development time – as Burgundy. All its wines seem to be very good, but it will be some time before it is known just what grapes should be grown there. Meanwhile, when the wines can be found and afforded, they can certainly be enjoyed. The Rieslings are quite exceptional, the 1980 showing great depth of fruit at three years old, with fruit sweetness rather than sugar. The nose was floral like a Moselle, the finish firm with a pH well below 3, the wine light and graceful yet promising long life. Subsequent wines have shown richer flavour, and it is very difficult to see how these wines can change except by getting better and better. The 1983 'Northern Slopes', for example, is a wine of extraordinary complexity of flavour, partly reflecting a moderate degree of noble rot infection. Fermented to dryness, it is difficult to compare with other Rieslings except some of Hickinbotham's. The cellar, however, seems to be seeking a more elegant style, as in their 1982 wine. They are too good to drink young. The Pinot and Cabernet wines are among the best in the nation in a good year, but Tasmania's vintages are much more variable than most of the mainland's.

Not every Tasmanian wine is outstanding; some are merely drinkable. The Heemskerk Traminer Sylvaner 1981, for example, though quite attractive with a firm acid finish, was so light that I could detect in it virtually no fruit character. Most Heemskerk wines are good, none the less, and the association with Louis Roederer to make sparkling wine seems likely to be successful, provided that the wines are allowed proper maturation time.

There can be said to be six wine districts in Tasmania: Piper River and Tamar Valley on the north coast; the east coast; the Coal River Valley; the Derwent Valley, and the Huon Valley. This, however, is somewhat misleading, as the map shows: Freycinet, Austwick and Bream Creek are indeed on the east coast but cover more than 100 kilometres of that coast and are further apart than the Barossa and McLaren Vale, or the Yarra and Goulburn Valleys. Only Piper River, with nine vineyards, and the Tamar Valley, with eight, can yet be expected to indicate regional styles, and there is so much to be learned about viticulture and wine-making in Tasmania that it would be a brave man who could claim to have identified these styles with certainty.

The wine-makers do not always help. From the Pinot Noir fruit of St Matthias on the west bank of the Tamar very close to Launceston, Graham Wiltshire makes a very good wine for the Wing family, but then, on the label, tells the drinker not to cellar the wine for more than two years. Yet the 1987 example in 1990 tasted, not like a 'DYA' past its prime, to use Hugh Johnston's adjuvant term, but like the early stage of a real wine in development.

The vineyards in the six 'regions' are as follows. Tamar: Buchanan, Cliff House, Glengarry (owned by Buchanan, 1980), Holm Oak, Marion's (1980, formerly Tamar Valley), Loira, Powercourt, Rotherhithe, St Matthias (1982); Piper River: Bellingham, Clover Hill, Delamere, Heemskerk, Idelwilde, La Provence, Pelion, Piper's Brook, St Patrick's; east coast: Austwick, Freycinet, Bream Creek; Coal River: Glen Ayr, Stoney, Uplands Estate; Derwent: Meadowbank (1974), Moorilla; Huon: Elsewhere, Panorama.

Frosts, birds and cold will certainly keep yields low, but for those who can find them Tasmanian wines are very fine. Because the Tasmanian industry has inherently high costs, problems will arise if the industry grows so large that the tourist market, the parochial island market and the highest-quality end of the mainland market all become saturated. As one of the Tasmanian growers put it to me, 'I rarely drink Australian wine when I can buy French anywhere near the price.' The higher the Tasmanian (or indeed any Australian) prices, the more French wines become competitive.

QUEENSLAND

In 1873 Anthony Trollope wrote:

> ... vineyards have been made, the owners of which make wine, and think that in a little time they will make good wine. I have drunk fairly good wine in Australia, but none made in Queensland. If on this head any wine-growing Queensland squatter should accuse me of falsehood – remembering the assenting smile with which I have seemed to acknowledge that his vintage was excellent – let him reflect how impossible it is for the guest to repudiate the praises with which the host speaks of his own cellar. All the world over it is allowed to the giver to praise his own wine – a privilege of which Australians avail themselves; but it is not allowed to the receiver to deny the justness of such encomium, except under circumstances of peculiar intimacy. Here, in these pages, truth must prevail; and I am bound to say that Queensland wine was not to my taste. I am delighted to acknowledge that their pineapples are perfect.

More than a century later, other Australians ('Southerners') tend to make similar comments, if perhaps rather less well expressed, about Queensland's wines. However, around Stanthorpe, 220 kilometres from Brisbane, at relatively high altitudes, a number of small wine-makers are bent on using the best techniques available to prove everyone else wrong.

Trollope tried wines made in the same general area, but where they were grown is not clear, since most authorities seem to trace wine-growing to Father Jerome Davadi, who planted his first vineyard at about the time of Trollope's visit. Davadi had learnt about horticulture and wine-making in his native Italy, and he is generally recognized to be the 'father of the fruit industry', as he saw that it would outlast the tin mines which had brought substantial numbers of settlers to the area. His first vineyard was the horse paddock of his presbytery, and he later planted another at the foot of Mount Marlay on the outskirts of Stanthorpe, a town originally called 'Quart Pot'.

Ballandean Station, where Angelo Puglisi's Sundown Valley

vineyard is now established, is regarded as having had the first planting of vines. In fact, a White Syrian vine planted in 1859 is still growing. However, the first Queensland wine industry collapsed in the 1880s and was not re-established until Italian immigrants began making wine in the late 1920s, the period of the Imperial Preference and export bounties. The first of these wineries was Zanatta's Biltmore, which suffered financial problems for a time after the Zanattas sold out in 1981.

Until the early 1970s all wines were made from table grapes, but Angelo Puglisi saw the need to grow wine grapes and planted Shiraz, Cabernet Sauvignon, Riesling, Sémillon, Chenin Blanc and Sylvaner, and since 1972 he has been producing a range of table wines from these varieties. Some, such as a 1988 Auslese Sylvaner with a surprising amount of fruit, are unusual. They are made with great care. I recall, after tasting a six-month-old Riesling, a very floral wine with considerable residual sugar and little acid, setting the bottle to one side for an hour or so. On re-examination, the wine had turned from a fresh greenish yellow to a clear, bright, pale pink.

As wine-makers and vineyard managers have paid ever greater attention to prevention of oxidation in grapes, by harvesting at night, cooling the must, fermenting at low temperatures, storing juice at low temperatures, blanketing harvested grapes and fermenting must with inert gas, they have protected some of the phenolic compounds which, when they oxidize, form pink coloration in a wine without affecting aroma or taste. In the past, sufficient oxidation normally occurred between harvest and the end of fermentation for pinking to be a relatively unusual problem. Now, however, it can be the most carefully made wines which are most susceptible to pinking. Furthermore, because it is a problem of slight instability in the wine, it is not predictable, and indeed a wine which has become pink in the bottle may lose this colour with time. Accordingly, wineries which have found this problem have sought aid from the Australian Wine Research Institute and elsewhere.

Because the compounds which cause pinking are phenolics, they can be removed with fining agents such as casein and polyvinylpolypyrrolidone (PVPP). However, this can lead to problems in itself since it has now been shown that many fining agents remove not just unwanted components but also some of the minor compounds which are very important in flavour.

Angelo's red wines are also well made, the 1982 Cabernet being

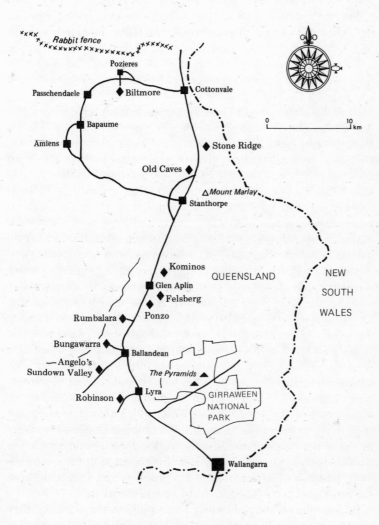

Granite Belt (Queensland)

a bright purple when a year old, with rather too much oak for the fruit but with sufficient acid to improve for a number of years.

Just north-east on a stony ridge is Stony Ridge, which has had an early success at a southern show and which may well be a vineyard to watch.

Bungawarra, one of whose proprietors is a dentist (rather than the usual medical practitioner), and which had its first crushing in 1979, is the winery which so far has produced the most notable Granite Belt wine, a 1981 Cabernet Sauvignon, deep crimson with a strong, stalky blackcurrant nose, reminiscent of young Penfold reds to some, deep fruit flavour, fine balance, enormous body, a compact and powerful wine that has developed as promised. It recalls the best of the older style of Clare wine and is a great portent to the future of the Granite Belt, which has as yet only intimations of an area character.

The Robinson family winery at Lyra, slightly south of Stanthorpe, is another winery already making wines with considerable potential. The proprietors are John and Heather Robinson; Heather was a Salter, of the family which established Saltram at Angaston in the Barossa Valley. The first label had a strange, almost Pre-Raphaelite family group on it, but the wines are well made, with a hint of hot-climate flavour about the reds, the Chardonnay generous to a fault. The 1987 Shiraz has a label claiming that it is a 'Cool Climate' wine, because of being made at 800 metres altitude; it is not but, tried at the trots over a high-protein smorgasbord, it was not disgraced by a 1986 Henschke Mount Edelstone, despite having had a malolactic fermentation in the bottle.

A winery with a peculiarly Queensland flavour to it is Old Caves, on the New England Highway, just to the north of Stanthorpe. It was set up by two members of the Zanatta family and is distinguished by a grotesque mural with spaces for tourists' heads to be pushed through and photographed by other tourists.

Though they are evidently from single vintages, not all the Old Caves wines have the year of vintage on the label. For example, wines labelled Riesling and Cervante consumed in late 1983 both showed considerable development, but probably this resulted mainly from the making. Drinking them with pork chops, we found that the Riesling had good colour, a Sémillon flavour and some bottle stink, showing considerable development, whereas the Cervante was slightly sweet with a hint of lime juice, rather an Italian wine, and much more drinkable, yet it too tasted old. In Australia, Riesling, as already mentioned, does not simply mean (as it should) the noble grape of the Rhine, the Mosel and Alsace, so that the Sémillon flavour was not surprising. Cervante, a table grape, carried with it no expectations.

Kominos makes a Cabernet Sauvignon that can be drunk very young but which has some prospect of development.

At present the total production of the area is less than 1,000 tonnes of wine grapes, compared with about 4,000 tonnes of table grapes. If the enthusiasm of the proprietors is matched by success in the marketplace, no doubt this crush will increase substantially. With the New England Highway passing through the area, these vineyards have the opportunity to capture a part of Queensland's enormous tourist industry. They have yet to capture a significant part of the Australian wine market, and have won few prizes at shows other than Brisbane's.

More than 1,000 kilometres north, near Herberton, not far from Cairns, is Foster's Wines. It makes a rich wine of the port type, smelling of stewed plums.

Near hot, though occasionally flood-bound Roma, some 500 kilometres north-west of Stanthorpe (but still more than 1,000 kilometres from Herberton – Queensland is a big place) is Bassett's Romavilla, established in 1863. It has produced good fortified wines for well over a century, and more recently, since the family sold out after more than a century of wine-making, has been making table wines as the market requires. But the climate is suitable for good fortified wines only, so the winery's second century will be no easier than its first.

NORTHERN TERRITORY

Table grapes are successfully grown 200 kilometres north of Alice Springs, in unpromising mulga country. Mulga is *Acacia aneura*, a nondescript small grey-green tree which with other related species and a range of tussocky grasses makes up the sparse shrubby cover of the infertile red soils of much of central Australia. Wine could be made from these table grapes, since the varieties grown include Muscat Gordo Blanco and Sultana. However, what is in some ways the most remarkable vineyard in Australia is closer to Alice Springs, on the Racecourse Estate just south of Heavitree Gap. Here, a pharmacist, David Hornsby, has established Château Hornsby, the Château being a converted orange-packing shed. In 1972 planting was begun, with the aim of growing some 8 hectares of Shiraz, Cabernet Sauvignon, Sémillon and Riesling, to yield, eventually, 100 tonnes. The yield is attributable to drip irrigation, without which no grapes could be grown. The first vintage was 1977, and the wines have been consistently drinkable, as would be expected from a hot area with no disease problems. The dry continental climate and altitude of 600 metres are of some advantage. However, the major charm of the Château is that it is so unlikely in the red heart. It is a tourist attraction with a restaurant in which the proportion of *vin du pays* consumed is very low, but to which that wine has drawn the drinkers.

8

The Future

During the 1970s annual consumption of wine per head in Australia doubled to about 20 litres, after which it hardly changed for another decade, then declined from 1988 to 1990. The earlier rapid increase was partly at the expense of beer, since bottled beer provides alcohol at about twice the price of wine in 'casks', as the bag-in-the-box devices are usually called, but also represented an actual increase in alcohol consumption. The decline at the end of the 1980s has been attributed to an increase in the consumption of low-alcohol (2.5 per cent or less) beer. Random breath-testing of motorists and blood-alcohol limits for drivers may also have been important.

Firmly ensconced in the folklore of the Geelong area is the story that rabid temperance advocates would sneak into wine cellars and add salt to the wine, or even smash the casks. Whether or not this happened, the temperance movement was certainly one of the factors involved in the collapse of the Victorian wine industry about the turn of the century. One of the changes that we are beginning to see is an increase in health-related criticism of all the alcohol industries. In the future it seems certain that labelling of the alcohol content of wine, beer and spirits will become mandatory, as it is in most other countries, that advertising in general will be further regulated and that certain types of advertising will be restricted or banned. Consumer pressure, indeed outrage, led in the mid 1980s to the withdrawal from sale of a Lindeman's wine-cooler product which seemed to everyone (except Lindeman's) to be aimed in its packaging at the young teenage market. Such ineptness is likely to hasten the introduction of legal restrictions on advertising, but these are unlikely to affect the consumption of wine as a normal adjunct to food unless the community as a whole changes its view of alcohol. This could happen, since over-simplification, self-righteousness and the urge to force others to do what is good for them are widespread traits; it is to be hoped that sanity is at least as common. The experiment of Prohibition makes one agree with Samuel Johnson: 'As man is a being very sparingly furnished with the power of prescience, he can provide for the future only by considering the past.'

Meanwhile, the bag in the box has become more and more important, at least in terms of sales of wine. It is a brilliantly simple idea to make a plastic bag with a simple tap opened by deforming a handle, fill the bag with cheap wine, and enclose the whole in a cardboard carton with a carrying strap at the top. It is ideal for outdoor drinking, and has changed the face of picnics (and their detritus). The device had teething troubles, mainly with leakage, but these have been mastered, and one can buy drinkable red wine for 60–90 cents a litre in bags and equivalent white for only a little more. The main drawbacks are twofold: only by counting can one assess one's consumption; and the price wars of the 1980s have made much of the increased production and sales unprofitable. Some large makers, such as Hardy, left the cask market in the early 1980s, though subsequent acquisitions have brought them back into it.

Appendices 3 and 4 show how wine sales changed in Australia from 1977 to 1989. A number of distinct trends may be seen. First, the bag in a box, which allows the drinker more control over ullage, has almost completely taken over the white wine market. (In 1984 boxed whites had over 60 per cent of the entire retail wine market, and this market share has hardly fallen since.) Secondly, sales of better red wines are slowly increasing. Thirdly, rosé consumption has been declining for some time, though it can hardly fall further without vanishing.

Australia has a substantial negative balance of trade in wine, but the figures conceal some of the most interesting facts. In the case of bottle-fermented sparkling wine, the share of the market held by imported wine is well over 10 per cent. Most of this is Champagne.

Exports have grown as Australian wines' distinctive qualities have been recognized, rather than with general increases in world trade, as there are no longer any markets like that in the United States in 1933 – under-supplied and undiscriminating. In any case, if there were such markets they would be supplied by the surplus of the world's two biggest producers, France and Italy. These countries have lower marginal costs of production, especially in their bulk-producing areas, quite apart from the possibility of subsidized export from the European Economic Community.

Exports to the United Kingdom, traditionally the largest importer of wine relative to its own production, are now well served, as I have already mentioned, by informed, interested importers. Alex Findlater of Suffolk, for example, has everything from Coldstream Hills to Penfold's Grange, from Cape Mentelle to Heemskerk. When the twenty-three exporters who form the 'Wine of Australia Campaign' held an Australia Day (26 January) tasting in London in 1988 as part of the celebration of the British settlement of Australia 200 years earlier, twenty-six importers participated; the tenfold increase to 5 million litres of Australian wine exports to the United Kingdom in the five years to 1988 was no accident. But it also reflected the collapse in the relative value of the Australian dollar over the same period, and future success depends on keeping costs down and quality up, now that the market knows what to expect. When the Australian currency was pushed up by high interest rates from 1988 to 1990, this was immediately followed by a fall in exports, showing the price sensitivity of the new markets.

Some of Australia's recent export success in Europe has been due to a particularly ill wind. When a nuclear reactor exploded at Chernobyl in early 1986, it blew radioactivity all over Sweden, rather less over the wine-growing areas of Europe, and virtually none over Australia. Hence, Sweden and to a lesser extent other European countries thought about buying 'clean' wine from Australia. When they found that it was good in both quality and value, they ordered more.

North America, South East Asia and Japan need more education about the merits of Australian wine than does Europe, but all are worthwhile markets for a small producer provided they are continuously attended to. Japan is now the largest single export market. Small producers who have made opportunistic exports to California have sometimes been successful, but frequently, because of variation in the size of the vintage and increases in home sales, they have failed to export continuously and have thereby lost their market.

Exporting has rarely been very profitable and is usually more time-consuming than selling in the domestic market. Yet for a country with few inhabitants which is in the top ten in consumption per head, but in the top twenty in total production, exports are necessary.

Turning from overseas trade to what may happen within Australia, consider again Tables 3 and 4. Extrapolation from these figures is very difficult; it is most unlikely that rosé will disappear completely, for example, or that no red wine will be sold in bulk in another ten years' time. There will always be home bottlers.

At the other end of the scale one finds that most secondary industries in Australia show a high degree of concentration, oligopoly being the norm. There are, for example, only six significant brewers: two public companies which are predominantly brewers and hoteliers, three which are successful parts of public companies, and one which is still run by the family that started it more than a century ago. However, even this one, Coopers, which is the smallest and best, has a large minority of its shares held by one of the others, which in turn has a large minority held by the largest of all, Foster's Brewing Company. In three states there is a regional monopoly of manufacture, and in most other states there are only two large brewers. What is available to the beer drinker is changing, as preservation, transport and storage of beer are not the problems they were when the regional monopolies were developing.

The wine industry is quite different. As the economists would say, it has low barriers to entry: while not at all profitable compared with most other manufacturing industries, it is in business terms cheap to establish a winery. Thus, it is a highly fragmented industry, dominated by less than a dozen large firms which between them sell about 90 per cent of all Australian wine. The pattern of control of these firms is, however, rather unusual. Penfold was the largest following its acquisition of Lindeman, Tollana and Wynn, and following its absorption into Seppelt within the South Australian Brewing company, will have almost 40 per cent of the retail market, perhaps twice the share of the next largest marketer, Orlando. (Wynn was until 1985 a part of Castlemaine Toohey, a large brewer, in which Allied Brewers of the UK had a significant minority holding until Castlemaine Toohey was acquired by the now collapsed Bond Corporation.) Berri-Renmano is probably the second largest in terms of production, and it is a grower-owned co-operative. McWilliam is a very large family company. Orlando is privately owned, following a 'management buyout' from Reckitt & Colman, but is controlled by a French aniseed-recycling company. Mildara Blass is a public company, in which William Grant & Son of Glasgow and Wolf Blass have large minority shares. Hardy is a large family company. Yalumba is a large family company. Brown Bros of Milawa is a family company. Of these firms, only Wolf Blass, Berri and McWilliam were started this century, and McWilliam began before the First World War.

In a submission early in 1990 to the Trade Practices Commission, the body meant to eliminate or prevent monopolistic and mono-psonistic behaviour by the corporate sector, the Winegrape Council of Australia claimed that Penfold had 39 per cent of the market for independent wine grapes, and was therefore in a position to dictate prices. The WCA claimed that Orlando was the second-biggest buyer in this part of the market, but had less than 10 per cent. Whatever the actual state of the market at that time, it was clearly unstable. Low barriers to entry cannot allow rogue-elephant behaviour, should it exist, to persist. Even if Penfold were to dominate the market, hundreds of smaller makers would survive. Wine is not a natural monopoly in a country with a tolerable climate.

The personal involvement that good wine demands in its manufacture may be the reason for the persistence of family connections. So, too, may be the very low profitability of wine, so that, while during the wine boom many large companies adventured into the wine industry, many of them have since left it. Furthermore, as fashion-following conglomerates have divested themselves of their wine interests, they have frequently sold them to the large, long-established wine firms, and when small but high-quality wine-makers have sold out to big companies, the family members most closely involved in the wine industry have in many cases started again on their own.

All these firms crush at least 15,000 tonnes a year, the largest over 50,000 tonnes. They are small by world standards, but because of the nature of wine there are only limited economies of scale in making it well, so the main need for growth is to combat the increasing buying power of the retail chains and mail-order wine 'clubs' that have come to dominate wine selling.

While a few other firms are of similar size to the smallest of these, and a few more slightly smaller, the history of the wine industry in Australia and the present state of the market together suggest that it may be much the same for the next fifty years: a mixture of foreign-controlled, market-orientated companies and long-established family companies. The introduction of a wealth tax, or the reintroduction of estate taxes, could change all this, but it is a mixture which makes for strong competition and good value for either the discerning or the heavy drinker. What will change is the composition of the 400 very small companies. Nothing is more certain than that a high proportion of these will be out of business by the turn of the century, though I doubt the prediction in early 1990 by a merchant bank, Dominguez Barry Samuel Montagu, that the number of producers will halve by 2000. (In rewriting this book for the second edition, I sadly deleted some twenty vineyards and happily added some sixty, but a few of the additions were embarrassing omissions from the first edition rather than new ventures, and I have without doubt missed a few deserving cases.)

In modern times, vineyard death occurs because vineyards are such poor investments; all other reasons are incidental. The Victorian Department of Agriculture in 1980 published a very thorough account of the establishment and development costs of a 4-hectare vineyard with an attached winery designed for cellar-door sales. Excluding the price of the land, the Department found that there would be negative cash flows for at least five years, during which time $170,000 would be spent. (The reason for not counting the purchase price of the land is that it should hold its value in the event of sale or closure of the business. The most of the land would vary widely, but would be within the range $1,000 to $10,000 per hectare, depending on region and merit within region.)

Again ignoring the cost of the land, over a twenty-year period the rate of return on capital would be between 5 and 10 per cent per annum. This is not good when one compares alternative investment, whether agricultural or otherwise. Under the most favourable conditions, the break-even point (the simplest though not necessarily the best investment decision criterion) would be thirteen years, and if there were adverse seasonal conditions and the wine market stayed over-supplied, the break-even point could be twenty years away from the start.

When this study was revised in 1989, the expected duration of negative cash flows and break-even point were the same, but all the other figures were worse: over twenty years the expected real rate of return was found to lie between −8 and + 20 per cent, a much wider and more risky range; and the peak outgoings, after five years, would be £1.23 million, a rise far greater than that of the Consumer Price Index.

Given these sound economic reasons for not investing in a vineyard, successful enterprises are likely to be ones where there is a significant cash flow from other sources, to get through these early years. This means people such as medical practitioners, who begin to establish their vineyards in middle age or earlier, or farmers, who can support their vineyard enterprise within their other more important farming activities. (The conservatism of farmers, combined with their willingness to try new technology if it will be more profitable or use less labour, forms a good basis for success in the wine industry, and characterizes big wineries as well as small, new ones.)

The successful establishment of a small winery requires more than just good viticulture, wine-making and accountancy: it requires brand identification. The small grower has to gain attention for his product and yet he is not in a position to advertise or to demand shelf space in bottle shops. He must rely on wine shows and wine writers, and is very vulnerable to early strong criticism and to shifts in fashion. Small wonder that he will tend to plant too many varieties and forget the less good ones on his labels.

There is much misleading labelling in the Australian wine industry. While writing the first edition of this book I was speaking with a wine-maker who had just lost his source of supply of high-quality white fruit, from a non-irrigated area, and had been seeking out irrigated fruit to replace it. He had made a verbal agreement with a grower on the River, who had then rung up in considerable embarrassment and said that another customer, in one of the eastern states, had increased his order for Chardonnay, and now there was none available. Now, the wine-maker in the eastern states does not sell Qualco Chardonnay, or Moorook Chardonnay, or even Cobdogla Chardonnay: his Chardonnay is labelled as if it came from the region where his winery is. The Tartar's home was wherever the Tartar's horse had trod; that wine-maker's wine was from where his winery was. It is very difficult to be more specific on account of the difficulty of getting written evidence of what one knows to be the case.

Given that such problems are occurring, what is the solution? Perhaps there is no one solution. The ability to detect wines from different areas by chemical means is improving, though it is still not very satisfactory, and this, and prosecutions under the various consumer protection laws, are perhaps all that government should do. In late 1989 the Federal parliament amended the Australian Wine and Brandy Corporation Act to empower this marketing body to administer a Label Integrity Programme, to deter fraudulent and misleading labelling. Relevant state and territory ministers have agreed to the scheme's introduction, so it should not founder on Commmonwealth–state rivalries, but will it supplant the various individual schemes?

Victoria, Tasmania and Western Australia have systems of guarantee of origin for their wines, and these are run by the Departments of Agriculture in those states. However, by no means all Victorian wineries avail themselves of the portrait of Queen Victoria on a 'Penny Black' stamp, which guarantees origin; the Tasmanian wine industry is tiny; and the Western Australian industry is remote from the main source of anonymous fruit, the River Murray. As noted earlier, one of the characteristics of the Australian wine industry is that enormous quantities of fruit are trucked around the country, and the controls necessary to ensure that every load of fruit is made into wine identified with its origin, not with its destination, would be horrendous. They could probably also be defeated, at least for the first century or so, given the brief success of some wine-shippers in Bordeaux, as recently as 1970, in defeating a system which had been in existence for a considerable time.

The wine-makers of the Mudgee area have a Society for the Appellation of Mudgee wines; such a co-operative venture, based on good-will and a recognition of the value of trustworthy labelling, is the best way for the industry to move. It is to be hoped that the new Label Integrity Programme does not become a ceiling for quality or a programme for the integrity of labels only, rather than wine.

Regardless of the success of the new scheme, the question of how one might introduce laws of *appellation d'origine* remains a vexed one. Consider the laws set down for Châteauneuf-du-Pape in 1923, and how they might apply to Australia.

First, it was suggested that grapes could be grown only on land capable of bearing lavender and thyme, as these plants, like the vine, were regarded as preferring similar poor soil. This regulation would affect few of the vine-growing areas of Australia, but would be very difficult to enforce should a grower be found to be growing grapes on other soil.

Second, only certain named varieties were permitted to be planted. Of the 400 wine-growers and makers in Australia, fewer than twenty do not grow Cabernet Sauvignon. More than half grow Riesling. More than half grow Shiraz. Thus, in every area one finds the most important grapes of the Rhine, the Rhône and the Medoc being grown together. It is difficult to see how one would start enforcing any relevant regulation.

Third, only specified methods of training and pruning vines were to be permitted. Viticulture has long been in a poor state in Australia, traditional practices reflecting what was workable with a minimum of labour in a country where land was not scarce and where the best vineyard areas were not defined. There is no reason to suppose that the best practices for each area have been determined, and although educators, researchers and enlightened growers are trying hard to discover these basic needs, there is far to go and not all growers want to make the journey.

Fourth, the alcohol content of the wine had to be 12 per cent of volume. It is usual to achieve this amount of alcohol in most Australian wine-growing areas, but not always possible in the coldest areas, and all too easy in the hot ones. Given current concerns about health, this stipulation might work against the interests of wine-growers, quite apart from interfering with the vignerons' decisions about when to pick, based on the balance of sugar and acid in the ripening grapes. Certainly a case could be made in the coldest areas that, when the red wines could not be made with more than, say, 10 per cent alcohol, they should not be sold as wines of that area, but this would be about as much as one might expect to achieve.

Fifth, the *triage*, whereby the grapes were sorted at harvest and at least 5 per cent had to be discarded as unfit for wine-making, would be impossible to introduce where there is mechanical harvesting. Where growers sell grapes to large wine-makers, such sorting occurs, but the basis is monetary rather than mandatory.

Sixth, no rosé wine was permitted to be made in Châteauneuf-du-Pape. Wine consumers' dislike of rosé is rapidly ensuring that this happens in most Australian wine-growing areas, possibly because the appropriate areas, varieties and vinification for good rosé have not been determined.

Finally, a tasting panel was to try all wine, and only that which passed could be sold as Châteauneuf-du-Pape. This seems a good idea, but given that the industry is already well established, it might well lead to corruption and litigation. (New South Wales has a certification scheme based on tasting, but it is voluntary and hardly used.)

The choice of the complex and arbitrary system for Châteauneuf-du-Pape as an illustration is deliberate; in its complication it reveals most of the difficulties which must arise in introducing mandatory guaranteeing of origin. One applauds the new Federal scheme and its acceptance by all the states, without necessarily being confident that the preparation for its introduction has been adequate.

Australia needs first to establish an acceptable nomenclature. The names 'Claret' and 'Burgundy' are slowly declining in favour of names related to varieties, as are some of the European white wine names, though to a much lesser extent. Only when, for example, Australian 'Champagne' is no longer called Champagne can Australian nomenclature be regarded as having come of age. French nuclear tests at Mururoa Atoll seem likely to delay this day. Imports of Champagne, however, continue to rise, Australians drinking more per head than any other customer nation, reflecting the limited success of Australian producers in meeting increasing demand. At Christmas in 1984, a discount war led to Australian wine made by the transfer process (i.e. fermented in bottle but then disgorged in bulk and rebottled after cleaning) being sold below $2.90 a bottle, barely covering costs, and basic Champagne such as Laurent Perrier NV for less than $14.00 a bottle. Case prices were even lower. Five years later, discounted prices for Australian sparkling wine had risen 15 per cent, for French 50–100 per cent, yet imports continued to rise. Margins on the Australian products are thin as a gnat's wing, with consequent temptations to makers to focus attention on cost rather than quality.

For many years Seppelt has been the undisputed market leader in the Australian bottle-fermented sparkling wine industry. At Great Western, in its kilometres of tunnels through the soft gold-bearing rock, it has a unique resource for maturation. In addition, as a family company it was able to pursue its own aims in a manner different from a public company or an arm of a huge overseas firm. Because of the enormous demand for its Great Western 'Imperial Reserve', Seppelt has tended to make this wine rather thin, light and characterless, but its better wines such as 'Salinger' are often exceptional, occasionally achieving the tiny bubbles, hint of aniseed and overtones of nuttiness that Champagne drinkers should be able to take for granted.

Because so many Australian wine-makers feel they must offer a full line of wines, many of the smaller companies buy sparkling wine from the Seaview Champagne Cellars in the Adelaide suburbs, just near the Grange Vineyard, and sell it under their own label. For this reason, Seaview and Killawarra brands are very frequently discounted, but they are good, serviceable sparkling wines, very suitable for Christmas. Possibly, now that Great Western, Minchinbury (Penfold), Kaiser Stuhl, Seaview and Killawarra are all Penfold – Seppelt sparkling wine brands, this discounting will become rarer or more predacious.

However, central and southern Victoria hold out much promise for quality as bargains become harder to find. It is perhaps at Château Remy and Taltarni in the Pyrenees district of Victoria and Yelloglen near Ballarat that the most Champagne-like sparkling wines appear to be made. It is hardly a coincidence that Château Remy is an offshoot of Remy Martin and both Yelloglen and Taltarni have French wine-makers, Dominic Landrigan of Yelloglen having worked previously at Great Western. All these wines are elegant, all show good yeast character, and some show considerable fruit, on account of varieties other than Pinot Noir and Chardonnay having been used in some years. Given the area's propensity to produce rich-fruit character in its grapes, even when Chardonnay and Pinot Noir are the dominant varieties, one expects the fruitiness to persist. They will be splendid wines, given sufficient time on lees. Domaine Chandon in the Yarra will also produce very good but rather different wines, as one would expect from its French parent and its Australian expert, Tony Jordan. In its 'Taché Brut' Taltarni has both made a pink sparkling wine of great charm and named it in a way which will annoy very few, although the name is French.

Because of the long influence of Imperial Preference and the English demand for fortified wines, good sweet fortified red wines of the port type are made in almost every wine-growing region of Australia. In addition, the initial bias at Roseworthy was towards wine-makers who could make good fortified wines. Thus, it is very hard to nominate where the best ports are to be found.

Over the years, the big companies with their enormous reserves of material have been the most consistent, and Seppelt, Stonyfell, Mildara, Yalumba, Hardy and Reynella are names which have always had substantial followings. Yet in each area smaller companies can compete: at Clare, Wendouree, Stanley and Clarevale have always made rich vintage ports, elaborations of their old heavy red wine; Clarevale no longer has any real existence, and Stanley is being revivified by Hardy, but Wendouree's port is better than ever, if one has lifetime enough to wait. In north-eastern Victoria, companies like Stanton & Killeen use their irrigated fruit to great advantage, and even in the Hunter one can find a firm like Saxonvale making a surprisingly good vintage port. Overall, these wines have fine fruit and adequate balance but very rarely have the smoothness of true ports or the scented complexity of the spirit used in Portugal.

It is very difficult to predict a future for Australian ports, given the recent absurdly designed tax on fortifying spirit and the glut of cheap fortified wines. Like the dry fortified aperitif wines, Australian port is a victim of a change in community attitudes as well as the Common Agricultural Policy of the European Economic Community.

Adaptability is needed, and may even be forthcoming.

Wine research in Australia has been much influenced by the problems of hot areas. I asked a number of senior wine researchers for their informal views of the current major problems, and they considered that oxidation and loss of flavour during wine-making were some of the most important. Past problems have also been dominated by hot-climate difficulties, as may be seen by a brief listing of them.

The technology of pure yeast culture is now well advanced, leading to reliable fermentation properties, especially when temperature is properly controlled. Similarly, control of hazes and deposits by fining, filtering and constant low temperature is now hardly a problem. Ion exchange, for pH control and prevention of potassium bitartrate precipitation in cheap wines, is also widespread. One feels there must be a better method than ion exchange, and that it relates mainly to control of excessive vigour and prevention of moisture stress in the vineyard, as substitution of sodium for potassium is hardly healthy for the drinker. Thus, good fruit from the cooler areas does not need ion exchange, and it makes the best wine. Reliable starting and completion of the malolactic fermentation has led to more consistent red wines from both cooler and hotter areas.

Temperature control in wine-making has been most vital in making good wine from cool areas and tolerable wine from hot areas, but it has hardly been a scientific advance, more an acceptance of technology developed in California and elsewhere, despite the pioneering attempts of Sydney Hamilton and others in the 1930s.

This emphasis on the correction of faults in wine-making carries over to consumer education. French and North American organizations have prepared kits which allow drinkers to detect the different fruits and flowers which contribute to the bouquet of wine, including lemon in Riesling and Muscat, pepper in Shiraz and Cabernet Sauvignon, green pepper in Cabernet, rose and orange blossom in Gewürztraminer, and violet in Pinot Noir. Roseworthy, on the other hand, has an excellent tasting pack which allows one to detect faults such as excessive sulphur dioxide.

There has been considerable recent work at the Wine Research Institute on the retention during wine-making of flavour compounds, mainly highly volatile esters and higher alcohols which contribute floral and fruity attributes to the wine. Such activities are moves in the right direction. In sum, however, little has been done directly for the cool climates, and few innovations in vineyard practice have arisen in Australia, despite their different appearance from those of the traditional European areas. Cool-climate wine-making and viticulture are the areas of concern to the makers and lovers of better wines, but to the major companies and the dominant wine consumers the problem is the shelf life of the bag in the box. The plastic bag is permeable to oxygen, despite the best efforts of the plastic makers, and air also creeps in through the tap as the box sits on the supermarket shelf. As sales of this undemanding and convenient product are now on a plateau, shelf life is all-important. Something must be done about it. But the cheap wines are reliable and good value as they are, and the best wines are already very good. Grange Hermitage, Petaluma Riesling, Moss Wood Cabernet, Bailey's Muscat, Wendouree Shiraz, Mount Mary Pinot Noir: one could add a score of names of wines which can be sought out with confidence of delight, showing the trait of disappearing from the market as soon as they are released.

In September 1983 some friends gave us the following dinner.

Sesame Asparagus with Avocado   Lindeman, Hunter
                                     River White Burgundy, 1967

Veal Goulash and Vegetables (green beans, new potatoes)	Lake's Folly, 1973 Mildara Coonawarra Cabernet Sauvignon, 1963
Exotic Fruits with Honey Rum Cream	Orlando Auslese Rhine Riesling, 1974

Coffee

'At least you shall say this of your host – he gave us splendid wine,' as Flecker wrote. In 1990, repeating the same excellent menu, the same host gave us, in order: Tulloch Sémillon 1974, Tyrrell 'Vat 70' 1978, Redman Claret 1969, Grange 1964, Penfold 'Bin 414' Sauternes 1962. Two Hunter wines, One Coonawarra wine, one Barossa wine each time, the Grange from everywhere: in another twenty years, will the best Australian wines come from these areas in these proportions? It seems unlikely, given the revival of the old Victorian areas and the promise of Tasmania and south-western Western Australia. Yet the big areas, the big companies and traditions still have much to offer. 'When we know our own strength, we shall then better know what to undertake with hopes of success,' as John Locke said. And the strengths are considerable: reliable climate, high average standards of production, and fruit with a superabundance of flavour. Carefully used, these strengths will mean better and better wines distinctive in their generosity and intensity of flavour.

Appendices

APPENDIX 1 Area and production of grape varieties, Australia* 1988–89

	Area of vines at harvest (hectares)			Grubbings ( ) (actual and/or intended)	Grape production (tonnes, fresh weight)			
	Bearing	Not yet bearing	Total		Wine-making	Drying	Table and other	Total
RED GRAPES								
Cabernet Franc	166	85	251	–	1,523	–	1	1,524
Cabernet Sauvignon	3,400	485	3,886	22	31,207	–	20	31,227
Currant (incl. Carina)	1,259	69	1,327	60	659	13,934	36	14,629
Grenache	2,196	26	2,222	51	33,656	–	94	33,749
Malbec	206	20	226	–	2,649	–	–	2,649
Mataro	655	4	659	16	10,107	–	93	10,200
Merlot	274	109	383	–	2,419	–	–	2,419
Pinot Meunier	24	4	28	–	169	–	–	169
Pinot Noir	654	277	930	–	6,011	–	–	6,011
Rubired	33	3	36	–	664	–	68	732
Shiraz	4,756	163	4,919	43	57,873	–	172	58,045
Other red grapes	2,427	383	2,811	93	7,904	142	11,853	19,898
Total red grapes	16,052	1,628	17,680	288	154,843	14,076	12,336	181,256
WHITE GRAPES:								
Chardonnay	2,788	954	3,742	12	28,419	–	6	28,425
Chenin Blanc	501	60	562	6	8,372	–	4	8,376
Colombard	574	67	641	–	14,773	–	–	14,773
Crouchen	488	2	490	33	7,394	–	–	7,394

	Area of vines at harvest (hectares)			Grubbings	Grape production (tonnes, fresh weight)			
	Bearing	Not yet bearing	Total	( ) (actual and/or intended)	Wine-making	Drying	Table and other	Total
Doradillo	965	4	968	56	23,145	—	39	23,184
Muscadelle	391	6	398	4	4,544	—	—	4,544
Muscat Blanc	482	7	489	9	6,736	—	36	6,771
Muscat Gordo Blanco	3,755	91	3,846	83	82,565	7,102	183	89,851
Palomino and Pedro Ximenez	1,362	10	1,372	57	22,401	—	70	22,471
Rhine Riesling	3,555	51	3,606	21	41,176	—	32	41,208
Sauvignon Blanc	700	191	891	9	7,315	—	1	7,316
Sémillon	2,578	135	2,713	32	40,232	—	88	40,321
Sultana	15,303	552	15,855	226	75,468	220,869	26,755	323,090
Sylvaner	126	—	127	1	2,414	—	—	2,414
Traminer	625	8	633	5	7,598	—	—	7,598
Trebbiano	1,330	8	1,338	30	23,829	—	178	24,007
Verdelho	111	24	135	—	1,012	—	—	1,012
Waltham Cross	1,059	15	1,074	56	4,073	6,111	2,560	12,744
Other white grapes	997	129	1,129	30	7,138	139	5,381	12,648
Total white grapes	37,693	2,315	40,008	671	408,595	234,218	35,334	678,147
Total grapes	53,745	3,944	57,688	959	563,438	248,294	47,670	859,403

* excludes ACT and NT

APPENDIX 2   Vintage chart (combined assessment of red and white wines) (scale 1–11: worst–best)

Year	Swan Valley	SW WA	River-land	Clare	Barossa	Southern Vales	SE SA	SW Vic	Yarra	Geelong	Central Vic	NE Vic	Hunter	Mudgee	Tas-mania	Qld
1962	9			9	10	9	10	6			9*	6	6			
1963	8			7	6	6	10	6			6	6	7			
1964	6			7	8	7	8	8			7	8	9			
1965	7			5	4	6	4	4			8	7	10*			
1966	7			7	7	4	8	8			7	8	7			
1967	8			9	8	10	8	8			7	9	9†			
1968	7			6	6	5	6	7			6	5	6			
1969	10			5	4	2†	6	6			5	7	9			
1970	7			8	8	7	7	7			7	7	8			
1971	9			5	5	7	6	7		5	8	8	4	4		
1972	7			9	10	6†	6	10		5	6	6	7†	9		
1973	6			7	7	7	8	8		5	7	7	8*	6		
1974	7	5		4†	3†	2†	8	5	5†	5	6	6	7†	9		
1975	8	7		7	5	7	6	10	4	5	4	8	6*	8		
1976	6	6*		7	9	9	8	7	8	6	7	7	6†	8		
1977	7	9*		9	7	8	7	4	6	7	8	9	7*	5		
1978	6	6		7	7	7	8	4	6	5	9	7	6†	8*		
1979	8	7		8	6	7	8	8	9	6	9	8	9	10		
1980	9	8		9*	7	6	9	9	8	7	10	7	7	9	8	6
1981	7	9		7*	8	7	7	7	9	7*	8	6	9	5	8	8
1982	8	9		9	9	8	9	7	10	9*	8	7	6	7	9	9

244

Year	Swan Valley WA	SW WA	River-land	Clare	Barossa	Southern Vales	SE SA	SW Vic	Yarra Vic	Geelong	Central Vic	NE Vic	Hunter	Mudgee	Tasmania	Qld
1983	8	10		4	4	4	5	6	7	6*	5	5	7	5	8	7
1984	8	8		9	7	8	7	9	9	9	8	7	8	9	7	7
1985	7	8*	7	8	7	9	8	9	9	9	9	8	9*	8	8	8
1986	8	9	7	8	9	8	9	9	9	9	8	9	9	8	8	8
1987	7	9	8	9	9	8	9	8†	7	9†		9	7	8	8	8
1988	7	9	9	9	8	9	8	8	9	9	9	8	7	9	9	8
1989	9	9	9	8	7	8	8	9	8	8	8	6	6	9	9	8
1990	8	9	9	8	8	7	7	9	8	8	9	7	7	8	8	8

* red better than white
† white better than red

245

	Table wine			Sparkling wine			Others*			Total			Exports
	Domestic	Foreign	Total	Domestic	Foreign	Total	Domestic	Foreign	Total	Domestic	Foreign	Total	
1977–78	116.6	5.2	121.9	23.7	1.8	25.5	54.3	0.8	55.1	194.7	7.8	202.5	4.6
1978–79	143.2	5.6	148.8	27.1	2.2	29.3	57.4	0.7	58.1	228.4	8.5	236.8	5.2
1979–80	160.9	5.1	165.9	29.9	1.4	31.3	54.3	0.4	54.7	245.0	6.9	251.9	6.9
1980–81	179.3	5.6	184.9	29.6	1.5	31.1	54.0	0.4	54.4	262.9	7.5	270.4	7.5
1981–82	197.9	6.7	204.6	27.7	1.7	29.5	52.9	0.5	53.5	278.6	9.0	287.6	8.6
1982–83	216.9	5.4	222.4	27.0	1.6	28.7	49.6	0.4	50.0	293.6	7.5	301.0	7.9
1983–84	227.8	6.8	234.5	29.0	2.5	31.5	49.0	0.4	49.4	305.8	9.7	315.5	8.9
1984–85	245.4	8.8	254.2	31.3	3.0	34.3	43.8	0.7	44.5	320.5	12.5	333.0	10.8
1985–86	253.4	8.5	261.6	30.4	3.0	33.4	41.7	0.8	42.5	325.2	12.3	337.5	21.2
1986–87	259.2	5.0	264.2	28.8	2.0	30.8	42.9	0.7	43.6	330.9	7.7	338.6	39.1
1987–88	255.8	5.7	261.5	32.6	1.9	34.5	42.1	0.6	42.7	330.5	8.2	338.7	46.1
1988–89	237.5	6.1	243.6	30.7	2.3	33.0	39.7	1.5	41.2	307.5	9.9	317.4	52.0

* fortified wine, flavoured wine, etc.

APPENDIX 4   Composition of table wine sales (in million litres; from the Australian Wine and Brandy Corporation 1989)

	Red				Rosé				White			
	Glass 1 litre or less	over 1 litre	Plastic	Bulk	Glass 1 litre or less	over 1 litre	Plastic	Bulk	Glass 1 litre or less	over 1 litre	Plastic	Bulk
1977–78	10.3	6.4	7.1	4.5	2.2	3.4	2.4	0.6	29.5	21.4	22.7	5.5
1978–79	10.3	6.7	7.5	3.8	1.9	3.4	3.1	0.7	31.5	28.0	37.9	8.4
1979–80	11.5	5.5	7.5	3.2	1.8	3.1	3.2	0.6	34.3	30.2	51.1	9.0
1980–81	12.5	5.4	8.9	2.5	1.7	2.5	3.6	0.4	36.7	28.7	69.5	7.0
1981–82	12.3	5.1	11.3	1.8	1.7	2.0	3.8	0.3	37.9	26.9	84.7	5.9
1982–83	12.7	4.9	12.8	1.5	1.3	1.9	4.3	0.2	36.8	27.8	103.6	5.0
1983–84	14.1	4.6	14.4	1.4	1.3	1.7	4.7	0.2	34.6	24.0	111.5	5.3
1984–85	16.8	3.7	1.67	1.2	1.3	1.1	4.9	0.2	39.6	18.3	137.8	4.5
1985–86	16.8	2.3	16.9	1.1	1.0	0.7	5.3	0.2	38.8	12.8	140.8	16.2
1986–87	19.0	1.8	17.7	1.8	1.1	0.5	5.4	0.2	36.6	7.1	110.4	22.1
1987–88	22.2	1.4	19.0	1.9	1.1	0.4	5.6	0.1	38.1	5.7	108.5	16.5
1988–89	22.8	1.3	18.2	1.6	1.1	0.3	5.6	0.1	41.8	9.5	102.6	10.9

APPENDIX 5 Total Australian wine production in megalitres, including wine for distillation (from Australian Bureau of Statistics)

Year	South Australia	New South Wales	Other states	Total
1980–81	225	92	58	375
1981–82	274	74	55	403
1982–83	203	76	61	340
1983–84	234	85	77	396
1984–85	263	107	81	451
1985–86	215	115	59	389
1986–87	197	113	62	372
1987–88	212	123	73	408

In 1788 over 200 Aboriginal languages were spoken in Australia, and the landscape bore names in these languages. Some of these names were retained by the European invaders, but most were lost. Many vineyards have Aboriginal names, but few of these were supplied by the Aboriginals who once lived in the vicinage; rather they have been taken from books like A. W. Reed's *Aboriginal Place Names* on account of their euphony or topographical or other suitability. I am greatly indebted to J. H. Simpson for the content of the following list, which is abstracted from her own list that details language, exact geographical location, and sources.

AKERINGA   Willunga, SA; *upon the plains*
ALKOOMI   Mount Barker (Lower Great Southern), WA; *very nice*
ANAKIE   Geelong, Vic.; *Anakie Youang twin hills*
BALLARAT   Vic.; *resting or camping place*
BAROOGA   Murray Valley, Vic.; *teal* [?]
BARWANG   Young, NSW; *nut tree*
BELBOURIE   Lower Hunter Valley, NSW; *creek with bushes*
BONNONEE   North-West Vic. [in Qld, perhaps '*dew*']
BOROKA   Great Western, Vic.; *warm*
BUNGAREE   Clare, SA; *dwelling place, seal, shade, go away*
BUNGAWARRA   Granite Belt, Qld [in WA, perhaps '*granite rocks and shallow water*']
BURONGA   Murray Valley, NSW; *bees*
COOLALTA   [?] Lower Hunter, NSW [coola can mean *angry, tree, koala, cooler*]
COOLAWIN   Clarendon, SA [in NSW, perhaps '*a big koala*']
COONAWARRA   SA; *swan, excrement, oyster, hill covered with honey-suckle* [i.e. *Grevillea* spp.]
COROWA   Riverina, NSW; *pine tree yielding gum, rocky river, swamp*
COWARAMUP   Margaret River, WA; *place of rat*
CUBBAROO   Namoi Valley, NSW; *head* [?]
DARINGA   Mclaren Vale, SA; *the half-way place, creek*
GNANGARA   Swan Valley, WA; *beard, yesterday, star*
KALIMNA   Barossa Valley, SA; *beautiful*
KARINA   Mornington Peninsula, Vic.; *white cockatoo*
KARRAWIRRA   Barossa Valley, SA; *red gum forest* [but Karrawirra was called Hoffnungsthal until World War I]
KILLAWARRA   NSW; *scrub*
KOOMBAHLA   Central Vic.; *girl*
KOONUNGA   Barossa Valley, SA; *place of excrement*

MALUNA   Hunter Valley, NSW; *nest*

MARRI   [*Eucalyptus calophylla*] tree in WA

MILAWA   Northern Vic.; *river*

MILDURA   Murray Valley, Vic.; *place of flies in the eyes*

MOONDAH   WA; *beyond*

MOORILLA   South-east Tasmania; *stony ridge*

MOOROODUC   Mornington Pen., Vic.; *dark and swampy place*

MULGA   [*Acacia aneura*] tree in NT and elsewhere

MURRUMBATEMAN   ACT; *good* [?]

MURRUMBIDGEE   NSW; *big water, ever-flowing*

NAMOI   NSW; *a particular acacia, a woman's breast*

NARANG   Margaret River, WA; *small, open, place of the big sheoaks*

NARRIKUP   Lower Great Southern, WA

NURIOOTPA   Barossa Valley, Sa; *the neck country* [derived from an Aboriginal legend concerning the neck of a great being]

PARINGA   Mornington Pen., Vic.; *by the river*

PARRAMATTA   Sydney, NSW; *head of the river, place where eels lie down, a dark jungle*

TANUNDA   Barossa Valley, SA; *many birds upon a creek*

TARCOOLA   Geelong, Vic. [in NSW, *a river bend*; the township of this name was called after the winner of the 1893 Melbourne Cup]

TARRANGA   [?] Murray Valley, Sa; *lagoon, billabong*

TUMBARUMBA   NSW high country; *a curl or fold, very soft, sounding ground*

WAIKERIE   Murray Valley, Sa; *anything that flies*

WILLUNGA   SA; *a place of green scrub*

WIRRA WIRRA   Mclaren Vale, SA; *forest, scrub, lightning*

YALDARA   Barossa, SA; *sparkling*

YARRA   Vic.; *running water*

YARRINYA   Yarra Valley, Vic.; *red gum on the river*

Bibliography

Antcliffe, A. J., 'Four new grape varieties released for testing', *J. Aust. Inst. Agric. Sci.* 41 (1975), 262–4.

– 'New CSIRO grape variety for irrigated regions', *Aust. Wine Brewing & Spirit Rev.* 99 (1979), 161–2.

Australian Bureau of Statistics, *Sales and Stocks of Australian Wine and Brandy by Winemakers*, Pub. No. 8504.0, 1984.

Australian Bureau of Statistics, 1988–89 *Viticulture Australia*, Pub. No. 7310.0, 1990.

Australian Wine and Brandy Corporation, *Annual Report 1988–89*, Adelaide, 1989.

Australian Wine and Brandy Producers' Association, *The Australian Wine and Brandy Producing Industry*, Adelaide, 1983.

Benwell, W. S., *Journey to Wine in Victoria* (2nd edn), Melbourne, 1975.

Bradley, R., *Australian Wine Vintages* (7th edn) Melbourne, 1989.

Brady, B. *Winemakers and Vignerons of the Southwest and Great Southern*, Perth, 1982.

Brien, C. J., Venables, W. N., James, A. T. and Mayo, O., 'An analysis of correlation matrices: equal correlations', *Biometrika* 71 (1984), 545–54.

Cox, H., *The Wines of Australia*, London, 1967.

Dakis, P., Hayes, P. and Noon, D., *The Profitablity of Investing in a Small Vineyard and Winery*, Victorian DARA Res. Rep. No. 87, Melbourne, 1990.

De Castella, F., 'Phylloxera-resistant vine stocks *vs* considerations governing the choice of a stock', *J. Agric. Victoria* 34 (1936), 303–9.

De Castella, H., *John Bull's Vineyard*, Melbourne, 1886.

Faith, N., *The Winemasters*, London, 1978.

Fornachon, J. C. M., *Bacterial Spoilage of Fortified Wines*, Adelaide, 1943.

Gaffney, D. O., 'Rainfall deficiency and evaporation in relation to drought in Australia', paper presented at 46th ANZAAS Congress, Canberra 1975 (available from Bureau of Meteorology, Melbourne).

Galbraith, J. K., *A Life in Our Times*, Boston, Mass., 1980.

Gladstones, J. S., 'The climate and soils of south-western Australia in relation to vine-growing', *J. Aust. Inst. Agric. Sci.* 31 (1965), 275–88.

– 'Temperature and wine grape quality in European vineyards', *Proc. III Tech. Conf. Aust. Wine Industry* (Albury, 9–11 August 1977), 1977.

Halliday, J., *Wines and Wineries of New South Wales*, Brisbane, 1980.

– *Wines and Wineries of South Australia*, Brisbane, 1981.

– *Wines and Wineries of Victoria*, Brisbane, 1982.

– *Wines and Wineries of Western Australia*, Brisbane, 1982.

– *Coonawarra*, Sydney, 1983.

– *The Australian Wine Compendium*, Sydney, 1985.

– *James Halliday's Australian Wine Guide*, Sydney, 1990.

Harslett, J. and Royle, M., *They Came to a Plateau: The Stanthorpe Saga*, Stanthorpe, 1973.

Heddle, E. M., *Story of a Vineyard: Château Tahbilk*, Melbourne, 1968.

Irvine, H. W. H., *Report on the Australian Wine Trade*, compiled at the request of the Victorian Minister of Agriculture, Robert S. Brain, Govt Printer, Melbourne, 1890.

Johnson, H., *World Atlas of Wine*, London, 1982.

Kelly, A. C., *Winegrowing in Australia*, Adelaide, 1861.

Kent Barlow, R., 'The "disloyal" grape: the agrarian crisis of late fourteenth-century Burgundy', *Agricultural History* 56 (1982), 426–38.

Labys, W. C., 'An international comparison of price and income elasticities for wine consumption', *Aust. J. Agric. Econ.* 20 (1976), 33–6.

Laffer, H. E., *The Wine Industry of Australia*, Adelaide, 1949.

Lake, M., *Hunter Wine*, Brisbane, 1964.

Livingstone-Learmonth, J. and Master, M. C. H., *The Wines of the Rhône* (2nd edn), London, 1983.

Mackay, G., *The History of Bendigo*, Bendigo, 1891.

Morrison, P. and Morrison, E. (eds), *Charles Babbage and his Calculating Engines*, New York, 1961.

Penfold, B. J., *Secret Wines of New South Wales*, Sydney, 1989.

Pike, D., *Paradise of Dissent: South Australia 1829–57*, Melbourne, 1957.

Powell, A., *Faces in My Time*, Vol. 3 of *To Keep the Ball Rolling*, London, 1980.

Ramsden, E., 'James Busby, the prophet of Australian viticulture', *J. Proc. R. Aust. Hist. Soc.* 26 (1940), 361–86.

Rankine, B. C., Fornachon, J. C. M. and Bridson, D. A., 'Diacetyl in Australian red wines and its significance in wine quality', *Vitis* 8 (1969), 129–34.

Rankine, B. C., Fornachon, J. C. M., Boehm, E. W. and Cellier, K. M., 'Influence of grape variety, climate and soil on grape composition and on the composition and quality of tables wines', *Vitis* 10 (1971), 33–50.

Rapp, A. and Mandery, H., 'Wine aroma', *Experientia* 42 (1986), 873–84.

Reed, A. W., *Aboriginal Place Names*, Sydney, 1988.

Sargent, S., *The Foodmakers*, Melbourne, 1985.

Schreier, P., 'Correlation of wine composition with cultivar and site', Centenary Symposium (ed. B. C. Rankine), Roseworthy Agricultural College (1983), 63–95.

Shaw, T. G., *Wine, the Vine and the Cellar*, London, 1863.

Simpson, R. F., Miller, G. C. and Orr, G. L., 'Oxidative pinking of white wines: recent observations', *Food Technology in Australia* 34 (1982), 44–7.

Somers, T. C. and Evans, M. E. 'April Red – one year later', *Aust. Grapegrower and Winemaker* 184 (1979), 2–4.

Starr, J., *Wines and Wineries of the Granite Belt*, Blackburn, 1982.

Sutcliffe, S., *André Simon's Wines of the World*, London, 1981.

Trollope, A., *Australia and New Zealand*, London, 1873.

Williams, C. H. and Raupach, M., 'Plant nutrients in Australian soils' in *Soils: An Australian Viewpoint*, Melbourne, 1983, 777–94.

Witcombe, R. K., 'Investing in wine grapes', *Agbulletin* AB1 (1980), Victorian Department of Agriculture.

Index